HUMANISM IN SOCIOLOGY: ITS HISTORICAL ROOTS AND CONTEMPORARY PROBLEMS

Aleksander Gella

Sue Curry Jansen and
Donald F. Sabo, Jr.

University Press of America

HM
101
.G33

Copyright © 1978 by

University Press of America, Inc.™

4710 Auth Place, S.E., Washington, D.C. 20023

All rights reserved

Printed in the United States of America

ISBN: 0-8191-0598-8

Library of Congress Catalog Card Number: 78-61394

This modest book is dedicated to all who--under diverse political systems--have suffered the results of anti-humanistic trends in our time, in our presence, throughout the world: from Aleksander Solzhenitsyn, the known warrior, to unknown victims like the Boat People.

ACKNOWLEDGMENTS

I would like to thank Harcourt Brace Jovanovich, Inc., for permission to use the quotation included here in Chapter I from <u>Selected Essays of T.S. Eliot</u>, "The Humanism of Irving Babbit." I am equally grateful to the Rand Corporation for allowing me to quote in Chapter X from Herbert Goldhamer (ed.), <u>The Social Effects of Communication</u>.

FOREWORD

This book has rather an unusual origin. It was conceived at the graduate student seminar on 'Humanistic Sociology' which I had led during the Spring Semester 1975 in the Department of Sociology, SUNY at Buffalo. The seminar had an experimental character. I proposed to a group of eight students that it would be more interesting to work together on one bigger essay or even a small book, than to have a conventional seminar.

Although the present book was actually completed during the next two years, its conception took place during this seminar. So, I am very happy to keep the promise I gave, to mention the names of all the participants of my seminar. They were: <u>David Gregorio</u>, <u>Sue Jansen</u>, <u>Elaine Lenkei</u>, <u>Dennis Lindberg</u>, <u>Don Mason</u>, <u>Paul Porter</u>, <u>Donald Sabo</u> and <u>Robert Wise</u>.

During fifteen meetings of this seminar, xeroxed chapters (or parts of them) written by me were distributed among the participants. They were the basis for our seminar discussions. My young collaborators were assigned to read and summarize some additional material or to prepare certain footnotes to particular points. However, one semester's seminar was too short a time to complete a book. After the seminar ended, I decided to continue working on it.

Three of my collaborators who wanted to keep working with me further were Sue Jansen, Dennis Lindberg and Donald Sabo. (Donald knew more of my ideas than the others because during the three previous years he worked as my teaching and research assistant.) Of these three, Dennis Lindberg prepared a first draft of a chapter on Max Weber but he had to leave Buffalo in the summer of 1975 for a teaching position in Davis and Elkins College, West Virginia, and our cooperation unfortunately ceased. Dennis was one of the most enthusiastic collaborators during my experimental seminar. The chapter on Max Weber on which he began to work was greatly enlarged and completed by me with the cooperation of Sue and Donald.

In my further work on this book I enjoyed the continuing help of Sue and Donald. He wrote a chapter on Sorokin, Sue largely con-

contributed to it and I had only to add some short remarks. She wrote a first draft on Mannheim of which ten typed pages are included in what I have finally prepared. Donald's greatest contribution was to Part Three. He wrote the first draft of both chapters X and XI. Then I worked on them and added only a few pages to chapter X but half the material in chapter XI. Sue has her valuable inserts in many other chapters written by me and worked as a manuscript reviser of all chapters. She is the exclusive author of the Appendix.

For all their help and contributions I have offered to these two young friends, Sue Jansen and Donald Sabo, the co-authorship.

I alone am responsible for all other chapters as well as the concept of this book, its main ideas as well as mistakes.

I would like to express my appreciation to Audrey Mang, my former assistant, for her skillful, careful and thoughtful typing of the manuscript in a very short time. I would also like to thank Anastasia Johnson, Assistant to the Chairman, for her coordinating efforts, and Rose Rabb, Margaret Holton, Diane Marlinski, and Edna Paine for their patient typing of the first drafts of this book.

Aleksander Gella

TABLE OF CONTENTS

HUMANISM IN SOCIOLOGY:
ITS HISTORICAL ROOTS AND CONTEMPORARY PROBLEMS

Acknowledgements		i
Foreword		iii
Introduction		vii

Part One — Humanism versus Positivism

Chapter I	Meanings of Humanism	1
Chapter II	Positivism: Idolatry in Academic Sociology	24
Chapter III	A Crack in the Idol: The Contemporary Crisis in Science	32
Chapter IV	The Search for a Humanistic Sociology	42

Part Two — Historical Roots

Chapter V	Humanistic Revolution in 19th Century Philosophy: Dilthey, Windelband, and Rickert	57
Chapter VI	Toward Interpretive Understanding: Max Weber	71
Chapter VII	Humanistic Sociology of Florian Znaniecki	91
Chapter VIII	Love has a Power of Its Own: Pitirim Sorokin	120
Chapter IX	Sociological Culture: Karl Mannheim	139

Part Three	Societal Problems	
Chapter X	Some Reflections on Techno-Scientific Optimism	159
Chapter XI	Education in the Techno-Industrial Complex	176
Chapter XII	Closing Remarks	192
Appendix	Humanistic Trends in Recent Sociology: A Guide to Literature and Issues	202
Index of Names		246

INTRODUCTION

The trend in sociological scholarship which is accurately labelled "humanistic" deserves particular attention during this period of great transformation through which humankind is now passing. Humanists in sociology recognize that man dwells in a hermeneutic circle: thus, they regard meaning and consciousness as the critical data upon which interpretations of social life are constructed. Because humanists in sociology have openly acknowledged the legitimacy of their kinship to philosophy, they have been able to provide a forum for the continuous reappraisal of sociological knowledge and the methods used to obtain it. Similarly, they have been sensitive to the role of values in society and in the scientific process itself. But, above all, humanism in sociology is distinguished by its commitment to the search for freedom of man in the machinery of social systems. It is also dedicated to the creation of a humane future.

This book has two aims: first, to contribute to the development of a greater awareness of the rich but neglected humanistic tradition in sociology which has a continuing significance for contemporary sociology; and, second, to demonstrate the relevance of the humanistic perspective for attempts to come to terms with the crisis in the modern world. To this end, various meanings of humanism are explored and their respective relations to the dominant currents in western thought are discussed. Humanistic elements in the works of Dilthey, Weber, Znaniecki, Sorokin, and Mannheim are systematically reconsidered.

Since recent developments in science underscore the need for a humanistic approach to societal problems, we will discuss humanistic sociology within this context. During the past decade the dominant sociological paradigm which is derivative of the natural scientific tradition has come under intensive critical scrutiny. The relevance of conventional methods and theoretical exercises has been severely questioned. Yet, the urgent need for a means of comprehending societal problems has not receded. Our age is shaking before a seemingly endless array of societal problems. The most compelling are: the increase in threats to the survival of humankind brought about by man's technological excesses as well as by the exhaustion of the world's resources; the transformation from the stage of independent and often autarchic national states to a global interdependence of nations; and the increasingly widespread dissatisfaction with modern science whose original character as a purely intellectual enterprise vanished in the parallel trends of subjugation by industry and growing service to and dependence upon technology. The ideas and energies of this work were born of this sense of social and professional urgency.

In considering contemporary world problems, we reached a disturbing conclusion concerning our own discipline. Much of the most prominent literature in sociology seems bereft of social relevance. Indeed, theoretical perambulations often exhibit a degree of abstract detachment from individual experience and social realities which make their earthly genesis suspect. We therefore decided to make an effort to defend the rights of citizenship in contemporary intellectual life of those sociological interests and studies which are suppressed by the domination of positivism and behaviorism.

It must be recognized that social science today, despite its substantive and technical advances, cannot offer solutions to or even significantly broaden our understanding of pressing world problems. The positivistic character of the dominant methodological models does not allow us to go beyond the limits prescribed by the principles on which these methods are founded. Often the specifistic inclinations and problematic foci of contemporary social science hinder formulation of the new conceptions of our humanity mandated by the imperatives of our shrinking globe. Many years ago, Robert Lynd warned social scientists, "Social science cannot perform its functions if the culture constrains it at certain points in ways foreign to the spirit of science; and at all points where such constraints limit the free use of intelligence to pose problems, to analyze all relevant aspects of them, or to draw conclusions, it is necessary for social science to work directly to remove causes of these obstacles".[1] Although the quantitative approach is often regarded as the only legitimate form of inquiry within sociology, there are important subject matters and intellectual concerns which cannot be reduced to the precise methodological specifications of this version of the scientific enterprise. Thus, the humanistic dimension of social reality cannot be fully encompassed within the conceptual boundaries shaped by the tools of positivism.

For a century, we have been told that sociology is still in its infancy and that we must not expect too much from it. Just as the development of a philosophy of science required the preexistence of science, the emergence of the sociology of sociology can be regarded as a step toward intellectual maturity. Through these modes of self-reflection and examination, we have learned more and more about the role of the human factor in the creation of social, scientific, and even technological realities. We may now begin to expect more from our hundred-year-old infant.

The twentieth century's faith in science was perhaps matched only by the zeal and respect the Enlightenment associated with reason. Faith seldom invites critical self-evaluation and, for many decades, the paradigmatic underpinnings and methodological assumptions of the natural sciences went essentially unquestioned. However, the situation has changed. The foundations of natural scientific knowledge are now being re-evaluated by contemporary thinkers.

Henryk Skolimowski, a philosopher and historian of science, points out that self-criticism within the philosophy of science during the past two decades has been so extensive that it has reached an impasse which has resulted in the dissolution of the traditional problems and boundaries of that discipline. He contends that the debate can no longer be regarded merely as an academic exercise--that, indeed, the future of an entire civilization depends upon the course of its resolution: "The survival of a civilization is more important than our attachment to the idols and icons of (traditional) science".[2] Skolimowski maintains that the work of Popper, Kuhn, Lakatos, and Feyerabend has been influential in "liberating" the philosophy of science from the constrictive dictates imposed upon it by the formalistic program of the Logical Positivists.[3] He describes the model of science constructed by the Logical Positivists as a "semi-logical system" and contends, "This logical reconstruction of science was so remote from the actual practice of science that scientists themselves often could not recognize science, as they practiced it, in the systems presented by logical positivists".[4]

The same facet of the positivistic ethos inspired Michael Polanyi's pioneering challenge to traditional notions of scientific knowledge. In _Personal Knowledge_, Polanyi demonstrates that scientific knowledge is personal--it necessarily involves judgment, commitment, connoiseurship, elegance, beauty, and faith.[5] Floyd Matson also addresses himself to the question of the crisis in science. He emphasizes the fact that scientific discovery itself has undermined the postulates of positivism. He maintains that the "Quantum Revolution" (particularly Heisenberg's principle of indeterminancy and Bohr's principle of complementarity) brought about "the total eclipse of mechanistic determinism and objectivism".[6] Matson calls for the development of a science of man in which man is the subject and not the object: "When man is the subject, the proper understanding of science leads unmistakably to the science of understanding".[7] However, "understanding" has only been accepted as a legitimate procedure within the humanities and social sciences by those authors who wanted to introduce the humanistic element into their disciplines. But the movement to "rehumanize" science has gained momentum in recent years. Thus, the late Abraham Maslow reported in _The Psychology of Science_:

>...in the last decade or two, a counter philosophy has been rapidly developing along with a considerable revolt against the mechanistic, dehumanized view of man and the world. It might be called a rediscovery of man and his human capacities, needs, and aspirations. These humanly based values are being restored to politics, to industry, to religion, and also to the psychological and social sciences....This change is part of a larger and more inclusive, more 'humanistic' world view. For the time being these two great philosophic orientations, the mechanistic and humanistic, exist simultaneously like some species-wide two party system.[8]

If paradigmatic re-examination has begun within the natural and social sciences, so also have we begun to look critically at the relation between science and societal problems. This self-reflection has been painfully disturbing for some and a source of new-found optimism for others.

Kurt Vonnegut's <u>Sirens of Titan</u> provides a literary key to the present dilemma of sociology as well as to the significance of a humanistic perspective.[9] The novel unfolds in the distant future. The tragi-comic protagonist is a robot, conceived and created by earth scientists as a means to carry out interplanetary missions and techno-scientific tasks without the hindrance of human imperfections. Marooned on a moon orbiting the planet Titan for several hundred years, the automaton experiences the first glimmerings of emotionality when he recognizes that he has been insensitively exploited by a despotic companion. Confused and without hope, the robot is overcome by suicidal logic and dismantles itself. A well-intended and altruistic earthman arrives on the scene and carefully reassembles the shattered fragments. The interaction between robot and repairman creates a sense of completeness and direction in his cybernetic soul. Technological consciousness merges with human awareness. The sociological vision was born of man's desire to exercise techno-scientific control over his environment. It was a humane vision impelled by noble motives: to relieve humankind of turmoil, starvation, violence, and misery, and to lay the foundations for a better life in the future. However, today we are confronted with the poverty of our means:

> The achievements of Western culture are materialized dreams, and since they were only made possible by the strangling of our feelings, they have increasingly materialized the evil in man--perverse brutality, whining arrogance, cruel obsessiveness, and devouring power-hunger. And when all these

>mangled impulses have been given physical form
>we will be unable to see the sky or the trees
>or any living thing, so inundated will we be by
>the machinery we have vomited up from our
>ulcerated insides.[10]

While we aspire to dominion, we face the possibility of demise. In our quest we have lost touch with our humanity. Like Vonnegut's robot, we are running the risk of dashing ourselves to pieces due to our inability to reconcile or even meaningfully perceive the relation between that part of us which is machine-like and technical and that part of us which is subjectively human. J. R. Bronowski succinctly captures the contemporary identity crisis of humankind:

>...The crisis of confidence which springs from
>each man's wish to be a mind and a person, in
>the face of the man's fear that he is a mechan-
>ism. The central question that I ask is: Can
>man be both a machine and a self?[11]

Sociologists can help mankind to get out of this identity crisis by reorienting social research from a dominating positivistic-behavioristic paradigm to a humanistic one. At the same time, however, we believe that the proper objective of a humanistic approach is to stimulate dialogue among fellow searchers, not to propound programs for others to follow. Therefore, in order to reorient our discipline from a positivistic-behavioristic paradigm to an interpretive one, Werner Pelz suggests that we must also reform our modes of discourse.[12] Dialogue rather than confrontation appears to be an appropriate form for humanistic sociology. We would also suggest that the sociologist surrender his or her professional hubris and accept the fact that the survival of the planet Earth is a communal project for "the global village". Like John O'Neill, "We may wish that our daily lives were more just, more honest and less violent. Some of us work towards that end, but in this none of us is at all special, least of all the sociologist. Indeed he should be the last to strike postures on this issue. For sociology has yet to earn the people's trust".[13]

Hopefully, in this way we may begin to rediscover our common humanity without surrendering our personal uniqueness.

INTRODUCTION FOOTNOTES

1. Robert Lynd, Knowledge For What? (Princeton: Princeton University Press, 1939), p. 249.

2. Henryk Skolimowski, "Science in Crisis," Cambridge Review, January 28, 1972, p. 70.

3. Ibid. Skolimowski suggests that the spade-work was done by Karl Popper, who in his The Logic of Scientific Discovery (1959) and Conjecture and Refutations (1963) showed the development of science as a continuing drama of old hypotheses being abolished by new ones. Thomas Kuhn's The Structure of Scientific Revolutions (1963) developed the thesis that a "paradigm" once established serves as a dominant frame in which science develops. However, since the publication of Kuhn's work, many other authors tried to amend the traditional views of science. Imre Lakatos' Criticism and the Growth of Knowledge (1970) offered the concept of "research programs" within which new scientific achievements are made possible. Paul Feyerabend's notion of "cognitive nihilism" describes the "simultaneously destructive and liberating" process which alters the traditional view of science by challenging the very notions of scientific "laws" and the inherent "rationality" of scientific method. See "Against Method: Outline of an Anarchistic Theory of Knowledge" in Minnesota Studies in the Philosophy of Science, vol. IV, 1971. It should also be noted that when the war disrupted the activity of the "Vienna Circle," the center of this intellectual movement was shifted to America where under the direction Carnap and Fleigl it continued to influence the philosophy of science (and philosophy in general). As a unified movement, Logical Positivism survived until the 1940's. However, even after the movement was largely disbanded, many of its ideas continued to exercise a strong influence upon the social sciences. Two key postulates of Logical Positivism which emphasize how far this viewpoint differs from the humanistic perspective of Dilthey may be isolated: (i) Physicalism, the belief "that everything can be said, in principle, in the language of physics"; (ii) The thesis of the Unity of Science which "holds that there is no fundamental cleavage between Geisteswissenshaft and Naturwissenschaft". (See: Abraham Kaplan, "Positivism" in International Encyclopedia of the Social Sciences, ed., David L. Sills (New York: Macmillan, 1968) Vol. 13, p. 393.)

4. Skolimowski, ibidem, p. 70.

5. Michael Polanyi, *Personal Knowledge* (Chicago: The University of Chicago Press, 1958).

6. Floyd Matson, *The Broken Image* (New York: Doubleday, 1964), p. 124. See also William Barrett, *Irrational Man* (Garden City: Doubleday, 1962).

7. Matson, ibidem, p. 247. Quoting Santayana, Matson also points to the fallibility of formal rationalizations of science provided by philosophers: "Unfortunately the supplements to science which most philosophers supply in our day are not conceived in a scientific spirit. Instead of anticipating the physics of the future they cling to the physics of the past. They do not stimulate us by a picture, however fanciful, of what the analogies of nature and politics actually point to; they seek rather to patch and dislocate current physics with some ancient myth, once the best physics obtainable, from which they have not learned to extricate their affections", p. 113.

8. Abraham Maslow, *The Psychology of Science* (New York: Harper and Row, 1966), pp. 2-3.

9. Kurt Vonnegut, *The Sirens of Titan* (New York: Dell Publishing Co., 1974).

10. Phillip Slater, *Earthwalk* (New York: Doubleday, 1974), pp. 121-122.

11. J. R. Bronowski, *The Identity of Man* (Garden City, N.Y.: The Natural History Press, 1965), pp. 8-9.

12. Werner Pelz, *The Scope of Understanding in Sociology* (London: Routledge and Kegan-Paul, 1974).

13. John O'Neill, *Sociology as a Skin Trade* (New York: Harper and Row, 1972), p. 219.

PART ONE: HUMANISM VERSUS POSITIVISM

CHAPTER I

MEANINGS OF HUMANISM

Before specifically considering the problems of humanistic sociology, some attention should be given to Humanism itself. The term is emotionally loaded. Its flexibility has resulted in many social movements and opposing schools of thought calling themselves humanistic. An examination of the problems of humanistic sociology, therefore, is better informed by a knowledge of the history of humanism as well as an awareness of the main contemporary ideological and philosophical controversies developing around the concept of Humanism.

Humanism in the Past

The tradition of humanism reaches back to China and Greece. The conflict between humanistic and anti-humanistic concepts and views of the nature of man and of knowledge began in the classical civilizations. Our contemporary discussions of humanism are antedated in China by Confucius' efforts to educate the self-controlled man who through a permanent self-improvement can achieve the sense of justice and respect for human dignity in himself and others. Confucius demanded that his followers be "always progressing and never come to a standpoint".[1] This was a requirement of personal and moral progress, neglected in modern times when the word "progress" became an idol of advanced and advancing nations.

The Hellenic approach to humanism has been outlined by Werner Jaeger, an unquestionable authority in studies of Greek culture, who wrote:

> By discovering man, the Greeks did not discover the subjective self, but realized the universal laws of human nature. The intellectual principle of the Greeks is not individualism but 'humanism,' to use the word in its original and classical sense. It comes from humanities: which, since the time of Varro and Cicero at least, possessed

> a nobler and severer sense in addition to its
> early vulgar sense of humane behavior, here
> irrelevant. It meant the process of educating
> man into his true form, the real and genuine
> human nature....Above man as a member of a
> horde, and man as a supposedly independent
> personality, stands man as an ideal; and that
> ideal was a pattern to which Greek educators as
> well as Greek poets, artists, and philosophers
> always looked.[2]

However, the Greeks are also the authors of another very different model of man: the brother of Varro and Cicero's ideal man who was fashioned of clay rather than spirit. Therefore, one can say that two opposite types of humanism originated in Greece. Protagoras, a sophist, marked the beginning of the first with his naturalist philosophy and the concept of man expressed in his famous saying, "man is the measure of all things". The second, which had its roots in Hellenic national traditions, was refined in Socrates' ethical intellectualism and was developed soon after Protagoras' teaching. The latter affirms as essentially human those aspects of man's life which lift him above nature. The former naturalistic humanism has an anthropocentric character, while the latter is searching for a point of gravitation over the earthly nature of man and is, therefore, often called theocentric. However, it should be made clear that non-naturalist humanism does not need to have religion as its background. Rather, the position need only affirm that what makes us "human" begins when we have moved beyond the needs of human-animal.[3] Sartre's definition of freedom succinctly illustrates this distinction: "What we call freedom is the irreducibility of the cultural order to the natural order".[4]

Though humanism has many dimensions, nonetheless, throughout the centuries these two concepts, naturalistic and non-naturalistic, have formed the underpinnings of humanistic movements, philosophies and trends. Thus, Martin Heidegger remarked:

> In general, one can understand Humanism as the
> effort to make man feel free in his manhood and
> by this to find his dignity, however, besides
> this the concepts of "freedom" and the 'nature
> of man' are determining the sense of humanism.[5]

Consequently, in each historical epoch and within each major intellectual trend, one finds that various "humanisms" are related to particular concepts of freedom and of human nature.

The ethos of Christianity was humanistic.[6] Its early period can be seen as a revolt against the decadence of human existence in the "affluent" society of the Roman empire. Historians have acknowledged that Christianity even in the Darkest Ages was a humanistic alternative to the barbaric conditions of life organized on the ruins of the Roman empire. Christian humanists argue that even in its moment of highest development Christianity involved humanistic elements of the Greek philosophical tradition.[7] When institutionalized Christian orthodoxy and the corruption of the Church hierarchy were making life in the Christian world more and more oppressed, one saint-revolutionist planted the seeds for the flowering of a new epoch. The Renaissance mentality and art were conceived over the grave of Saint Francis of Assisi. Saint Francis and his legend became the source of Christian humanism for the ensuing centuries. Although his movement was institutionalized by the church, the seeds of the humanistic turn toward nature and the appreciation for the beauty of earthly life flourished on the Italian soil of the 15th and 16th centuries. It was a secular reaction against the social, cultural, and political domination of the Medieval Church expressed by the literary activity of the 14th, 15th and 16th century "humanists". They were men of letters educated in <u>litterae humaniores</u> at a time dominated by scholasticism and marked by the first steps towards the modern natural sciences.[8]

The next great wave of humanism was in the 18th century when the radically naturalistic and anthropocentric approach purported to be "scientific", and tried to liberate man from transcendental feelings and religion. A historian of science called the 18th century "The Age of Humanism".[9] The term <u>humanism</u> is of relatively recent origin. The word 'humanist' was first applied in fifteenth century Italy.[10] Renaissance authors from Petrarch to Erasmus called themselves humanists. Nineteenth century historians of philosophy broadened the meaning of the term by using it to refer to both late ancient authors of the philosophic life (Cicero) as well as Renaissance authors.

Until the twentieth century, there was no ambiguity regarding the meaning of a humanistic education. It referred to an esteem for and cultivation of classical ideas and patterns of life through studies of ancient history, philosophy, and languages. The architects of western aesthetic and intellectual culture were faithful to this tradition. It was not until the second half of the twentieth century that western civilization began to produce generations of educated people whose virtues are no longer molded on the patterns of Homer's heroes and according to Plutarch's "Lives".[11]

Early Twentieth Century Philosophies of Humanism

During the twentieth century, three basic trends of modern

humanism crystallized: first, a naturalistic and anthropocentric humanism advocated by anti-religious intellectuals; second, a non-naturalistic and personalistic humanism defended mainly by Christian philosophers; and third, a socialist humanism discussed mainly by Marxists. However, in spite of the great differences between the first and the third, both are rooted in the same philosophical naturalism. Whereas the second humanism stands fundamentally apart from the first and the third by rejecting the naturalistic outlook as well as with regard to the basic question of man's nature.

The naturalistic concept of humanism is held by both Marxists and most liberal philosophers who have protested against the belittling of the importance of man's natural conditions, the neglect of his earthly cravings, and the rights of his body. In European history this protest was fully justified in the 18th century as a reaction against the domination of religious dogmas and the expansion of Church authority.

The liberal naturalists and Marxist naturalists (except Marx himself) tend to see man as a product and continuation of nature, merely a step in the evolutionary process. The opposite view formulated by non-naturalists (religious or a-religious) emphasizes that the human animal is becoming _human_ just when he tries to transcend the limits of his earthly nature, at that moment when he tries to lift himself over the compulsions and cravings of his body and understands that personhood is a product of culture and not of nature. This is what Marx expressed in saying the "root of man is man".[12]

The representatives of naturalist humanism say: "The varieties and emphasis of naturalistic humanism include 'scientific', 'ethical', 'democratic', 'religious' and 'Marxist' humanism. Free thought, atheism, agnosticism, skepticism, deism, rationalism, ethical culture, and liberal religion all claim to be heir to the humanist tradition".[13] Nevertheless, this humanistic orientation was in general anti-religious, materialistic or agnostic. In certain cases it presented a proposition of secular "religion". R. W. Sellars wrote at the beginning of the century: "The Humanist's religion is the religion of one who says yes to the life here and now, of one who is self-reliant, fearless, intelligent and creative..."[14] Naturalistic humanists began to idolize humanity as an absolute value with which they have tried to replace the idea of God. Almost all intellectual circles of the 19th and first half of the 20th century believed that scientific and economic progress was unavoidably leading toward a civilization of happiness, that it was approaching the great humanitarian goal of affluence and of a democratic paradise of equality and freedom. They identify humanitarianism with humanism.

The early phase of these contemporary humanistic controversies took place at the very beginning of the 20th century when the triumphant development of capitalism displayed a total sacrifice of human values for the achievement of material welfare and when the opposite ideology of communism blindly followed the same direction. Then, several thinkers independently raised the problem of humanism. F.C.S. Schiller, founder of the humanist philosophy, wrote "Humanism is really in itself the simplest of philosophical standpoints: it is merely the perception that the philosophic problem concerns human beings striving to comprehend a world of human experiences by the resources of human minds".[15] Schiller assumed that Protagoras, because of his views summarized in the famous saying Man is the measure of all things, "should be regarded as the first recorded ancestor, not merely of the strictly humanist theory of knowledge, but also of the humanistic attitude towards life in general".[16] Schiller's naturalistic humanism soon met sharp criticism.

In America, Irving Babbitt was the most articulate twentieth century champion of humanistic education.[17] But Babbit was also an outstanding adversary of the naturalistic-anthropocentric type of humanism. At the beginning of the 20th century he published Literature and the American College, subtitled: "Essays in Defense of the Humanities".[18] For our present discussion on humanism, the distinction he made between humanism and humanitarianism is highly interesting. He wrote:

> The humanist, then, as opposed to the humanitarian, is interested in the perfecting of the individual rather than in schemes for the elevation of mankind as a whole. [The second is represented by the] humanitarian busybody with whom we are all so familiar nowadays, who goes around with schemes for reforming almost everything - except himself.[19]

Babbitt is so interesting to us today as an author, because he was one of the first who sounded the alarm regarding the lost balance between the humanities and natural sciences in the educational system of modern industrial societies. He argued that:

> The humanities need to be defended today against the encroachments of physical science, as they once needed to be defended against the encroachments of theology. But first we must...try to trace from its origins that great naturalistic and humanitarian movement which is not only taking the place of the humanistic point of view, but actually rendering it unintelligible for the men of the present generation.[20]

Although we may not agree completely with Babbitt's views on humanitarianism because there is an inner relation between these two notions and social trends, it is at the same time highly important to realize that humanitarians do not need to be humanists in the essential sense of the term, and that the reverse is also true. Humanitarianism is compatible with materialism, utilitarianism and scientism, while humanism could be related, independent or opposed to these philosophies.[21] Babbitt saw humanism as an effort to find a way between extremes. He affirmed that historically a humanist is one who "moved between an extreme of sympathy and an extreme of discipline and selection and became humane in proportion as he mediated between these extremes".[22] Following Blaise Pascal, he said that the true mark of excellence in man "is his power to harmonize in himself opposite virtues and to occupy all the space between them".[23] In his personal life as well as in his intellectual endeavors, man is a being who is "foredoomed to one-sidedness, yet who becomes humane only in proportion as he triumphs over this fatality of his nature, only as he arrives at that measure which comes from tempering his virtues, each by its opposite".[24] Marx could sign this statement.

Babbitt had good reason to disagree with the views of the other well-known advocate of humanism of his generation, F.C.S. Schiller.[25] For Schiller labeled as "humanism" his own philosophical views which were very close to a crude pragmatism and the assumptions of common sense realism. "Humanism", he wrote, "is really in itself the simplest of philosophical standpoints".[26] Babbitt saw humanism as an elevation of man over his own nature, while Schiller's humanism was deeply naturalistic and anthropocentric. He treated his philosophy as "humanistic" basically because he accepted without qualifications Protagoras' dictum "man is the measure". Today we are sharing Babbitt's reservation concerning Schiller's humanism which was indeed not much more than an "intellectual impressionism of a Protagoras".[27]

In spite of the fact that Babbitt presented a deeply penetrating analysis of the essential meaning of humanism as well as an astute understanding of political processes,[28] his works have been largely neglected and are today almost forgotten. To some extent, Babbitt may have been a victim of behaviorism because during the nineteen-twenties, under the flamboyant leadership of John Watson, that school of psychology generated a great deal of excitement and was regarded by many as the intellectual wave of the future. In addition, Babbitt's erudite style (which is sometimes pejoratively referred to as 'priggish') probably did little to endear him to Americans whose ears were accustomed to more equalitarian fare--even from professors. However, the most significant reasons for the premature demise of Babbitt's humanistic movement were the intellectual excesses of his less able followers and the formidable stature of his critics who included George Santayana and T. S. Eliot.

In essence the critics have charged Babbitt with advocating a kind of aristocratic authoritarianism. Santayana charges the humanism of Babbitt with propounding "ethical absolutism".[29] He describes the humanists of the Babbitt school as censorious minds "designed by nature to be the pillars of some priestly orthodoxy".[30] Santayana maintains that these people are not "humanists" in the old sense but rather Calvinists who hope to impose their absolutism upon others.[31] T. S. Eliot's remarks regarding Babbitt's humanism are even more alarming from our point of view as he accused him of combining positivistic tendencies with a Calvinist spirit.[32] Eliot also charged Babbitt with inconsistency:

> The great men whom he, Babbitt, holds up for our admiration and example are torn from their contexts of race, place, and time. And in consequence, Mr. Babbitt seems to me to tear himself from his own context. His humanism is really something quite different from that of his exemplars, but (to my mind) alarmingly like very liberal Protestant theology of the nineteenth century: it is, in fact, a product--a by-product--of Protestant theology in its last agonies....If I have interpreted him correctly, he is thus trying to build a Catholic platform out of Protestant planks. By tradition, an individualist, and jealous of the independence of individual thought, he is struggling to make something that will be valid for the nation, the race, the world.[33]

Eliot acknowledges the value of true humanism which he distinguishes from the humanism of the "zealots" of the Babbitt school. He lists the following functions of "true" humanism:

> I. The function of humanism is not to provide dogmas, or philosophical theories. Humanism, because it is general culture, is not concerned with philosophical foundations; it is concerned less with 'reason' than with common sense. When it proceeds to exact definitions it becomes something other than itself. II. Humanism makes for breadth, tolerance, equilibrium and sanity. It operates against fanaticism. III. The world cannot get on without narrowness, bigotry and fanaticism. IV. It is not the business of humanism to refute anything. Its business is to persuade, according to its unformulable axioms of culture and good sense. It does not, for instance, overthrow the arguments

or fallacies like Behaviourism: it operates by taste, by sensibility trained by culture. It is critical rather than constructive. It is necessary for the criticism of social life and social theories, political life and political theories. V. Humanism can have no positive theories about philosophy or theology. All that it can ask, in the most tolerant spirit, is: Is this particular philosophy or religion civilized or is it not? VI. There is a type of person whom we call the Humanist, for whom Humanism is enough. This type is valuable. VII. Humanism is valuable (a) by itself, in the 'pure humanist', who will not set up humanism as a substitute for philosophy and religion, and (b) as a mediating and corrective ingredient in a positive civilization founded on definite belief. VIII. Humanism, finally, is valid for a very small minority of individuals. But it is culture, not any subscription to a common programme or platform, which binds these individuals together. Such an 'intellectual aristocracy' has not the economic bonds which unite the individuals of an 'aristocracy of birth'.[34]

It is important to note that both Santayana and Eliot are themselves correctly labelled humanists. Santayana identifed with a naturalistic form of humanism while Eliot's humanism was of the non-naturalistic or transcendent variety. Neither challenged the value of the humanistic ethos itself, only Babbitt's elaboration of it. Since Babbitt and Eliot belong to the same class of intelligence, to the same category of broad minds and high spirits, their disagreement shows the depth of the problem as seen from two different perspectives within the same non-naturalistic camp of humanists.

We take the position that even if all of these criticisms are adequate and justified, Babbitt's ideas merit reconsideration in light of today's radically changed social climate. In the present technocentric world, the philosopher is not likely to become king. Rather it has become problematic whether philosophy itself will survive. And, at a time when scientists speak of humanizing technology, humanists too often are attempting to make their disciplines more scientific.[35] Similarly, when the newspapers regularly report the declining quality of higher education in America,[36] we can no longer regard an elite of talent and learning as a serious threat to democracy. In an overcrowded world a humanistic self-control may be the only means of avoiding imposition of external controls which would usurp personal freedom.

* * * * * *

Three Ideologies of Humanism

Naturalistic and anthropocentric humanists usually assume that religion is an obstacle to the development of human capacities. Therefore, they seek to replace duty to God with duty to man. Their goal is the humanitarian and utilitarian mastery of natural resources and human capacities. They believe in the possibility of a secular ethics which is autonomous and situational in character. The advocates of this type of humanism published their first Manifesto in 1933. This document was signed by thirty-four intellectuals who called themselves "religious humanists". We can only speculate as to the motives for the use of the adjective 'religious'. But the first points of the Manifesto show that it was simply an abuse of the term.[37]

In 1973 the next generation of naturalistic humanists set forth their Humanist Manifesto II, in the conviction "that humanism offers an alternative that can serve present-day needs and guide humankind toward the future".[38] The one hundred forty-four intellectuals who signed it (plus many others who signed it ex post) do not essentially differ from their predecessors. They share with them basically the same naturalistic views but did not use the term "religious". In the works of some of the naturalistic humanists a continuation of Comte's "Religion of Humanity" could be easily traced. One of these humanists wrote: "Modern Humanism is the immediate successor to the Positivist 'Religion of Humanity' ...though the Positivist Church is moribund, the modern Humanist feels, with Gilbert Murray, that what Comte was trying to say 'is not only sublime but true'".[39]

We assume, on the contrary that the humanist sociologist should warn people against the model of secularized theocracy with which Auguste Comte wanted to make us happy. In our view, it would be a total misunderstanding to treat Comte as a humanist.

By addressing ourselves to the points made in Manifesto I and II, we inevitably over-emphasize the unity of the position of these contemporary humanists. They themselves emphasize their diversity in their many publications--and correctly so! Even though the label 'naturalistic' may capture the general philosophic tenor of the manifestoes, it does not accurately describe the intellectual outlook of some of the individual supporters of this movement. Thus, for instance, one of the movement's most widely circulated publications is The Humanist Alternative. This book consists of thirty essays by different authors who attempt to define humanism. It is if anything eclectic including such diametrically opposed individuals as B. F. Skinner and Floyd Matson. Matson is certainly one of the most outspoken and effective critics of behaviorism and, in our opinion, one of the most able defenders of the sort of humanism we wish to advocate. In The Humanist Alternative, he sharply condemns many recent forms of naturalism in social science:

> The behaviourist view of man as a helpless pawn in the fell clutch of circumstance is paralleled in its anti-Humanism by the recurrently popular doctrine which traces human conduct to blind instinctive urges, notably that of aggression, arising from a primordial and predatory ancestry. From social Darwinists through classical Freudians to the new school of ethological determinists led by Konrad Lorenz, the instinctive theory of aggression has served to reinforce a fashionable pessimism concerning the human potential for rationality, responsibility and resourcefulness. The extraordinary acclamation which has been accorded this viewpoint in recent years (not, to be sure, among life-scientists, most of whom repudiate it, but among the literary intelligentsia and reading public) suggested the emergence of an intellectual and cultural backlash which expresses a desire for externally imposed constraint, discipline and authority...To the widespread 'distrust of reason' which Reinhard Bendix discerned among the social scientists a score of years ago must now be added the distrust of man himself-- the inclination to see him only as the victim or villain, never as the victor, in his personal drama of existence.[40]

The naturalistic humanism has been criticized by those authors who maintain the non-naturalistic view on the nature of man. They are mainly represented by Christian philosophers, but one can find them among philosophers of any world religion. However, it would be misleading to assume that one has to be religiously oriented to accept a non-naturalistic concept of man. Babbitt's humanism was a-religious although not anti-religious.[41] And Marx, in so far as he can be treated as a non-naturalistic humanist, can serve as another example of the fact that non-naturalism does not need to be linked with religion. The naturalists emphasize the anthropocentric character of the humanism they defend, and theocentric character of the humanism of their opponents. The non-naturalists, however, stress the point that their humanism is an attempt to arrive at a synthesis of the natural and supernatural (or natural and cultural). The core of this conflict of opinions is the definition of human nature.[42]

The long dispute between naturalistic humanism and Christian humanism was highly elevated in the 20th century when a large number of Christian thinkers began their counterattack against the anti-religious humanists, who since the end of the 18th century victoriously dominated intellectual life forming a climate of atheistic snobbery comparable to the snobbery of religious piety in the Middle Ages. The twentieth century's naturalistic humanism evoked a strong response from Christian intellectuals as well as from those who in general appreciate the social and/or moral significance of religion. Max Scheler's practical ethics[43] and the personalism of Emmanuel Mounier[44] were important contributions to the dialogue of Christian humanism. In 1932, T. S. Eliot wrote: "If you find examples of humanism which are anti-religious, or at least in opposition to the religious faith of the place and time, then such humanism is purely destructive, for it has never found anything to replace what it has destroyed".[45]

Among Christian philosophers who challenged the appeal of naturalist humanisms the most significant was the voice of Jacques Maritain whose directly responsive title, Humanisme Integral, was published in 1936.[46] For the contemporary discussion of humanism, his view on the need of pluralistic cooperation among peoples in search for common good has a particular significance. The social ideas of Christian humanism have been socially more advanced than those of the "naturalists". Maritain wrote: "From the point of view of integral humanism, it appears that this bourgeois type of humanity is seriously endangered and that its condemnation is deserved....in the eyes of the new humanism of which I am speaking, it is necessary to change bourgeois man...."[47]

It should be clear that the non-naturalistic, anti-anthropocentric, and non-Marxist humanism does not need to be Christian. Humanism does not even need to be religious in order to define man as different from all other species by virtue of his heroic efforts to transcend the limits of natural existence. These efforts are as old as civilization itself.

Thus, at the present time we are witnesses to three main types of humanism: naturalistic, non-naturalistic and Marxist.[48] Summarizing our considerations we should repeat: the first and the third humanisms basically accept the same concept of man. The second (in the case of Christian humanism) and the third have certain common social ideas. So, the fundamental philosophical line of division lays between the non-naturalistic humanism on one side, and the two naturalistic types, the liberal (bourgeois) and Marxists humanisms on the other side. The basic social contradiction divides liberal (bourgeois) humanism from that of Christian and Marxist (socialist) humanism. The exchange of opinions among these three groups of humanists shows that a dialogue is possible if not always fruitful unless the social attitudes of the interlocutors have something in common. Thus, the Marxists and the

Christians are leading an interesting dialogue which is modernizing the views of both sides, while a dialogue between naturalist-liberal humanists on the one hand and the Christian and Marxist humanists on the other hand did not develop at all.

After World War II the most interesting voice in the Christian-Marxist dialogue was that of Emmanuel Mounier, whose philosophy of personalism was one of the expressions of Christian humanism. Particularly his views on property and possession offered an understanding of these notions which raised a bridge between early Christian philosophers and some elements of Marxian thought.[49]

To understand the implications of the Marxist-Christian dialogue one has to recognize that there exists an important kinship between Christianity and communism, which has been denied until recent times by both sides. The Marxist movement rejected the transcendental and metaphysical elements of any religion but took over the ideas of Social Gospel and expressed them in a strictly materialistic way.[50] Therefore, in the capitalist West, the decline in transcendental feelings has been accompanied by a growing church emphasis upon the social gospel; in the communist countries where the state is attending to the realization of social gospel, this usurpation by the state of the traditional role of the chruch led to the resurgence of transcendental interest among Christians, and forced intellectuals on both sides to rethink their social attitudes.[51] The ideas of humanism appear to provide a common platform of discussion.

Some Christian ideas lay at the very heart of the socialist movement. Saint Simon, the aristocratic father of early socialism which was later called Utopian Socialism, joined socialist ideas with social elements of Christian thought and gave to his last work the title, New Christianity.[52] Lenin asserted in "Socialism and Religion": "Unity in this truly revolutionary struggle of an oppressed class for creating a paradise on the earth is more important to us than the identity of views among proletarians on the question of paradise in heaven".[53]

In their struggle to fashion a "socialism with a human face", modern Marxists have returned to the ideas of Utopian Socialism repeating the old statement of Saint Simon concerning happiness. A converted Stalinist, Adam Schaff, built an international reputation by discovering human elements in Marxism. In his Marxism and the Human Individual, he wrote that the followers of various ontological and epistemological views can "proclaim with conviction the principle of social eudaemonism, it means the view that the aim of life is to tend towards the greatest happiness of the broadest masses of people and that only in this way the personal happiness is achievable".[54]

The dialogue between the representatives of Christian and Marxist humanisms became worldwide during the pontificate of John XXIII.[55] However, the Magna Charta of the dialogue is Paul VI's Ecclesiam suam.[56] For communist leaders the opportunity for a dialogue has a strictly political character. It reinforces communist propaganda among the believers. On the other hand, Christians believe they can influence their adversaries' philosophical standpoint.[57]

One Marxist philosopher, summarizing modern Christian views, wrote:

> Progressive Christian thought in the West is attempting to separate religion from capitalism. Many 'leftist' theologians maintain that Marx's criticism of religion is fully justified with respect to Christianity of the past ages, when it was 'distorted'. In their opinion, however, this criticism does not apply to 'true' Christianity. Marxism allegedly became atheistic only for 'reasons of a passing nature'.[58]

From the Christian point of view, one anecdote attributed to the outstanding philosopher, I. M. Bochenski, is noteworthy. Sometime during the 1940's he supposedly stated, "After a few hundred years people will say 'Marxism...?' oh yes it was such a heresy in the 19th and 20th century".[59] The dialogue is a symptom of times when more and more people realize that only the blending and blurring of old ideological and religious antagonisms can help the earth's dwellers to face the problem of survival.

Because we affirm the importance of tradition, this does not mean that we wish merely to resurrect "a noble anachronism".[60] Rather, we would like to point out that it is difficult to know where you want to go unless you know where you have been. We are living in a new age with new problems and priorities. We require a humanism which can meet the challenges of this age.

We can learn from the 'humanisms' of the past--not only by examining the great ideals which they embodied, but also by frankly acknowledging and confronting the limits of those ideals as they have been articulated in historical forms of humanism. Our discussion of humanism would therefore be less than candid if we did not attempt to deal with the question of elitism.

The eminent art critic, Herbert Read, cheerfully observed, "Humanism is for the happy few".[61] Since Read considered himself to be among the elect, he was not much disturbed by the implications of his statement. Others have been less able to accept this premise so facilely. In Humanism and Terror, Maurice Merleau-

Ponty argues that: "no matter how real and precious the humanism of capitalist societies may be for those who enjoy it...it is the privilege of the few and not the property of the many".[62]

He asks:

> who dares to say that, after all, humanity has always progressed in the hands of a few and been sustained by its delegates and that we are the elite and the rest have only to wait their turn? Yet, this is the only honest reply. But this would mean acknowledging that Western humanism is a humanism of comprehension--a few mount guard around the treasure of Western culture; the rest are subservient. It would mean that Western humanism, like the Hegeliam State, subordinates empirical humanity to a certain idea of man and its supporting institutions. It would imply that in the end Western Humanism has nothing common with a humanism in extension, which acknowledges in every man a power more precious than his productive capacity, not in virtue of being an organism endowed with such and such a talent, but as a being capable of self-determination and of situating himself in the world.[63]

Similarly, Karl Mannheim was genuinely disturbed by what he regarded as a "sharp conflict" between the cultural ideals of humanism and democracy.[64] The last years of Mannheim's life were devoted to an effort to devise a means of translating those elements of humanism which are "indispensable for a full and rich life" into a cultural ideal of a "more universal appeal".[65] Or, in Merleau-Ponty's terms, Mannheim sought to integrate Western humanism and "humanism in extension".

Just because the dons of Eaton and Cambridge appointed themselves guardians of the treasures of Western humanism, this does not mean that we must accept their hubris or regard them as the only legitimate heirs of our common legacy. One does not need an advanced degree to appreciate the marvelous legend of Saint Francis and the virtues it inspired. Similarly, one does not need a bachelor of fine arts to be awed and humbled in the presence of an original Rembrandt or Breugle. Indeed, one might pause and reflect upon the fact that the most esoteric forms of art are themselves products of the age of science and specialization--for as Roger Shattuck has pointed out the "average perception" was the norm for Western art until the latter part of the nineteenth century, "from Leonardo to Caurbet, painters painted a tree as everyone sees a tree--or thinks he does".[66] Unquestionably today, there are tastes which must be educated, but this does not mean that only the educated have taste. Samuel Beckett is not for everyone,[67] but perhaps it is legitimate to ask if the values which inspired the folk art of Appalachia don't have as much to say about our common humanity as the dialogue of Vladimir and Estragon in Waiting for Godot?

But these are relatively frivolous matters in a world divided by hunger and ideological strife. Humanism has been implicated in a more serious form of elitism by virtue of its association with two other 'isms'--capitalism and liberalism. One of America's greatest presidents called himself a 'humanist' and kept slaves.[68] The record is no better abroad. In Europe humanistic education flourished. And who were the colonial administrators who denied the humanity of the subjugated races? They were products of this education. Sartre expressed this sentiment well during the Algerian crisis when he addressed his fellow Frenchmen:

> You, who are so liberal and so humane, who have such an exaggerated adoration of culture that it verges on affectation, you pretend to forget that you own colonies and that in them men are massacred in your name.[69]

Those who stood outside the Western tradition harbored this sentiment long before Sartre: it is present in muted form in Rabindranath Tagore's essays on Nationalism and in agonized outrage in Frantz Fanon's The Wretched of the Earth. Liberalism has given its response. When Europeans were massacred in Algeria and Angola, Sartre reports the liberals were "stupefied":

> ...they admit that they were not polite enough to the natives, that it would have been wiser and fairer to allow tnem certain rights in so far as this was possible; they ask nothing better than to admit them in batches and without sponsors to that very exclusive club, our species...[70]

Humanism has not responded. We respond, the face of true humanism--humanism-in-extension--is black, red, and yellow, not merely white. It is not just a male face but a female face as well. It is perhaps important to briefly address the last point. Until this century, the humanistic education was a male preserve as Virginia Woolf so skillfully documented in A Room of Her Own and Three Guineas. Humanism was born of the 'old boy tradition'. Thus, for example, George Santayana's biographers saw no contradiction in the fact that they could simultaneously describe him as a 'humanist' and a 'misogynist'. Recently, some feminists have expressed a concern that the growing interest in humanism may be used as a means of ideologically undermining women's demand for equality. As Robin Morgan puts it, "'humanism' is a word often misused as a bludgeon to convince women that we must put our suffering back at the bottom of the priority list".[71] We agree with Morgan that this is a <u>misuse</u> of the term humanism. A "humanism in extension" must include the feminine experience just as it must encompass the multi-racial experience--and this inclusion cannot be merely rhetorical.

We do not delude ourselves about humanism. We endorse it in full recognition of the fact that it is not a pure vessel. It is tainted by its past associations but it is also ennobled by its past achievements. Albert Salomon admonishes us not to forget western humanism's greatest contribution to world civilization:

> Freedom is a way of life, incorporated in our political and legal institutions, is an accomplishment of the world of the West. Regardless of the profoundities and sensitivities of Chinese and Indian philosophies for them freedom was never a moral, intellectual, or spiritual problem. When we agree with opponents that imperialism and colonialism have corrupted the postulate and image of freedom that the people of the West have fought and suffered for, we may tell them something else.......<u>Freedom was an accomplishment of the West--and we should not forget it.</u>[72]

For us, humanism is merely the least flawed hope we have in a less than flawless world. We acknowledge that "humanism in extension" is still a utopian ideal. However, we will once more risk the charge of elitism by subscribing to

> ...Bell and Mau's dictum (1971) that intellectuals have a responsibility to create utopian images of the future, so they may act as virtuous cycles, as self-fulfilling prophecies.[73]

For sociologists <u>humanism</u> is not one of the several social theories nor a hypothesis; rather, it is a philosophical perspective which centers on man; it is an attempt to defend the human realm against the demands of society, state, church, science, technology and any other force, organized or not, which threatens man's dignity, freedom and/or free self-realization.

CHAPTER I FOOTNOTES

1. See: Irving Babbitt, <u>Democracy and Leadership</u> (Boston, Mass: Houghton Mifflin Co., 1924), p. 3.

2. Werner Jaeger, <u>Paideia, The Ideals of Greek Culture</u> [transl. from German by Gilbert Highet] (New York: Oxford University Press, 1962), p. xxiii-xxiv.

3. Werner Jaeger assumes that Protagoras is the root of the anthropocentric while Plato of the theocentric humanisms. <u>Humanism and Theology</u>, Milwaukee, 1943. Some humanists might object to our assertion that non-naturalistic humanism does not need religion as its background. T. S. Eliot writes: "...the humanistic point of view is auxiliary to and dependent upon the religious point of view". Eliot, "The Humanism of Irving Babbitt" in <u>Selected Essays of T. S. Eliot</u> (New York: Harcourt, Brace and World, Inc., 1932), p. 427.

Babbitt speaks of "co-operation" between humanism and Christianity. While Babbitt denies humanism is "either precarious or parasitical", he acknowledges, "Religion indeed may more readily dispense with humanism than humanism with religion..." Irving Babbitt, "Humanism: An Essay at Definition" in Norman Foerster, ed., <u>Humanism and America</u> (New York: Farrar and Rinehart, 1930), p. 37 and pp. 43-44.

4. Jean-Paul Sartre, <u>Search For a Method</u> [translated with an Introduction by Hazel E. Barnes] (New York: Random House, 1963), p. vii.

5. Martin Heidegger, <u>Uber den Humanismus</u>, Vittorio Klostermann, Frankfurt A-M., 1947, p. 11.

6. One critic, George Santayana, would suggest that it was perhaps too humanistic: "In the Old Testament and even in the New, there were humanistic maxims, such as that the Sabbath was made for man, and not man for the Sabbath. Epicurus had crept into Ecclesiastes, and Plato into the Gospel of Saint John; and by a bolder stroke of humanism than any one had yet thought of, God himself had been made man". Santayana sardonically remarks, "the voice that reverberates from the heavens is too clearly a human voice". <u>Santayana on America</u>, p. 145.

7. Werner Jaeger tried to outline his views "of the situation of humanism with regard to medieval tradition and the problem of theology" in particular in three parts:

   1. The humanistic aspect of St. Thomas' theocentric view of the world;

   2. The position and special character of his age in the historical series of revivals of classical culture to which it belongs;

   3. The position of humanism with regard to the theological problem or the two basic forms of humanism.

   <u>Humanism and Theology</u> (under the auspices of the Aristotelian Society of Marquette University: Milwaukee, 1943), p. 5.

8. Leonardo da Vinci, who is the greatest mind of that age, was never treated as a humanist because of his lack of training in classics, despite his contribution to the 'naturalistic humanism' in modern ages.

9. "Perhaps the most adequate designation of it would be the Age of Humanism. It was the century in which the knowledge acquired was made known to far wider circles than had ever been the case previously, and was applied, moreover, in every possible direction in order to improve the conditions of human life. All the intellectual and moral forces of the age were harnessed to the chariot of human progress as they had never been harnessed to it before". <u>A History of Science, Technology and Philosophy in the 18th Century</u> (New York: Harper and Brothers, 1961), Vol. 1, p. 27.

10. Irving Babbitt, "Humanism: An Essay at Definition" in <u>Humanism and America</u>, edited by Norman Foerster (New York: Farrar and Rinehart, 1930), p. 26.

11. This ideal undoubtedly had broader circulation in Europe than in America where more pragmatic interests shaped higher education (particularly, the Land-Grant Colleges). The humanistic ideal was, however, preserved in America by the more elite universities which, of course, were also the most prestigious.

12. In the Marxist camp the chief advocate of naturalist view was Engels. See: L. Kolakowski, "le Marxism de Marx et le Marxism d'Engels", <u>Philosphie Contemporaine</u>, Paris, 1971.

13. *Humanist Manifestoes* I and II. (Buffalo: Prometheus Books, 1973), p. 15.

14. R. W. Sellars, *The Next Step in Religion, An Essay Toward the Coming Renaissance* (New York: The Macmillan Company, 1918).

15. F.C.S. Schiller, *Studies in Humanism* (London: Macmillan & Co., 1907), p. 12.

16. F.C.S. Schiller, *Our Human Truths*, (New York: Columbia University Press, 1939), p. 18.

17. Irving Babbitt (1864-1933), literary critic and independent philosopher. Professor of comparative literature in Harvard, became a leader of the "new-humanism" movement. For the discussion on our present problems, three of his works deserve a particular attention: *Literature and American College*, 1908, *Rousseau and Romanticism*, 1919, and *Democracy and Leadership*, 1924.

18. I. Babbitt, *Literature and the American College, Essays in Defense of the Humanities* (New York: Houghton, Mifflin and Co., 1908).

19. *Ibidem*, p. 8 and 9.

20. *Ibidem*, chapter "What is Humanism?", p. 31.

21. In ancient times science had a humanistic character in the sense that it provided a way for the intellectual development of the individual but it did not have the *social consequences* which today are threatening both our individual and social existence.

22. Babbitt, *op. cit.*, p. 22.

23. *Ibidem*, p. 22.

24. *Ibidem*, p. 23.

25. F.C.S. Schiller (1864-1937), Oxford professor, main works: *The Riddles of the Sphinx* (1899), *Humanism* (1903), and *Studies in Humanism* (1907).

26. F.C.S. Schiller, *Studies in Humanism* (London: Macmillan & Co., 1907), p. 12.

27. Babbitt, *Literature*........., p. 26.

28. See Irving Babbitt, Democracy and Leadership (Boston: Houghton Mifflin Co., 1924).

29. George Santayana, "The Genteel Tradition at Bay" in Santayana on America, edited by Richard Colton Lyon (New York: Harcourt, Brace & World, 1968), p. 138.

30. Santayana quoted in Lyon's "Introduction" to Santayana on America, p. xxix.

31. Ibidem.

32. "It is Humanism's positivistic tendencies that are alarming. In the work of the master, and still more in that of the disciples, there is a tendency towards a positive and exclusive dogma. Conceive a Comtism from which all the absurdities had been removed--and they form I admit, a very important part of the Comtist scheme--and you have something like what I imagine Humanism might become". T. S. Eliot, "Second Thoughts About Humanism".

33. T. S. Eliot, "Second Thoughts About Humanism" in Selected Essays of T. S. Eliot (New York: Harcourt, Brace & World, 1932), p. 430.

34. T. S. Eliot, "The Humanism of Irving Babbitt" in Selected Essays..., p. 422. Eliot, "Second Thoughts...", pp. 436-437.

35. John Wilkinson, "The Civilization of the Dialogue" in The Dissenting Academy, edited by Theodore Roszak (New York: Pantheon Books, 1967), p. 172.

36. As measured by student scores on standardized nationwide tests.

37. Perhaps they wished to avoid being labelled 'atheists' or 'agnostics' during the somewhat repressive religious climate of the era, i.e., the Scopes trial had taken place only a short time earlier. Authors explained their religious views as follows: "First: Religious humanists regard the universe as self-existing and not created. Second: Humanism believes that man is a part of nature and that he has emerged as a result of a continuous process. Third: Holding an organic view of life, humanists find traditional dualism of mind and body must be rejected". Humanist Manifestoes I and II (Buffalo, N.Y.: Prometheus Books, 1973).

38. Ibidem, p. 13.

39. Hector Hawton, "Humanism: The Third Way", *The Humanist*, 1951, (quoted from Margaret Knight, ed., *Humanist Anthology*, 1961, p. 170).

40. Floyd Matson, "Toward a New Humanism" in *The Humanist Alternative*, edited by Paul Kurtz (Buffalo, N.Y.: Prometheus Books, 1973), pp. 95-96.

41. Babbitt was not hostile to religion but it was not a primary focus of his concern.

42. A. Etcheverry, *Le conflict actual des humanismes*, Paris 1955, p. 7.

43. Max Scheler (1874-1928), German phenomenologist. See: *Der Formalismus in der Ethik und die materiale Wertethik, Vom Ewigen im Menschen in Werke*, A. Francke AG, Berne 1954.

44. Emmanuel Mounier (1905-1950) was one of the most outstanding French founders of Personalism.

45. T. S. Eliot, "Humanism of Irving Babbitt" in *Selected Essays*, 1932.

46. Jacques Maritain, *Integral Humanism* [trans. by J. W. Evans] (New York, 1968).

47. J. Maritain, op. cit., pp. 88 and 89.

48. The old Marxists lost their struggle for the recognition of their ideology as a science. The younger generation of Marxists, particularly after the "discovery" of crimes (justified by Lenin's views on the usefulness of mass terror, and totally exploited by Stalin), began to turn toward the humanistic elements in their scripture, and they found and are emphasizing certain common points in social ideas of Christianity and communism.

49. See: Emmanuel Mounier, *Vom Kapitalistischen Eigentumsbegriff zum Eigentum des Menshen.* (Vita Nova Verlag) Luzern 1936.

50. See: Franz Henrich (ed.) *Humanismus Zwischen Christentum and Marxismus* (Rasel-Verlag) Munchen 1970.

51. See: A. Gella, in a panel discussion (held at the Third Congress of the Polish Institute of Arts and Sciences in America, McGill University, Montreal, on May 16, 1975): "Poland in the Last Quarter of the Twentieth Century, *Slavic Review*, Dec. 1975.

52. Henri de Saint-Simon, *Nouveau Christianism*, Paris 1825; first English translation, 1834.

53. Lenin, "Sotsialism a relighia" (quoted from Janusz Kuczynski, "The Marxist-Christian Dialogue" in *Dialectics and Humanism*, Warsaw 1974, vol. 1, no. 2, p. 118).

54. Adam Schaff, *Marksizm a jednostka ludzka*, Omega, Warzawa 1965, pp. 173-4.

55. See: Frederick J. Adelmen, S.J., *From Dialogue to Epilogue*, The Hague 1968, p. 61.

56. *Ecclesiam suam*, the first encylcical letter of Paul VI (Aug. 6, 1964).

57. This influence became particularly visible in communist countries, where the old anti-religious attitudes of the proletariat was undermined by the fact that the Church in these countries is no longer an ally of the exploiters and the ruling class but just the reverse. It is on the side of the oppressed societies.

58. J. Kuczynski, *op. cit.*, p. 119.

59. I. M. Bochenski, O.P., Professor of Philosophy in Fribourg, Switzerland.

60. Babbitt admits he was accused of this. Irving Babbitt, "Humanism: An Essay at Definition" in *Humanism and America*, edited by Norman Foerster (New York: Farrar and Rinehart, 1930), p. 27.

61. Herbert Read, "Julien Benda and the New Humanism", an introduction to Benda's *The Betrayal of the Intellectuals* (Boston: The Beacon Press, 1930), p. xxxii.

62. Maurice Merleau-Ponty, *Humanism and Terror* (Boston: Beacon Press, 1969), p. 175.

63. *Ibidem*, pp. 175-176.

64. Karl Mannheim, *Essays On The Sociology of Culture* (London: Kegan-Paul, 1962), p. 230.

65. *Ibidem*.

66. Roger Shattuck, *The Banquet Years* (Garden City: Doubleday & Co., Inc., 1961), pp. 40-41.

67. Beckett enthusiasts might even dispute this point. Thus Martin Esslin reports that Waiting For Godot has been successfully performed for prisoners at San Quentin and poverty-stricken illiterate children in Mississippi as well as Parisian cosmopolitans. The Theatre of the Absurd (Garden City: Doubleday and Co., 1961).

68. Thomas Jefferson.

69. Jean-Paul Sartre, "Preface" to Frantz Fanon, The Wretched of The Earth (New York: Grove Press, Inc., 1968), p. 14.

70. Ibidem, p. 20.

71. Robin Morgan, "Rights of Passage", Ms. Magazine, Sept. 1975, p. 98.

72. Albert Salomon, In Praise of Enlightenment (Cleveland: World Publishing, 1962), p. 400.

73. Cited by Pauline Bart, "Sexism and Social Science" in Journal of Marriage and the Family, Vol. 33, No. 4, Nov. 1971, p. 742.

CHAPTER II

POSITIVISM: IDOLATRY IN ACADEMIC SOCIOLOGY

   An almost symphonic sense of order seems to emerge as one traces the development of scientific rationalism in western thought. Many thinkers from the ancient philosophers through Hegel and Marx to some contemporaries agreed that man's facility to reason would enable him to understand the true nature of reality--perhaps Hegel's famous proscription, "The Real is rational and the rational is real", is the classic expression of this attitude.[1] Rationalism and empiricism, the main currents of thought in the seventeenth century, found reconciliation and expression in the philosophy of the Enlightenment. It was believed that by learning the laws of the universe and of society, man's social behavior could be ordered in accordance with these laws. The faith in man's ability to initiate progress--the major intellectual hallmark of the Enlightenment--was fused with the mechanical, observable, predictable Newtonian conception of the universe. In short, the eighteenth-century belief in the perfectibility of man grew out of the seventeenth-century belief in a rationally understandable and predictable universe. As much as man reasoned, however, societal problems remained. The French Revolution and consequent rapid social change did much to disturb the placid intellectual optimism of previous centuries, but the commitment to order and rationality remained paramount in the minds of men. This is most vividly portrayed by the positivist philosophy of Auguste Comte.

As a general tendency of modern science, positivism is understood here as a background of many schools of 19th and 20th century thought, though they formally rejected "positivism" as it was envisioned by Auguste Comte. This tendency appeared in European thought much earlier than Comte verbalized it and still dominates our intellectual life under some new names like behaviorism, neopositivism, logical empiricism and to some extent pragmatism.[2] Even Marxism, which is so officially opposite to positivism, bears an imprint of the positivistic tradition.

   In the popular sense of the word positivism includes at least three basic philosophical tendencies in modern sciences: <u>positiv-</u>

ism in the narrower sense of Comte's philosophy; empiricism of the British tradition; and both traditional and dialectical materialism.[3] We place primary emphasis upon the origin and impact of Comte's positivism, because this marked a formal beginning of sociology. We also focus on one particular form of the positivistic orientation, behaviorism, because of its pervasive influence upon modern social science.

The consideration of social problems, which we today call "sociological", can be found in all ancient religious and philosophical traditions. A first attempt to present a systematic analysis of social life, its laws and institutions, in the form of a new science was made by Auguste Comte. His mentality was shaped by two revolutions. On the one hand he reacted against the chaos brought to social life by the upheavals of the French Revolution, and on the other hand, he took for granted the promises of the industrial revolution and some optimism related to the subsequent growth of capitalism. His educational background separated him from the canons of the traditional philosophy of the time. Comte did not have a classical or humanistic education. He was the first, though not the last man in the formative age of sociology, who was trained in polytechnic sciences. Hence, his knowledge and understanding of human history was limited and often naive. His greatness, however, depended upon the fact that he perfectly understood, an essential need of his time, the need for the liberation of science from the burdens of traditional philosophy. Sociology[4] was deemed by him to be the crown of all sciences. Although he proposed that sociology should not only use all the methods of the natural sciences but also an historical approach, the general principles underlying his sociology were the same as those which applied in the natural sciences. Rejecting epistemological and metaphysical problems and concerns, he tried to build a new philosophy geared to practical aims and natural scientific methodologies. For the further development of the social sciences, Comte's total rejection of psychology was imperative because he assumed one could not be an observer and the observed, or in other terms, the object as well as the subject of an investigation. Since then, for a long period, positivistic sociologists have avoided problems of motivation, value, attitude, intuition, judgment, and introspection which are tied on the one side to sociology but on the other side to psychology.

The influence of Comte's views went far beyond sociology. Criticizing the method of introspection, Comte paved the way for behaviorism in psychology. A hundred years later many sociologists began to adopt behavioristic concepts from psychology. They contended that sociology could be provided with a stable claim to scientific status only if it concentrated on the study of "behavior" rather than "action" which has a voluntaristic connotation. The mechanistic concept of man and phenomena, a notion which was already outdated in physics, reached its highest expression within the social sciences in the twentieth century. In spite of this, some historians used to say that the nineteenth century began in 1830 with the publication of Comte's Cours de Philosophie Positive.[5]

Many of the intellectual streams of the tradition of scientific rationalism found confluence in Comte's thought. It is well known that many natural scientists worked on essentially positivistic principles long before Comte verbalized them. Comte himself saw the beginning of the positive orientation in the thought of Francis Bacon, Rene Descartes, Galileo, and David Hume. We have to recall here the fundamental concepts of those great men of the past which became the components of Comte's philosophy and sociology. Under the name of positivism, these ideas shaped all that has been great as well as some that now appear to be fundamentally dangerous in the development of modern science. From Bacon, Comte borrowed the concept of science as a power;[6] from Descartes, the method of analysis;[7] from Galileo, the conviction that the task of science is a quantitative description of measurable phenomena;[8] and from Hume, the conviction that the world of science is and should be free of value judgments, because there does not exist any logical transition between facts and values.[9]

All these ideas were in circulation before Comte. He used them to build a philosophical system and in consequence helped these ideas to dominate intellectual life in the modern world. Although today nobody can question the fact that the rapid development and great achievements of natural science and subsequently that of modern technology have been possible specifically due to the ideas of great founders of modern science, they are also responsible for the development of "technical ideologies" and a robot mentality easily manipulated by technocrats of the positivistic school.

The principles of positivism contain a set of directives for scientific procedure together with certain ideological commandments. Therefore, to understand the drama of science and our participation in it, one would have to consider them carefully. They suggest that science should be concerned: (1) with real subjects, i.e., those which are available to our intellect, (2) with problems of a utilitarian character, (3) with certain (unquestionable) subject matters, and (4) with precise questions only.[10] With the triumph of these principles, science ceased to be a purely intellectual endeavor. In agreement with Bacon's view that "knowledge and human power are synonymous", science had become an instrument for a subjugation of the natural environment and organization of the human world. Since Comte laid the foundation of positivism, Bacon's old idea was revitalized: "the real and legitimate goal of the sciences is the endowment of human life with new inventions and riches".[11]

What is under criticism today is the ideological ethos tied to the general positivistic outlook and concept of science.[12] Today the error of authors who believed that the impact of modern science brought the "End of Ideology" is embarrassingly evident.[13] Therefore, any criticism of positivism should be informed of its complexity and should not deny the value of those of its elements which are essential for scientific inquiry and for achievement in the natural sciences.

When Marx launched his attack on Comte's philosophy and sociology, his criticism was limited only to the social, above all, the class bias of this philosophy and sociology. Marx rejected the positive philosophy of Comte and his disciples asserting, "Positive philosophy means ignorance of everything positive" and condemned the theological spirit and prophetic fervor of Positivism claiming that it is "profoundly rooted in Catholic soil".[14] The essential difference between Marx and positivistic sociologists such as Saint-Simon, Comte, and Durkheim was ideological. As Nicholas Regush succinctly states, "Whereas Karl Marx believed the developing bourgeois society contained the seeds of its own destruction, Academic Sociology was to develop a science determined to perfect the new society", however, both traditions subscribed to the notion that "a sociological search can bring knowledge valid enough to be systematically applied".[15] Thus Marx's criticism is only marginal to the contemporary negative attitude toward the tradition of positivism in the social sciences. Marx wanted to use science in a similar manner as Comte, but for different social goals. Comte and Marx both sought to develop a 'science' of society following the natural science model. As H. Stuart Hughes has pointed out, Marx shared the positivistic "conviction of the inevitable limitation on human freedom--whether by physical circumstance or through emotional conditioning which has become the unstated major premise of contemporary social science".[16] Marx, like Pareto and Freud, thought that what is "deepest" in human conduct, for the most part, falls into a pattern or mere repetition. Marx believed this repetition could be studied empirically. His empirical studies were to provide a 'scientific basis' for socialism. In the Economic and Political Manuscripts of 1844, Marx expressed his early ideas on the nature of an empirical 'science of man': "Sense experience (cf. Feuerbach) must be the basis of all science. Science is only genuine science when it proceeds from sense experience, in the two forms of sense perception and sensuous need, that is, only when it proceeds from Nature. The whole of history is a preparation for 'man' to become an object of sense perception, and for the development of human needs (the needs of man as such). History itself is a real part of natural history, of the development of Nature into man. Natural science will one day incorporate the science of man, just as the science of man will incorporate natural science; there will be a single science".[17] Marx, like Comte, wanted to use his philosophy for practical goals. The effective use of scientific methods was, at that time, most clearly verbalized in positivism and Marx saw no other way but to apply them to his concept of political and social action.[18] Thus, any contemporary criticism of positivistic ideology should go much further than that born as a direct response to Comte's thought.

CHAPTER II FOOTNOTES

1. Hegel quoted by William Barrett, *Irrational Man* (Garden City: Doubleday and Company, Inc., 1963), p. 159.

2. Leszek Kolakowski in his *Alienation of Reason: A History of Positivist Thought* (Garden City: Anchor Books, 1969) described the positivistic characteristics of the main philosophical systems from Hume to the Vienna Circle.

3. Comte's positivism, Mill's empiricism, and Marx's dialectical materialism were formulated subsequently in three decades between 1830 and 1860 but their united influence lasts to our days.

4. The term "sociology", which Comte coined, was offensive to the linguistic taste of scholars with humanistic backgrounds because the conjunction derived from the Latin *socio-* with the Greek *-logy* sounded monstrous and absurd.

5. Wladyslaw Tatarkiewicz, *Historia Filozofii*, Warszawa, 1950, vol. III, p. 7.

6. Francis Bacon (1561-1626) in *New Atlantis* developed the idea of technocracy; in his *Utopia* scientific technicians were fully in charge of state matters. See: V.C.G. Trew, *The Influence of Francis Bacon on Modern Thought*, 1948, and B. Farrinsten, *Francis Bacon, Philosopher of Industrial Science*, 1951.

7. Rene Descartes (1596-1650) suggested three kinds of operation for mathematical procedure: intuition, deduction and enumeration. In the positivistic tradition, only the *enumeratie* procedure survived. See: L. J. Beck, *The Methods of Descartes: A Study of the "Regular"*, 1952.

8. Galileo Galilei (1564-1642). Since the time of Pythagoras and his sect, Galileo was the first who assumed that the book of nature is written in mathematical language. See: *Discoveries and Opinions of Galileo*, ed. by Stillman Drake, 1955.

9. David Hume (1711-1776), in his analysis of causality, and in *An Inquiry Concerning the Principles of Morals* (1751), laid the groundwork for this statement.

10. Wladyslaw Tatarkiewicz, op. cit., vol. 3, p. 25.

11. Francis Bacon, Novum Organum (Chicago: Britannica Great Books, 1952), p. 120.

12. See: Henryk Skolimowski, Zmierzch Swiatopogladu Naukowego (London, 1974) and the review article by A. Gella, "On the Crisis of Science, Technology and Ideology", Polish Review, New York, No. 4, 1975.

13. Daniel Bell's recent justitication of his The End of Ideology (Glencoe, 1960) in Contemporary Sociology (3:2, p. 107) is revealing: "...I did not say 'ideology was ending' in the fifties. I was writing of the erosion and 'exhaustion' of the mood in the fifties, and made the specific point that intellectuals, particularly young ones, would always hunger for ideology. And I indicated further the new forms of Third World ideology that would arise". Ignoring the question of whether or not Bell is guilty of misrepresentation in titling his book "The End of Ideology" when that book, in his words, did not say 'ideology was ending', it is still clear that ideology to Bell is something hungered for by intellectuals who are either immature or from 'backward' nations. The ending of ideology coincides with the triumph of positivism (whether or not it is called that), which, of course, is to Bell without ideology or values of its own.

14. Marx quoted from Capital, Vol. 1, 1st ed; and a letter to Engels, Mar 20, 1869, T. B. Bottomore and Maximilian Rubel, Karl Marx: Selected Writings (New York: McGraw-Hill, 1964), p. 13.

15. Nicholas Regush, Introduction to Visibles and Invisibles: A Primer for a New Sociological Imagination (Boston: Little, Brown and Company, 1973), p. 10.

16. H. Stuart Hughes, Consciousness and Society (New York: Random House, 1961), p. 4.

17. Bottomore and Rubel, Karl Marx: Selected Writings, op. cit., p. 70. Hilde Weiss shows how Marx attempted to attain "an exact description of actual social conditions" through the technique of survey analysis in "Karl Marx's 'Enquete Ouvriere", in T. Bottomore, ed., Karl Marx (Englewood Cliffs: Prentice-Hall, Inc., 1973), p. 173. Marx thought of himself as a scientist and a political activist. In his view, theory grew out of action and action out of theory in an inseparable dialectical relationship. Therefore, Hughes contends Marx regarded "'bourgeois' social science as 'patently a fraud'". Nevertheless, Hughes argues that a careful examination of Marx's own writings reveals that "the entanglement of scien-

tific investigation and practical precept was not so tight as he imagined"--"In the vast, overlapping, disparate corpus of Marxian writings...there were certain sequences of doctrine that could be separated from those with which they had originally been aligned, and were hence capable of independent application". Consequently, many elements of Marxian social theory have been assimilated by academic sociology. Hughes, Consciousness and Society, op. cit., p. 68. By the 1890's 'critical' Marxism was so subordinate to messianic Marxism that Hughes reports, "Marxism was to figure in the intellectual renovation of the 1890's as an aberrant, and peculiarly insidious, form of the reigning cult of positivism. It loomed on the cultural horizon as the last and most ambitious of the abstract and pseudoscientific ideologies that had bewitched European intellectuals since the early eighteenth century". Hughes, ibidem, p. 42.

18. Seymour M. Lipset remarked, "Karl Marx was a rationalist and positivist who believed that political action must be based on scientific knowledge. He spent twenty years in the British Museum working every day to analyze the nature of the capitalistic society. Some years later, when young Marxists began to turn out books, explaining that everything was related to economic factors--art, culture, political events--Marx said, 'if this be Marxism, then I am not a Marxist'. Friedrich Engels said that if these young Marxists thought all one had to do was have inspiration and theory, what did they think Marx had been doing in the British Museum for twenty years". Seymour M. Lipset, "Are Rationality and Reason Dead?" The Humanist (March/April), 1975, p. 10.

CHAPTER III

A CRACK IN THE IDOL: THE CONTEMPORARY CRISIS IN SCIENCE

Today we are facing totally new problems which were unknown for those who laid the foundations of modern science. We are, therefore, compelled to reconsider the relation between science and society in a rudimentary new way with implications which extend far beyond both the positivist concept of "value free" science and the Marxist focus on its class aspect. The narrow empirical approach within the scientific ethos of the western world has been carried to such an extreme that it now produces "large-scale detrimental consequences for our entire civilization".[1]

The role of science as an independent intellectual inquiry was gradually ended during the twentieth century when it became a component of all social enterprises.[2] Since the beginning of the nineteenth century, science has become necessary for industrial and technological development as well as for military purposes. Therefore, science has enjoyed industrial and military support, but it also soon found itself dependent upon this "patronage". In this circumstance, science lost much of its independence and was reduced to a component part of the techno-industrial growth of our civilization.

Even the American Physical Society was forced to consider this fact in 1969 when a group calling themselves Scientists and Engineers for Social and Political Action introduced a "No war research" resolution at their annual convention. The resolution stated:

> Fundamentally, we have come to view the problems of science as flowing from the basic problems of political and economic control in the society. We have learned that technology follows the logic of profit and that control of funding dominates the direction of scientific work. In short, <u>scientific activity is not value-free in this or any</u>

other _society_.[3]

The great prestige of science, won during the seventeenth, eighteenth, and nineteenth centuries, caused a process which we can call the inflation of scientific production. From the fact that almost 60,000,000 pages of "scientific" work is published per year, many authors proudly emphasize that more scientists are living now than during all previous centuries. This is a great exaggeration. Ninety percent or more of those who enjoy the privilege of calling themselves "scientists" are as a matter of fact only "technicians" in various fields of science.

An interesting insight into this problem may be found in mathematics. The common man has an impression that the greatest mathematical geniuses lived in our century and opened the Atomic Age by their achievements. However, mathematicians are of a different opinion. At least some of them assume that the last actual mathematical genius was Riemann (1826-1866), while Albert Einstein, John von Neuman, David Hilbert, and Herman Weil belong to the first generation of great "engineers" who pushed mathematical inquiries toward specialization.[4] This marriage of technical orientation and specialization is killing the possibility of the kind of free flow of thought which typified the geniuses of the past. The process of specialization, which narrows the horizon of a scientist, diminishes his intellectual possibilities to search for new aspects of the studied subject, to achieve a new insight by comparing and combining various questions, problems, and findings, and to stimulate and refresh his own intellectual intuition by contact with ideas apparently unrelated to his own interests. The negative effects of specialization are known in all fields of science.

Modern specialists are occupied not so much with intellectual inquiry, but with "producing information" based on the available data. Their achievements, however, are largely the products of well-established "machinery" of scientific methods and techniques. In a figurative way we can say, they only turn the winding-key of a tremendous machine which was built by the greatest minds of the past. Its mechanism is rather simple. First, it selects available material with a blissful feeling that this can be done independently of human and social values, because one of the grandfathers of positivism, David Hume, imposed upon us a conviction that there is no logical passage between the world of values and the world of facts.[5] Then, the cog-wheels, following Galileo's idea, quantitatively fragment this "freely" selected subject matter. "Freely" in this context means to have the right to follow the principles of utilitarianism, practicality, pragmatism and class interest which were successfully programmed into our scientific mind respectively by Bentham, Comte, James, and Marx, together with Pareto. From the next turn of our winding-key we get further results generated by the famous Cartesian analytical method which are important for man's conquest of nature. For the last three hundred years it mattered little that the results were predicated upon a tenuous assumption that all entities are simply a sum total of their parts. Nonetheless, we achieved something important for the further realization of Francis Bacon's program which suggested that we treat science as a power in our conquest of nature. Further methodological steps such as induction, reduction, representation, and verification are additional links in the chair of accepted scientific procedure.[6]

In the nineteenth century most of the greatest achievements of science possessed a highly humanitarian character. Medical discoveries and the rapid growth of hygienics contributed to the control of epidemics. Technological inventions based on empirical and experimental research in the natural sciences seemed to be ushering mankind into a millenium of peace and happiness. The development of science shaped by the ideas of positivism, empiricism, and dialectical as well as mechanical materialism had no outstanding adversaries. However, there were internal struggles among those who shared the enthusiasm for science but wanted to harness her to different chariots.

For a long time, people did not notice that science began to change its goal. From its very beginnings, more than two and a half millennia ago, men of science as well as philosophers were undertaking a search for truth. They believed that truth as a full knowledge about our universe is available and only our limited collection of data, our far from perfect methods, and the weaknesses of our intellect prevented us from possessing its full light. The great hope that each new discovery, each new invention in methodology, and each new theory approaches a final knowledge of truth, was a powerful motive in the development of science.

However, in the 19th century, the very concept of the search for truth was undermined by new theories in mathematics, physics, and logic. First, the idea of truth was questioned in mathematics by Georg F. B. Riemann and Nicholas Ivanovich Lobachevski when they discovered that the axioms of Euclidian geometry might be replaced by others. Then physicists delivered the explanation of the nature of light which was the next step in questioning the concept of truth. In logic, L.E.G. Brouwer challenged the belief that the laws of classical logic of the Aristotelian tradition have an absolute validity, and J. Lukasiewicz's studies of alternative logics added the next step in the developing suspicion concerning the achievability of truth. In accord with these revelations in science, philosophers began to change their views of the tasks of philosophy and its goal. The methodological analysis of the Vienna Circle led to the conclusion that only hypotheses about reality but not truth itself is obtainable.[7] Parallel to these developments in mathematics, natural science, and philosophy, the social sciences began their trek upon the "road to suspicion", to use the title of Gunther Remmling's book.[8]

The twentieth century **crisis of science** as a new component of human existence became evident just at the moment when the highest achievements of science as a servant of human struggles and desires were realized, e.g., when man touched the secret of the internal structure of matter, when science delivered the power of total annihilation of humankind and its planet, when discoveries led him to understand the natural limits of cognition, when his scientific knowledge promised to achieve a divine control even over human nature, and when he overstepped the orbit of his own planet.

The values, goals, and procedures of the scientific enterprise are presently undergoing a radical re-evaluation. It is no longer possible to view science as a hermetically sealed realm of pure cognitive activity as the mythsmiths of logical positivism would have had us believe. We are forced to acknowledge the rather simple sociological fact that science is a human activity which is shaped by powers and interests within the scientific community.[9]

Today the cult for fixed methods of scientific procedure is being critically challenged by philosophers of science. Probably the most radical view on the subject has been presented by Paul K. Feyerabend:

> The idea of a method that contains firm, unchanging and absolutely binding principles for conducting the business of science gets into considerable difficulty when confronted with the results of historical research. We find then, that there is not a single rule, however plausible, and however firmly grounded in epistemology, that is not violated at some time or other. It becomes evident that such violations are not accidental events, they are not the results of insufficient knowledge or of inattention which might have been avoided. On the contrary, we see that they are necessary for progress.
>
> It is clear, then, that the idea of a fixed method, or of a fixed (theory of) rationality, arises from too naive a view of man and of his social surroundings. To those who look at the rich material provided by history, and who are not intent on impoverishing it in

> order to please their lower instincts, their
> craving for intellectual security as it is
> provided, for example, by clarity and preci-
> sion, to such people it will seem that there
> is only one principle that can be defended
> under all circumstances, and in all stages
> of human development. It is the principle:
> anything goes.[10]

The dialogue inspired by the "crisis" in science can have a humanizing effect upon our discipline. Kathleen Gough has pointed out that:

> ...social science, like all science, becomes
> morally and socially either meaningless or
> harmful unless its skills and knowledge are
> periodically referred back to the question,
> 'Science for what purpose and for whom?' If
> we cease to ask this question, we cease to
> seek wisdom and cease to be intellectuals in
> any meaningful sense of the word. With the
> loss of responsibility for our learning, we
> also cease to be fully social, and therefore,
> human.[11]

If in this and the previous chapter, it seems that we have been more concerned with what humanistic sociology _is_ _not_ rather than what _it_ _is_, this exigency is a reflection of the present unfortunate state of our discipline which has so thoroughly sacrificed humane learning in its reckless pursuit of the idols of scientism. With Santayana we identify with the suppressed sides of human nature. Within our discipline that means identifying with the forces of tolerance and common sense in the pursuit of knowledge of humankind. We do not reject science but merely reject its inappropriate and sometimes fictitious applications. We, therefore, find ourselves in the paradoxical position of staking a _radical_ claim for the forces of _moderation_! We wish merely to reintroduce man--the conscious, viable, willing, acting, creating, loving, laughing, lamenting, grieving, despairing, sciencing, wishing, triumphant, human being--back into the _sciences_ of man.

T. S. Eliot cautions:

> The function of humanism is not to provide
> dogmas, or philosophical theories....When it
> proceeds to exact definitions it becomes
> something other than itself.[12]

We believe that there is merit in Eliot's statement. Yet, we also believe that it is possible to recognize humanism when it is manifested in the scholarly enterprise. It has been possible for us to reach an unanimous agreement that the names of Wilhelm Dilthey, Max Weber,[13] Florian Znaniecki, P. A. Sorokin, and Karl Mannheim can be placed on a list of those <u>sociologists</u> <u>who</u> <u>were</u> <u>humanists first</u>. Some of us would perhaps wish to give other names a prominent place in such a list--names like George Herbert Mead, Alfred Schutz, George Simmel, Alfred Weber, W. I. Thomas, Robert MacIver, Albert Salomon, and Charles Horton Cooley, but all such lists are necessarily selective and woefully incomplete. We must therefore find solace in the saying of Cardinal Newman:

> Nothing would be done at all if a man waited until he could do it so well that no one could find fault with it.

CHAPTER III FOOTNOTES

1. Skolimowski, "Science in Crisis", Cambridge Review, Jan. 28, 1972, p. 74.

2. Skolimowski, Zmierzch Swiatopogladu Naukowego, provides an interesting illustration of the change of science in relation to its social sub-stratum. There is a story concerning the observation of the eclipse that took place in 1780 during the War of Independence. The place for best astronomical observation was a small island in Maine. This was, however, in British hands. But it was enough that Professor Williams, as a representative of the American Academy of Arts and Sciences, wrote a letter to a British commander Colonel Campbell, to receive permission for a group of Harvard scientists to make their scientific observations in the territory of a foreign power in the state of war with the Americans. P. 38.

3. Report from Science For The People, China: Science Walks on Two Legs (New York: Avon Books, 1974), p. 37.

4. For these views I am in debt to Dr. Andrzej Ehrenfeucht, a mathematician, logician and computer science professor at the University of Colorado, Boulder.

5. In 1968 Aleksander Gella made on Hume's view the following remarks: "David Hume, being a follower of the subjective conception of values also wrote: 'When you pronounce any action or character to be vicious, you mean nothing, but that from the constitution of your nature you have a sentiment or feeling of blame from the contemplation of it'. Hume's moral philosophy was of great significance. It liberated the development of modern science from religious and ideological burdens. His point of view became generally accepted in European philosophy. After him, another British thinker. Edmund Burke, expressed the same idea in these words: 'Nothing universal can rationally be affirmed of any moral or any political subject'. Contemporary followers of the objective value theory can easily challenge these opinions. Statements such as 'a beautiful thing is that which I like' and 'a good thing is that which I crave for' are simplifications only. The adjectives 'beautiful', 'true', 'good', and 'bad', are, on the morphological level, similar to predictors, but on the level of syntax they are something else. Maybe it will be more comprehensive if I add that such terms as necessity, beauty, goodness, possibility, are not the

characteristics of a given subject, but they belong to the subjects as their designations which can be certified in model sentences". (A. Gella, "Can Our Search For Social Values Be Supported by Science?" Organon, 1968, p. 90.) Two years later Paul K. Feyerabend observed: "According to Hume, theories cannot be derived from facts. The demand to admit only those theories which follow from facts leaves us without any theory. Hence, a science as we know it can exist only if we drop the demand and revise our methodology". Paul K. Feyerabend, "Against Method: An Anarchistic Theory of Knowledge", in Michael Radner and Stephen Winokur (eds.) Analysis of Theories and Methods of Physics and Psychology (Vol. IV of Minnesota Studies in the Philosophy of Science, Minnesota: University of Minnesota Press, 1970), p. 43.

6. A more fundamental criticism of the positivistic conception of social science is made by C. Wright Mills in The Sociological Imagination. He contends that in mimicking a supposed 'scientific method' positivists in the social sciences distort and trivialize the actual methods of the natural sciences. "What they have done, in brief, is to embrace one philosophy of science which they now suppose to be The Scientific Method". In contrast, "Polykarp Kusch, Nobel Prize-winning physicist, has declared that there is no 'scientific method', and that what is called by that name can be outlined for only quite simple problems. Percy Bridgeman, another Nobel Prize-winning physicist, goes even further: 'There is no scientific method as such, but the vital feature of the scientist's procedure has been merely to do his utmost with his mind, no holds barred'. The mechanics of discovery, William S. Beck remarks, 'are not known...I think that the creative process is so closely tied in with the emotional structure of an individual...that...it is a poor subject for generalization...'" C. Wright Mills, The Sociological Imagination (New York: Oxford University Press, 1958), pp. 57-58. The methodology of positivism then is the methodology of engineering and applied science, not the methodology of pure science (which is held to be a-methodological and based on the intensive use of the creative mind). Habermas shows that Charles Sanders Peirce put forth a similar criticism. Unlike the positivists, Peirce understood "that the task of methodology is not to clarify the logical structure of scientific theories but the logic of the procedure with whose aid we obtain scientific theories". (p. 91) Peirce argued that neither deduction nor induction, the traditional forms of scientific reasoning, extend knowledge. Instead science progresses through what Peirce called abduction or the invention of hypotheses. A hypothesis is then tested using the other two forms of reasoning. Jurgen Habermas, Knowledge and Human Interest (Boston: Beacon Press, 1971).

Here then is an explanation for Mills' contention that 'Abstracted Empiricism' (read positivism) in the social sciences has not produced substantive propositions or theories. The positivist conception of science, even natural science, is inadequate in that it provides for methodologies of prediction and testing, but not of discovery.

7. For a discussion on the problem of truth in mathematics and natural science I am thankful to Professor Andrzej Ehrenfeucht.

8. Gunther Remmling, Road to Suspicion, A Study of Modern Mentality and the Sociology of Knowledge (New York: Appleton-Century-Crofts, 1967).

9. Within the philosophy of science Popper, Kuhn, and Polanyi are the most influential advocates of this view. A humanistic sociologist might take note of the fact that long before these views gained currency, Karl Mannheim expressed a similar view. He met with strong criticism during his lifetime for holding this view. Mannheim's editor pointed out in 1953, "Karl Mannheim always maintained that science does not develop in a vacuum but is part and parcel of the social process, with its concrete content of clash and strife of real interest groups". P. Kecskemeti, "Introduction" to Essays On Sociology and Social Psychology (London: Kegan-Paul, 1953), p. 9.

10. Feyerabend, op. cit., pp. 21-22 and pp. 25-26.

11. Kathleen Gough, "World Revolution and the Science of Man" in The Dissenting Academy, ed. Theodore Roscak (New York: Pantheon Books, 1967), pp. 148-149.

12. Eliot, op. cit., p. 436.

13. Some Critical and/or Radical sociologists may take exception to the inclusion of Max Weber on our list on the grounds that his much-abused doctrine of "ethical neutrality" contributed to the ascent of the scientistic mentality within sociology. Wolfgang Mommsen, Herbert Marcuse, Alvin Gouldner, and a number of others have suggested this. For an account, see Arthur Mitzman, The Iron Cage: An Historical Interpretation of Max Weber (New York: Alfred A. Knopf, 1970), pp. 307-314. Weber's defenders might reasonably argue that Weber assumed this position in an effort to defend the freedom of scholarly inquiry within the repressive political climate of Imperial Germany. In regard to his commitment to and superhuman pursuit of humane learning, we believe we are standing on the shoulders of a giant! In a different context, Weber might

be regarded as a humanist. Merleau-Ponty describes Weber's refusal to choose between an 'ethics of faith' or 'conscience', which places value on the unconditional respect for ends regardless of consequences. Being no Machiavelli, he refuses to sacrifice the ethics of faith. Yet, he also refuses to sacrifice the result apart from which action loses all meaning. There is a 'polytheism' and 'struggle of the gods'". <u>Humanism and Terror</u> (Boston: Beacon Press, 1969), p. xi.

CHAPTER IV

THE SEARCH FOR A HUMANISTIC SOCIOLOGY

What is Humanistic Sociology? Is it merely a set of noble, if somewhat nebulous, sentiments justifying a value-committed or activistic sociology? Or, does the adjective "humanistic" connote a concern that is more strictly academic, i.e., suggesting a particular relation between sociology and the humanities or the traditions of sixteenth-century Humanism or perhaps some sort of a sociological renaissance of the ideas of the Enlightenment which some historians describe as the Age of Humanism? There are no easy answers to these questions. However, we believe that the words of two great "humanists" of another generation can guide us in our quest for answers. George Santayana maintained that "The humanist would not deserve his name if he were not in sympathy with the suppressed sides of human nature (sometimes, as today perhaps, the highest sides of it); and he must change his aversions as the ruling convention changes its idols".[1] And T. S. Eliot warned that humanism is concerned more with "common sense" than with exploring the formal canons of reason or aligning itself with a particular school of philosophical thought".[2] We might, therefore, say that within the discipline of sociology, "humanism" is a somewhat ambivalent label that has been attached to almost all those currents of thought which have tried to oppose the excesses of positivism, empiricism, and scientism in nineteenth and twentieth century social thought. Thus it has been possible for one of the leading advocates of empirical sociology in the socialist countries, Jan Szczepanski, to list six applications of the term "humanistic" within Western social thought.[3] Szczepanski offers his own definition of "humanistic science" as "science about the behavior of man and the products of his activities".[4] He is convinced that humanistic doctrines can only influence scientific methods indirectly because the "accuracy of scientific method depends exclusively upon the logical accuracy of reasoning, exactness of observation, and precision in establishing and measuring facts".[5] Presumably this statement reflects the attitude of those sociologists who would like to promulgate behavioristic methods and positivistic empiricism by identifying them with humanistic goals. However, sociology does not become

42

humanistic merely be making a declaration that a highly developed behavioristic methodology serves humanistic ends when the ends themselves are established by ideologists.[6] This is a separate problem which urgently requires solution in our time. However, the issue which we can and must deal with more directly in this essay and more generally in our teaching and research in sociology is the fact that the pretensions of the "science" of "behavior" are crippling our ability to create and disseminate knowledge about man and society.[7] We need to extend the scope of sociological concepts and methods beyond the sphere of external behavior.

Many sociologists retain a faith in the possibility of a techno-scientific solution to philosophical problems. Perhaps, they can share Szczepanski's conviction that "the construction of an electronic apparatus which can translate or analyze content is based on the researchers showing that the 'understanding' assumed by many methodologists as a boundary between the humanistic and natural sciences is not an action proper to the mind but only has as its equivalent clearly mechanical operations".[8]

There is, however, an increasing number of sociologists who are returning to a consideration of the fundamental problems involved in the distinction between the natural and social sciences. They recognize that an electronic apparatus translates or analyzes content only in so far as the scientific ingenuity of human intelligence allows man to program his apparatus. Sociologists who reject the positivistic and behavioristic heritage are not united by any single program either positive or negative. The term "humanistic sociology" is more frequently invoked by those who in one way or another are in opposition to the dominating tendencies of our discipline. However, examination of the respective premises and substantive researches of some of these individuals suggests that perhaps they may be abusing the flexibility of the adjective "humanistic".[9] In fabricating the conceptual clockworks of humanism, many sociologists wind a pattern too abstract or too nebulous to provide a tangible guide to this area. The results of their labors has been more form than substance.[10]

When the positivistic-behavioristic paradigm was recognized as the only legitimate or orthodox form of sociology in America, a few brave souls refused to surrender their humanistic perspectives.[11] However, their defense of humanism was largely one of example rather than exhortation. There were some notable exceptions.

C. Wright Mills was not the only American sociologist who spoke out against the dominance of the positivist-functionalist paradigm during the nineteen-fifties, but his voice was the most resonant. In his 1954 essay, "I.B.M. Plus Reality Plus Humanism = Sociology", Mills stated the case he would develop more fully in

The Sociological Imagination.[12]   He argued that American sociology was divided into three camps: The "Scientists" (later anointed "Abstracted Empiricists"), the "Grand Theorists", and sociologists who have acquired "the humanistic concern". Mills identifies with the last group and defines its major task as consistently and relentlessly asking these questions:

> (1) What is the meaning of this--whatever we are examining--for our society as a whole, and what is this social world like? (2) What is the meaning of this for the types of men and women that prevail in this society? And (3) how does this fit into the historical trend of our times, and in what direction does this main drift seem to be carrying us? No matter how small-scale what he is examining, the sociologist must ask such questions about it, or he has abdicated the classic sociological endeavor.[13]

Echoing the sentiments of Karl Mannheim who had described a "sociological culture" as the surrogate for humanism in industrial society,[14] Mills also considered the possibility that sociology could become the "common denominator" of contemporary intellectual life, but he warned:

> ...for such a salutary development to get fully under way, theorists are going to have to do their work with a sense of reality as well as with scope and insight. Research technicians are going to have to go about their work with more imaginative concern for its larger meanings, as well as with mathematical ingenuity. Both are going to have to drop their trivialization of subject matter and their pretensions about method. Both are going to have to face up to the realities of our time. And both are going to have to acquire the humanist concern--which some American historians have retained--for excellence of clear and meaningful expression.[15]

Mills' essay, "On Intellectual Craftsmanship", provides a practical and yet eloquent account of the everyday working practices of a sociologist motivated by the humanistic concern.[16] It remains unsurpassed as a pedagogic example for the humanistic sociologist.

In the early 1960's a growing number of outstanding scholars called for the development of a more humanistic sociology. In his 1960 Presidential Address to the American Sociological Association, Robert Bierstedt urged sociologists to affirm their discipline's status as a form of "humane learning". Claiming that Webb, Thomas, Znaniecki, Veblen, Sumner, and Tocqueville, were great sociologists because they were humanists first, Bierstedt maintains that, "whether or not sociology is or ought to be a science it owns a rightful place in the domain of humane letters and belongs, with literature, history, and philosophy, among the arts that liberate the human mind".[17] Although he acknowledges that sociology ought to be as "scientific" as possible, Bierstedt nevertheless argues that the scientific method does not exhaust the resources of scholarship in sociology" "I think we ought to take much more seriously and literally the view that sociology can also serve as a bridge between the sciences and the humanities and that in a very important sense it belongs to the realm of humane letters".[18]

Another major figure in American sociology who helped lay the foundations for the emergence of a humanistic sociology is Robert Nisbet. Although he has since repudiated American sociology's recent "plunge into subjectivism" whether in the guise of "ethnomethodology, consciousness-, reflexive-, or egocentric-sociology",[19] in 1963 Nisbet contributed to the criticism of the "folklore of scientism" which "apotheosizes the routine and insignificant".[20] In an essay with the provocative title, "Sociology as an Art Form", he pointed out that the "key ideas" of the most remarkable sociological minds of the nineteenth century--Tocqueville, Weber, Simmel, Tönnies, and Durkheim--are not only "unrelated to prior 'scientific' ideas", but they also "have their closest affinity with an art movement, Romanticism".[21]

In the same year the most direct and best-known celebration of the humanistic perspective, Peter Berger's <u>Invitation to Sociology</u>, was published. Berger describes the irony implicit in the "methodism" of the social sciences--the desire to emulate the procedures but not the spirit of the older and more prestigious sciences--he points out that, "The irony of this process lies in the fact that natural scientists themselves have been giving up the very positivistic dogmatism that their emulators are still striving to adopt".[22] Berger believes that one very important lesson sociologists can learn from natural scientists is to develop a "sense of play" in approaching their discipline.[23] He points out that:

> Natural scientists, on the whole, have with age, acquired a degree of sophistication about their methods that allows them to see the latter as relative and limited in scope. Social scientists still tend to take their discipline with grim humorlessness, invoking terms such as "empirical", "data", "validity" or even

> "facts" as a voodoo magician might his most
> cherished hobgoblins. As the social sciences
> move from their enthusiastic puberty to a
> mellower maturity, a similiar degree of detach-
> ment from one's own game may be expected....
> so that one can afford not only tolerance but
> even an interest in other people's epistemo-
> logical entertainments.[24]

Berger regards the mere presence of such an "ironical skepticism concerning its own undertakings" as the hallmark of the humanistic character of an intellectual discipline.[25] Although he makes no reference to it, Nietzsche's classic, <u>The Gay Science</u>, might be seen as a philosophical exemplar of this attitude.[26] Like Bierstedt and Nisbet, Berger also affirms the link between humanistic sociology and the humanities. He points out that:

> Sociology is vitally concerned with what is,
> after all, the principle subject matter of
> the humanities--the human condition itself.
> Just because the social is such a crucial
> dimension of man's existence, sociology comes
> time and again on the fundamental question of
> what it means to be a man in a particular sit-
> uation. The question may often be obscured by
> the paraphernalia of scientific research and
> by the bloodless vocabulary that sociology has
> developed in its desire to legitimate its own
> scientific status. But sociology's data are
> cut so close from the living marrow of human
> life that this question comes through again
> and again, at least for those sociologists
> who are sensitive to the human significance
> of what they are doing.[27]

He therefore believes that a humanistic sociology requires an "openness of mind" and "a catholicity of vision"--"Openness to the humanistic scope of sociology further implies an ongoing communication with other disciplines that are vitally concerned with exploring the human condition".[28] Berger especially emphasizes the importance of a knowledge of history and philosophy to the humanistic sociologist. He describes the role that the humanistic sociologist can play in the contemporary world situation with a Machiavellian metaphor:

> One can think of the sociologist as a
> <u>condottiere</u> of social perception. Some
> <u>condottieri</u> fight for the oppressors of
> men, others for their liberators. Espec-
> ially if one looks around beyond the

> frontiers of America as well as within
> them, one can find enough grounds to be-
> lieve that there is a place in today's
> world for the latter type of condottiere.29

Berger's book is undoubtedly required reading for all sociologists with humanistic sympathies. However, it is intended merely as an "invitation" addressed to a general audience. Berger himself makes only this modest claim for his extraordinary little volume.

In the scope of The Social Construction of Reality, Berger and Luckmann attempt to delineate the prerequisites for the development of a humanistic sociology.30 They contend sociology must take its place among the disciplines that "deal with man as man; ...it is, in that specific sense, a humanistic discipline".31 In their view sociology's "proper object of inquiry" is

> ...society as part of a human world, made by
> men, inhabited by men, and, in turn, making
> men, in an ongoing historical process. It
> is not the least fruit of a humanistic socio-
> logy that it reawakens our wonder at this
> astonishing phenomenon.32

However, they maintain that their conception of sociology "does not imply that sociology is not a science, that its methods should be other than empirical, or that it cannot be 'value-free'.33

Berger also dealt directly with the topic of humanistic sociology in his article, "On Conservative Humanism". Since we have described humanistic sociology primarily as a movement against the main currents of sociological thought, Berger's article is of special significance for it underscores an important point. Sociologists professing a humanistic perspective are a diverse group. They do not necessarily share common ideological roots although their work is as vulnerable to ideological critique as that of their colleagues.34 Humanistic sociologists include conservatives, liberals, and radicals. They share a common conception of social reality as a human creation and a conviction that sociologists must respect the integrity of the phenomena they study. Among them, such as meritorious historian of sociological theories, Don Martindale, underscores the ideological diversity of humanistic sociology.

In this respect Severyn Bruyn's The Human Perspective represents an essential contribution in the recent movement toward the development of a humanistic sociology.35 Bruyn provides a detailed analysis of the most widely used qualitative method in sociology, participant observation. He sees the social sciences as "interlocuters" between the extremes of the sciences and the humanities.

Recently the intensity of interest in humanistic sociology has accelerated. John Glass approaches the topic by asking, what does the human potential "revolution" in psychology mean for sociology?[36] Glass contends that the image of man prevailing in contemporary (functionalist) sociology is that of a passive "product" of society. He points out that while sociologists have manifested a great deal of concern with pathological deviations (crime, mental illness, alcoholism, etc.), they have almost completely ignored deviations in the other (healthy) direction, i.e., creativity, self-fulfillment, and their institutional requisites. Glass sees existential or phenomenological sociology, ethnomethodology, symbolic interactionism, and participant observation, as offering humanistic alternatives to conventional sociology.

Particularly interesting, from our viewpoint, are views of those who are demanding the rights and place for philosophical considerations in sociological research. Maurice Roche is a good example. He approaches humanistic sociology from a philosophical perspective because he believes "sociology coexists with...humanistic philosophy in a common context".[37] Roche asserts that two self-styled "revolutions" in philosophy, phenomenology and conceptual analysis (or ordinary language philosophy) have certain "humanistic" features in common which have important consequences for the development of a humanistic sociology:

> ...phenomenology and conceptual analysis...are opposed to the application of natural scientific procedures, theories, analogies and aspirations in the human and social sciences. They are particularly opposed to the mechanism and reductionism of philosophical standpoints like logical positivism or empiricism. Both advocate a descriptive approach to human experience as an important method for philosophy and the social sciences. And finally both can be seen to rely on virtually the same theory of man.[38]

Roche argues that whereas psychological theories tend to be mechanistic and reductionistic, sociological theories (at least those in the "classic" tradition) tend to be anti-psychologistic and humanistic.[39] He maintains that although classical sociology had significant humanistic elements "in spite of its too common positivistic and scientistic veneer"; these elements were largely repressed by the professionalization of sociology.[40] However, he contends that the emergence of a fully articulated humanistic sociology can be greatly facilitated through a dialogue with humanistic philosophies.

The former President of the American Sociological Association, Alfred McClung Lee, also contributed to the dialogue by arguing for an activist sociology which he identifies with the problems of suppressed groups in modern societies.[41] Lee also champions the cause of literacy in sociology following Mills' opinion that all significant work in sociology can and should be reported in language which any intelligent member of society can comprehend. Lee makes clear that in Toward Humanist Sociology he is recording his personal version of humanistic sociology and specifically notes that he makes no claims to any particular alliances with other present or historical forms of humanism.

While Mills, Bierstedt, Berger, Bruyn, Glass, Roche, and Lee have been primarily concerned with indicating what a humanistic sociology should be, few authors have made a direct effort to define the scope, subject, methods, and concepts of humanistic scholarship as it has actually been practiced within sociology. Don Martindale in the States, and Edmund Mokrzycki, a younger generation sociologist in Poland, made some efforts in this direction.

Martindale argues that a humanistic sociology could only develop after sociology "became indubitably established and had made its way into the universities as one of the basic academic disciplines".[42] Earlier rejections of the physical science bias of the dominant schools of sociology entailed a rejection of sociology altogether rather than attempts to formulate an alternative school of sociology. He contends that the "humanistic impulse" in sociology has manifested itself in (i) the "social behaviorism" of Tarde, Le Bon, Giddings, Ross, Weber, MacIver, Commons, Veblen, James, Cooley, Mead, and Thomas; (ii) phenomenological, formalistic, and existential sociology; (iii) the sociology of C. Wright Mills; and (iv) mainstream Catholic sociology (Thomistic).[43] Martindale classifies the first two as individualistic, with the first impelled by Rationalism and the second rooted in neo-rationalism. The third and fourth types of humanistic sociology are characterized as collectivist with left- and right-wing orientations, respectively.

Edmund Mokrzycki, in his articles and book, provides some rather comprehensive reflections on the concepts and methods of humanistic sociology.[44] He distinguishes humanistic sociology as a contemporary trend opposed to "technical", plainly empirical and "manipulatory" sociology, and points out that its historical roots can be traced to two sources, Dilthey's meta-sociological ideas and the Chicago School of sociology. Mokrzycki's efforts are worth emulating in that he attempts to at once define the term with conceptual clarity yet place it within its larger historical and philosophical context.

At the end of this review of the present search for humanistic sociology, the ongoing efforts of the Humanist Sociological Association should be mentioned.[45]

* * * * * *

What we understand by the term "humanistic sociology" needs a systematic explanation. Therefore, we have to analyze systematically those elements in the works of great classical sociologists which allow us today to call them the fathers of humanistic sociology.

Such an analysis is also related to our views on the particular significance of studies in the history of sociology for the further progress of our discipline.[46]

In short, the development of sociology and related social sciences differs in its very nature from that of natural and exact sciences. For the student of the latter, a separate study of his discipline's historical development is incomparably less important than for the student of a social discipline, particularly sociology. This is because the relationship between natural sciences and their social substratum are weak. There is not a direct influence of political, social, economic and other external factors on the immanent, autogenetic development of mathematics, physics or biology. External factors may play a role in accelerating or hampering natural sciences' development but do not interfere in the sequential growth of their interval logic. In natural sciences, new theories are constructed on the firm ground of old theories. Every verified theory creates a link in the progress of a given discipline. In addition, every mistake is noted and is never repeated. Therefore, we can say that the natural sciences are historical in the sense that the whole chain of their past discoveries creates a united basis for every new discovery, and this is the reason why historical knowledge about the circumstances of the development of physics or biology is not necessary, in a direct sense, for their students. The representatives of natural and exact sciences very often make light of the history of their own sciences. However, they forget that the whole past of a given science is included in the present intellectual horizon of their studies.

In all the social sciences, and sociology above all, the matter is quite different. The development of these sciences is responsive to their social substratum in a degree which could never be observed in the natural sciences. Permanently active, immanent, logical determinants which rule their development do not exist. In other words, new social theories have not resulted from the logical evolution of old theories. The consequences of previous developments are not unavoidable, as is the case in the natural sciences. The appearance of new theories in sociology and related sciences cannot be explained without turning our attention to the social and historical background which directly affects the development of these sciences. Of course, in many narrow sociological researches we can observe an autogenetic development similar, to a certain degree, to that in the natural sciences. However, the history of sociology as a whole supplies us with an uninterrupted chain of examples illustrating how much its ideas and trends have been responsive to social, economic, and political background. In this situation, knowledge of the history of sociology plays (as well as in other social sciences) a very important role. Only a serious knowledge of the history of sociology can protect sociologists from repeating old errors and "discovering" old ideas. Therefore, we can observe a paradox: the more the history of sociology is neglected, the more sociology becomes responsive to the social environment and suffers all the consequences of its responsiveness; the more historical consciousness sociology possesses and the greater allowance it makes for its own legacy, the more autogenetic it becomes.

CHAPTER IV FOOTNOTES

1. George Santayana, "The Genteel Tradition at Bay" in <u>Santayana on America</u>, edited by Richard Colton Lyon (New York: Harcourt, Brace and World, 1968), p. 129.

2. T. S. Eliot, "Second Thoughts About Humanism" in <u>Selected Essays of T. S. Eliot</u> (New York: Harcourt, Brace and World, 1932), p. 436.

3. (1) Philosophical doctrines derived from Protagoras and the sophists which were later developed by F.C.S. Schiller and F. Znaniecki, as well as the existential humanism of Irving Babbitt; (2) The philosophical and political views formulated during the renaissance by Machiavelli; (3) The intertwining of the concepts of humanism and humanitarianism derived from the views of Herder and Humboldt as well as from utopian French communists; (4) Socialist humanism which Gorki named 'truely universal proletarian humanism; (5) In common language the terms 'humanistic attitude' or 'humanistic content' are used to designate the elements of different doctrines which are directed by the needs and interests of individuals and communities; and (6) 'Humanism' is used as a slogan fulfilling the role of Pareto's derivations. See: Jan Szczepanski, <u>Odmiany Czasu Terazmiejszego</u>, Kiw, Warszawa 1971, pp. 556-558.

4. <u>Ibidem</u>.

5. Szczepanski, <u>ibidem</u>, p. 564.

6. Ten years ago Aleksander Gella considered this problem: "The idea of excluding the consideration of values from scientific activity sometimes leads to a conflict between the needs of society and the behavior of scientists, as is clearly shown in the following example recorded by Howard Selsam during the Roosevelt administration. The U. S. Department of Agriculture organized a series of conferences to solve certain problems of the national society and of rural life with a participation of representatives of all branches of the social sciences. However, these specialists were willing to discuss questions concerning the selection of desirable social objectives because, they maintained, they were competent to discuss only matters of fact, not of value, which lie within the domain of philosophy and religion. In result of this

situation, the Department of Agriculture rallied together philosophers and religious leaders to resolve agricultural problems. Therefore, Selsam asked: 'How can philosophers and religious leaders determine the desirable objectives of our national society or our rural life?' They must do so by deduction from some abstract principles concerning either man's ultimate good in this world or the prerequisites for his salvation in the next, or else they must become social scientists and seek to do the job that those who are technically better trained and equipped have so woefully neglected.'" A. Gella, "Can Our Search for Social Values Be Supported by Science", Organon, 1968.

7. In The Human Condition, the late Hannah Arendt explores the existential consequences of the distinction between 'action' and 'behavior' within the historical context of Western civilization: "Society replaces action with behavior and it equates the individual with his social status (which determines his behavior)--rank in the eighteenth-century half-feudal society, title in the nineteenth-century class society, 'or mere function in the mass society of today.'" She argues that the pretentiousness of the 'behavioral sciences' contributes to the process of reducing humans into mass-men who are expected to behave like conditioned animals. See Kurt Wolff, "Men's Historicity and Dualism" in Trying Sociology (New York: John Wiley and Sons, 1974), pp. 226-227 and Hannah Arendt, The Human Condition (Chicago: University of Chicago Press, 1958), pp. 41-45. It is perhaps useful if at this juncture we also consider the deformations which two other key concepts, 'knowledge' and 'science', have been subjected to in the era of scientism. The rapid progress of natural science introduced a significant change into use of the two terms knowledge and science. It is well known that modern languages differ in the scope which they offer to these words. In English-speaking nations Francis Bacon "substituted for the contemplative, the practical ideal of knowledge". Then science in in English became this prestigious part of knowledge, which offered man the promise of dominating and manipulating nature, and not merely the enjoyment of cognition. Thus, in English the growing prestige of science changed the content of the term knowledge, which is not often understood as a designate of all learning and cognition, which lies beyond the scope of science. This separation of knowledge and science is not so straightforward in other languages. For example, in German, das Wissenschaft (knowledge in general) was divided on die Naturewissenschaften and die Kulturwissenschaften, with their subgroups: Sozialenwissenschaften, Historischewissenschaften and Schonenwissenschaften. In Polish and Russian the term Nauka (science) embraces all intellectual endeavors which have been organized in forms of academic disciplines. Thus, the

humanistic disciplines in Central and Eastern Europe never so decisively lost their citizenship in the realm of science as in the West.

8. J. Szczepanski, op. cit., p. 563.

9. On October 14, 1974 Dr. Aurelie Pocoei, executive committee spokesman of the Club of Rome warned that only a new "humanistic philosophy" could ward off worldwide social and political chaos. Speaking at the opening of the four-day conference on problems of world development, Dr. Pocoei stressed the necessary role of a "new humanism" in solving world problems such as overpopulation, insufficient food production and growing inequality between rich and poor.

10. Harold M. Hodges in "The Humanistic Intelligentsia" listed 27 contemporary sociologists "who have championed a humanistic approach", A. Gella (ed.) The Intelligentsia and the Intellectuals (Sage Publication, 1976).

11. The name of P. A. Sorokin looms large here of course; but the names of Robert MacIver, Willard Waller, Ernest Becker, Herbert Blumer, Irving Goffman also come immediately to mind. In the sense which Santayana gives to the term "humanism", those American sociologists who would later label themselves "radicals" might be recognized here insofar as they opposed the excesses of the positivistic-behaviorist establishment which was held to be aligned with the interests of the American as well as with any other state establishment.

12. C. Wright Mills, "I.B.M. Plus Reality Plus Humanism = Sociology" in Mills' Power, Politics and People, edited by Irving Louis Horowitz (New York: Ballantine Books, 1963), pp. 568-576.

13. Ibidem, p. 572.

14. Karl Mannheim, Essays on the Sociology of Culture (London: Routledge, Kegan-Paul, 1962), p. 230.

15. Mills, op. cit., p. 576.

16. An earlier version of this essay was published in Symposium on Sociological Theory edited by Llewellyn Gross (New York: Harper & Row Publishers, 1959).

17. Robert Bierstedt, "Sociology and Humane Learning", American Sociological Review, 25 (February, 1960), p. 4.

18. Ibidem, p. 7.

19. Robert Nisbet, The Sociology of Emile Durkheim (New York: Oxford University Press), p. vi.

20. Robert Nisbet, "Sociology as an Art Form" in Sociology on Trial, edited by Maurice Stein and Arthur Vidich (Englewood Cliffs: Prentice-Hall, Inc., 1963), p. 154.

21. Ibidem, p. 156.

22. Peter L. Berger, Invitation to Sociology (Garden City: Doubleday & Co., Inc., 1963), p. 13.

23. Ibidem, p. 165.

24. Ibidem.

25. Ibidem.

26. Although the editor and translator of a new edition of this work, Walter Kaufmann, noted the particular relevance and importance of this volume for sociologists, there is little evidence that they have given it the attention it deserves.

27. Berger, op. cit., p. 167.

28. Ibidem.

29. Ibidem, p. 170.

30. Peter L. Berger and Thomas Luckmann, The Social Construction of Reality (Garden City: Doubleday & Company, 1966).

31. Ibidem, p. 189.

32. Ibidem.

33. Ibidem.

34. See Peter Berger, "On Conservative Humanism" in Berger and R. Neuhaus, Movement and Revolution (New York: Doubleday Anchor, 1970).

35. Severyn T. Bruyn, The Human Perspective in Sociology: The Methodology of Participant Observation (Englewood Cliffs: Prentice-Hall, Inc., 1966).

36. John Glass, "The Humanistic Challenge to Sociology" Journal of Humanistic Psychology, Fall 1971, pp. 170-183.

37. Maurice Roche, Phenomenology, Language and the Social Sciences

(London: Routledge and Kegan-Paul, 1973), p. 326.

38. Ibidem, p. vii.

39. For example, psychological explanations of mental illness see the etiology of the ailment in terms of genetic abnormality, or inborn personality traits, or environment conditioning (S R), or fixation of the personality at a certain stage in sexual or ego development, or as some combination of these factors. Explanations of such factors can be made only from the perspective of the detached scientific observer. The actor's experience as well as his account of it are regarded as symptoms. However, sociological explanations accord the actor's account some explanatory value as meaning dimensions in his developing situation. Ibidem, p. viii.

40. Roche writes, "I would include in the repressed humanism, Weber's concept of an interpretive sociology, Schutz's elaboration of this and his own contributions in more recent years, and symbolic interactionism and the whole influence of George Herbert Mead's thought", p. 316.

41. Alfred McClung Lee, Toward Humanist Sociology (Englewood Cliffs: Prentice-Hall, Inc., 1973).

42. Don Martindale, "Humanism, Scientism, and the types of Sociological Theory" in Sociological Theory and the Problem of Values (Columbus, Ohio: Charles E. Merrill Publishing Company, 1974), p. 236.

43. Ibidem.

44. Edmund Mokrzycki, "Two Concepts of Humanistic Sociology", Polish Sociological Bulletin, Warsaw, No. 2, 1969. "The Operation of Verstehen", ibidem, No. 2, 1970 and Zalozenia Sociologii Humanstycznej, PWN Publisher, Warszawa 1971.

45. This group centered at Miami University in Oxford, Ohio under the sponsorship of Charles Flynn and Ann Davis has published a journal of humanistic sociology, Humanity and Society. Also indicative of the growing popularity of the movement toward a humanistic sociology is the publication of two introductory sociology textbooks which explicitly embrace the humanistic theme: Robert M. Glass, Ronald E. Roberts, and Dean S. Dorn, Sociology - With A Human Face: Sociology As If People Mattered (St. Louis: Mosby, 1976) and Thomas Ford Hoult, Sociology Readings For A New Day (New York: Random House, 1976).

46. Aleksander Gella, "The Significance of the History of Sociology", Actes, Histoire des Science de L'Homme, Vol IX Paris 1971.

PART TWO: HISTORICAL ROOTS

CHAPTER V

HUMANISTIC REVOLUTION IN 19TH CENTURY PHILOSOPHY:
DILTHEY, WINDELBAND, AND RICKERT

The reaction against the simplifications of Comte's positivism was almost immediate. Among the critics was Karl Marx. He totally rejected Comte's philosophy because he fully grasped its ideological significance for the growth and maintenance of capitalism. But Marx also wanted to be "scientific" and therefore silently accepted positivistic principles of science.

Comte discussed the nature of sociology and its methodological problems in a general and superficial way. He was convinced that his new discipline could be patterned after the natural sciences. He separated social phenomena into a class by itself but he was confident that the methods of the natural sciences could be applied to all aspects of social phenomena. Although he realized that the most significant method for the new science of "sociology" should be the historical method, Comte nevertheless pushed its development into a strictly materialistic framework by insisting that sociology should be based directly on biology (with the total omission of psychology). This was the original sin committed by the "sire" of sociology.[1]

The formidable attack on positivism in the social sciences was launched by German philosophers and historians and not by sociologists themselves.[2] Methodologists felt a certain incongruity in relation to humanistic disciplines. The alternative for them was either to make humanistic studies as precise, exact, and empirical as the natural sciences or to deny them the status of sciences.[3] As the natural sciences gathered together an ever-expanding knowledge of the empirical world, traditional German scholarship with its roots in the soil of Idealistic and Romantic philosophy was called into serious question by Anglo-French positivism.

A dichotomy, latently inherent in the German Idealist heritage since the Kantian synthesis, emerged between the natural sciences (<u>Naturwissenschaften</u>) and historical and cultural studies

(Geisteswissenschaften and Kulturwissenschaften). The positivists claimed that man is subject to the same modes of scientific scrutiny as natural phenomena.[4] The historicists, however, argued that, because the activities and cultural creations of man are endowed with meaning, a truly comprehensive understanding of man cannot be derived solely by the use of positivist methods. Therefore, they searched for a link between historicism and transcendant (or non-naturalistic) humanism which insists that man is something more than nature. Most sociologists struggled to make their discipline as similar to the natural sciences as possible, so that they might win the status of "scientist".

The great debate on the character and relationship of the natural sciences and the humanities was most intense in Germany because the spread of French positivism and English empiricism and utilitarianism met greater resistance there due to the strong tradition of Kantian idealism and dualism. The tradition of transcendent humanism better survived the storm of positivist empiricism in agricultural countries than in highly industrialized nations. Polish sociology offers an excellent example. A strong humanistic tradition was drowned by the growth of empiricism which paralleled the industrialization of the country.[5]

There were three German philosophers, Wilhelm Dilthey, Wilhelm Windelband and Heinrich Rickert, whose reactions to the positivist conceptions of social studies generated a standing discussion on the relationship between the natural sciences on the one hand and the social, cultural, and historical on the other. We pay particular attention to Dilthey as his contribution seems to have had the most decisive influence on the development of the humanistic sociology during the following generation.[6]

Among those who influenced the development of sociology, there were two outstanding figures who held low regard for sociology itself--Marx and Dilthey. Their criticisms came from divergent viewpoints and were inspired by different causes. While Marx rejected sociology as the bourgeois ideology of Auguste Comte, he was unaware of accepting positivistic procedures. However, Dilthey launched his attack against positivism precisely because he objected to the assertion that positivistic methodology could be used in socio-historical studies. Though Marx enriched that discipline with new concepts and fields of studies, it was Dilthey whose criticism penetrated to the very basis of positivist and evolutionary ideology. Dilthey wrote:

> My polemic against sociology concerned the stage of its development which was characterized by Comte, Spencer, Schaffle, Lilienfield. The conception of it which was contained in their works was that of a science

>of the common life of men in society, including among its objects also, law, morality, and religion....My rejection of sociology... applies to a science which aims at comprehending everything which happens de facto in human society in a single study....in the end sociology is the name for a number of works which have handled the facts of society according to a great principle of explanation, or for a tendency in explanatory procedure. It is not the name of a science.[7]

It should perhaps be noted that even Max Weber, who did so much in an effort to establish sociology as a reputable academic discipline in German, held much of the sociology of his day in low esteem. Karl Jaspers quotes Weber as stating, "Most of what goes by the name of sociology is a fraud".[8] However, Dilthey made one exception in his condemnation of sociology. This was in the case of the work of George Simmel. In his <u>Einleitung in die Geistewissenschaften</u>, a criticism of the pseudo-science of Comte and Spencer in which he denied the possibility of developing a scientific sociology, he made "explicit laudatory reference to Simmel".[9] This sympathetic attitude toward Simmel might be explained as suggested by George Lichtheim who notes that:

>Dilthey and Simmel represented a reaction against the positivism of the natural sciences, but also against the Marburg school which denied the possibility of insight into the veritable nature of reality...they had to come to believe that real essences were cognizable through an act of intellectual intuition.[10]

In his later years, however, Dilthey softened his attitude toward sociology. H. A. Hodges points out that Dilthey prepared some notes toward a future revision of <u>Einleitung</u> many years after its original publication. In these notes, "Dilthey made it clear that he had no objection to sociology if it meant merely a comparative study of different forms of social groupings and stratifications".[11] In spite of his views, Dilthey made the first decisive step toward the development of humanistic sociology. But his contribution to sociology was done only in an indirect way. His aim was to offer a critique of the cognition of humanistic knowledge comparable to Kant's critique in the field of natural sciences.[12] He decisively separated natural sciences and humanities on the basis of their different subject matter. Sociohistorical reality, the subject matter of the humanities which in his view included social studies has a dual nature: spiritual and material. Therefore, a researcher of socio-historical reality cannot blindly follow the methodological patterns of the natural sciences. In socio-historical studies (or as he called them the "human studies") we are searching not only for *facts* and laws, as in natural sciences, but also for *values*. When positivists try to remove or ignore values, they distort the picture of social reality.

Dilthey defended the human studies as true sciences, but asserted that they are basically different from the natural sciences. The human studies are "those fields of investigation in which the chief aim is to understand some portion of mental life through the interpretation of its outward expressions in individual or social histories, in economic, political, or religious processes and institutions, or in the creative activities and products of the fine arts".[13] The essential element of cognition in the human studies is *Erlebniss*, used by Dilthey in the sense which is most closely translated as "unmediated experience".[14]

Dilthey was the first proponent of an independent scientific status for the human studies. He severely criticized the assumed homogeneity of the natural sciences and human sciences, arguing that the methods and presuppositions of the former were not appropriate for the specific requirements of the latter. He therefore contended that the human studies must adopt a new and independent method of inquiry. Since the natural sciences study phenomena which are alien to the scientist himself, he cannot "understand" his subject matter, but only explain it in terms of causal laws. Hence, Dilthey argued, the student of human phenomena has a great advantage: "The fact that the investigator of history is the same as the one who makes it, is the first condition which makes scientific history possible; here we have the first significant element for the solution of the epistemological problem of history".[15] The human studies, he argued, must use empirical inquiry to gather information objectively, and simultaneously use subjective intuition, empathy and compassion to understand the meaning which the collected data and observations have to the studied human beings: "When the two functions of consciousness (empirical inquiry and subjective intuition via *Erlebniss*) central in human studies, finally coincide, then we grasp the essence of human development".[16]

The use of empathy in understanding is analogous to what is called 'taking-the-role-of-the-other' in Meadian social psychology[17] and is thus not essentially mystical, but rather grounded in the reality of daily life. As Rickman points out, "understanding" for Dilthey "is not a matter of penetrating intuitively into the minds of others, but of realizing what their expressions mean ....The understanding of expressions is based on familiarity with the social and cultural context, in which they occur. This... Dilthey called the 'objective mind' or the 'objectifications of life'".[18] "If sufficient evidence is available we grasp, with some degree of objectivity, the meaning which life had for the person we are describing, the inner organization or pattern of his life....When he grasps the relations between intention, action and the ensuing actual consequences the historian understands the historical pattern of events".[19] The process of understanding is spiral, as the examination of documentary and other physical evidence leads to an attempt to empathetically take the role of the other, which leads to a greater understanding of the evidence, in turn leading to a more accurate empathetic understanding. Only in this way we can grasp the meaningful relations of the active agents. However, we should be aware that for Dilthey the term "understanding" had a very definite meaning. It was for him as H. P. Rickman pointed out a technical term. Dilthey assumed that "Understanding is the rediscovery of the I in the Thou".[20]

Dilthey argued that inner experience or consciousness has an immediate, indubitable presence, which is more objective and more universally valid than sensory perceptions of the external, physical world. Self-awareness is far more secure and generally valid for Dilthey than the awareness of the external appearance of physical phenomena.[21]

This appreciation of the inner experience, perhaps a central characteristic of humanistic sociology, is reflected in the broad educational background of many humanistic sociologists.[22] Dilthey himself strongly emphasized the importance of poetry, literature, and autobiography. On the significance of poetry he wrote:

> Thought produces concepts, art creates <u>types</u>....None of us would possess more than a meagre part of our present understanding of human conditions if we had not become used to seeing through the poet's eyes, and beholding Hamlets and Gretchens, Richards and Cordelias, Marquis Poas and Philips in the men around us....<u>Poet</u>s are our organs for the understanding of men, and they influence the way in which we lead our lives in love, in marriage, and with friends....There is a philosophic attitude which has nothing to do with the profession of a philosophical specialist. In every poet who rises to an ideal of life and a Weltanschauung, even though it is expressed only in the system of images which he sets before our fancy, we commonly believe that there is a streak of philosophy. For there is in him a capacity to make oneself conscious of life in its wholeness, in

> its universal meaning, a capacity based on the practice of facing every phenomenon of life with a heightened degree of reflection. That is why the philosopher is born, the true philosopher, like the true poet, has a touch of genius....[23]

On the importance of the literary form of autobiography Dilthey wrote:

> ...autobiography is the highest and most instructive form in which the understanding of life comes before us....history does indeed know of various assertions of something unconditional as value, norm, or good. Such assertions appear everywhere in history - now as given in the divine will, now in a rational concept of perfection, in a teleological order of the world, in a universally valid norm of our conduct which is transcendentally based. But historical experience knows only the process, so important for it, of making these assertions: on its own grounds it knows nothing of their universal validity....The question whether it can be shown with logical cogency that the subsumption of experience under such unconditional principles, which is undoubtedly a historical fact, must be referred to a factor in man which is universal and not limited in time - this question leads into the ultimate depths of transcendental philosophy, which lie beyond the empirical circle of history, and from which even philosophy cannot wrest an assured answer. And even if this question were decided in the affirmative, this could be of no service to the historian in selecting, understanding, and discovering connections, unless the content of this unconditional principle can be determined.[24]

Dilthey's work in attempting to establish the objective and universal validity (<u>Allgemeingultigkeit</u>) of historical understanding led him to an awareness of and concern with the uniqueness of historical inquiry, particularly as it was related to what Dilthey termed the "human sciences". In this matter, Howard Nelson Tuttle rightly noted that "This question of the objective validity of historical judgment demands a sustained philosophical inquiry, for the attempt to establish this validity is the key to Dilthey's unique approach to the study of man, and to his important attempt to secure the human studies on an autonomous foundation".[25]

Because Dilthey emphasized the uniqueness of historical and/or individual events and works, H. A. Hodges contended that Dilthey triumphantly embraced a "radical relativism".[26] However, John E. Sullivan argues that Hodges overstates Dilthey's relativism. Sullivan maintains Dilthey never rested secure in his relativism. He cites Dilthey's own testimony on this point. In a lecture delivered on his seventieth birthday, Dilthey asserted there are three types of philosophical worldviews: materialism or positivism; classical or objective idealism; and the idealism of liberty and freedom. Dilthey himself was personally most sympathetic to the latter type but he argued:

> Every world view is conditioned historically and therefore limited and relative. A frightful anarchy of thought appears. The very historical consciousness that has brought forth this absolute doubt, however, is able to set limits for it. The world views are divided by an inner law....These types of world views exist alongside each other through the centuries. The liberating element here is that the world views are grounded in the nature of the universe and in the relationship between the finite perceptive mind and the universe. Thus each world view expresses within its limitations one aspect of the universe. In this respect each is true. Each, however, is one-sided. To contemplate all the aspects in their totality is denied to us. We see the pure light of truth only in various broken rays....Historical consciousness shatters the lost chains that philosophy and the natural sciences could not break. Man has now achieved freedom....Confidently we may recognize in each of these views an element of truth. And if the course of our life brings us closer to a particular aspect of the incomprehensible harmony, if the truth of the world view which this particular aspect expresses fills us with creativity, then we may quietly surrender. For truth is present in them all.[27]

Dilthey therefore does not claim that we can never find truth--we may occasionally glimpse a "broken ray" of eternal truth.[28] He merely rejects the pretensions of the positivistic claim that we can fully capture all truth, dissect it, label it, and store it in air-tight containers for all future generations to venerate.

In "human studies", the researcher, Dilthey assumed, is striving not merely for the explanation of causal relations as in natural science, but also for understanding and interpretation.[29]

Dilthey's criticism of positivism and the emphasis which he placed upon "meaning" as the primary dimension of socio-historical phenomena resulted in the introduction of the concept of "verstehen" into the vocabulary of sociology. But the interpretation of the term itself created a longstanding dispute among sociologists of the 20th century. The controversy is rooted in the fact that, at times, Dilthey used the term to refer to the process of understanding, while, in other instances, he used it to denote the result of the process. Almost every historian and/or theoretician of social sciences has discussed the concept of verstehen.[30]

It is important to note that in Dilthey's view we do not know ourselves through verstehen but only another. For our own experience is self-evident. Also the verb verstehen becomes a noun in Dilthey's thought and acquires a technical meaning which is narrower than "understanding" in the normal English or German usage. It primarily refers to the observation and theoretical interpretation of subjective states of mind of given actors. But Dilthey used the term to refer to a plethora of different kinds of understanding: individual gestures, words, art, textual interpretations, society, historical eras, biographical data, psychological states, etc.

Thus we can identify at least three major uses of the concept of verstehen in Dilthey:[31]

1. It can refer to the inner rational content of an act; e.g., the understanding of symbolic content of intellectual symbols, like mathematics or science.

2. It can refer to understanding by an empathic projection of one's self into another's emotional state; e.g., we can understand the sorrow caused by a death of another's father.

3. The last and highest form of verstehen is in the understanding of an artistic symbol--here the entire cognitive, emotional life of the artist must be relived.

The intellectual passage spanning from Dilthey to Max Weber includes two other outstanding thinkers, as well as many others less known, who should be at least mentioned here, to present a sequence of the development of ideas. Dilthey's distinction of sciences according to their subject matter clashed with the concept of Wilhelm Windelband. Although fifteen years younger, he published his first significant work almost simultaneously with Dilthey.[32]

Windelband did not accept Dilthey's classification of sciences according to their subject matter. Instead he assumed that reality is indivisible. He therefore proposed a division based on difference in methods which are used in research. In other words there is a difference between sciences and not between their subject matters. Because the same reality is approached by researchers from two different points of interest, some want to achieve a generalized knowledge of phenomena, others are interested in a strictly individualized approach. Windelband introduced two terms which describe those approaches, terms which permanently enriched our scientific terminology: "nomothetic" and "idiographic". Studies developed by those who seek "laws" and general relationships are of a <u>nomothetic</u> character, while studies by those who search for the uniqueness of phenomena are <u>idiographic</u>. In nomothetic sciences we are looking for that which is repeatable and unchanging; in idiographic studies we focus on the unrepeatable and individualized phenomenon.

However, Windelband realized that the same subject matter may be studied from two angles: generalizing or individualizing. Although natural phenomena are usually approached nomothetically, each of them can be a subject of idiographic studies. Some disciplines of the natural sciences possess, by nature, an idiographic character, e.g., geology. Nonetheless, Windelband contended in the humanities the idiographic method dominates--this was perhaps more true for his time than for our own.

Heinrich Rickert continued this discussion. He presented a compromise which incorporated elements from the approaches of both Dilthey and Windelband. Thus, he offered a dual classification of the sciences. From the standpoint of the subject matter, he distinguished natural sciences and cultural sciences. From the methodological standpoint he differentiated nomothetic and ideographic sciences. Like Windelband, he assumed that the subject matter of both the natural sciences and the "cultural sciences"[33] was the same. The methodology of natural science is justified in both fields. But in order to decide to which group a particular study belongs, one needs intersecting divisions of methods and subjects. "All scientific work is carried on in an <u>intermediate</u> region between the two polar <u>extremes</u> of a <u>generalizing</u> method and an individualizing method".[34] For example, psychology's subject matter belongs to the sphere of human cultural life, but studied by the nomothetic methods of the natural sciences and therefore this discipline belongs to natural rather than cultural sciences. It is so because "A decision on this depends only upon the <u>point of view</u> they take toward the objects that constitute their subject matter, i.e., whether they regard them merely as part of nature or relate them to cultural life".[35]

Rickert rejected the alleged irrationalism of intuitive cognition and tried to rationalize the concept of humanistic studies by stressing the objectivity of historical analysis. However, his historical methodology was limited to the description of individual phenomena and subjects. He did not believe in a possibility of historical generalization or formulation of historical laws. In his view, history as well as the cultural sciences are "concerned with objects which are related to general cultural <u>values</u> and which can therefore be understood as meaningful".[36] Rickert influenced Max Weber not only in terms of his criterion for the classification of science but also through his views on the meaningfulness and significance of values. He assumed that in historical studies the changes in cultural values serve as the historian's "criterion of relevance...."[37]

CHAPTER V FOOTNOTES

1. George Simpson used this term to identify Comte as the original progenitor of sociology. See <u>Auguste Comte: Sire of Sociology</u> (New York: Thomas W. Crowell, 1969).

2. The intrusion of positivistic empiricism affected the institutional make-up of the universities. Holborn points out, "As the sciences amassed an ever growing knowledge, the departments of study proliferated, and the individual could call only a relatively small field his own". Hajo Holborn, <u>A History of Modern Germany: 1840-1945</u> (New York: Alfred A. Knopf, 1969), p. 396.

3. Wladyslaw Tatarkiewicz, <u>Historia Filozofii</u>, Warszawa, 1950, Vol. III, p. 188.

4. Man is seen by positivists as a part of nature, not essentially different from other natural phenomena. Hence the tie between positivism and naturalistic humanism, as discussed earlier.

5. A. Gella, "Past and Present Polish Sociology", <u>East European Quarterly</u>, Vol. II, No. 2, 1968; and "Current Development of Sociology in Poland", in D. Martindale and R. Mohan, <u>Current Development of World Sociology</u> (in press); and J. Szczepanski (ed.), <u>Empirical Sociology in Poland</u>, P.N.W. Warszawa 1966.

6. Dilthey was born near Mainz in 1833, the son of a pastor of the Reformed Church. He received his doctorate from Berlin in 1864 and was named Professor of Philosophy at Basel in 1867 where he was a colleague of Jacob Burckhardt. He taught at Kiel and Breslau and was called to the Chair of Philosophy at Berlin in 1882 where he remained until his death in 1911.

7. Wilhelm Dilthey, "Selected Passages from Wilhelm Dilthey", tr. H. A. Hodges, in Hodges, <u>Wilhelm Dilthey: An Introduction</u> (New York: Howard Fertig, 1969), pp. 139-40 and 141.

8. Karl Jaspers, <u>Three Essays</u> (New York: Harcourt, Brace and World, 1964), p. 191.

9. Quoted by M. Mauss,"Simmel in German Sociology" in <u>Essays on Sociology, Philosophy and Aesthetics</u>, Kurt Wolff, ed. (New

York: Harper and Row, 1959), p. 191.

10. George Lichtheim, <u>George Lukacs</u> (New York: Viking Press, 1970).

11. H. A. Hodges, "Wilhelm Dilthey" in <u>International Encyclopedia of the Social Sciences</u>, David L. Sills, ed. (New York: Macmillan and The Free Press, 1968), Vol. 4, p. 186.

12. H. A. Hodges describes Dilthey's philosophical approach as the result of a mingling of British and French Empiricism and the German transcendental philosophy of the post-Kantian period. He characterizes Dilthey's work as "critical" philosophy in the Kantian sense because it is primarily concerned with epistemological issues and the logic and methodology of the sciences. Hodges lists "the apostles of romantic humanism", Lessing and Goethe, as Dilthey's spiritual ancestors. In describing Dilthey, Hodges writes: "He carried over something of the spirit of the age of romanticism into the age of scientific humanism, and brought the enthusiasm of Goethe into the midst of the bewilderment of the twentieth century". Hodges, <u>An Introduction</u>..., pp. 1-2.

13. Wilhelm Dilthey, <u>The Essence of Philosophy</u>, trans. by Stephen A. Emery and William T. Emery (Chapel Hill: University of North Carolina Press, 1954), p. x. Dilthey's use of the term 'human studies' (sometimes less adequately translated as 'cultural sciences') should alert us to the fact that the tension between humanism and positivism is not limited to sociology. The psychologist Gordon Allport sees virtually all modern psychological theories as being based in a view of the mind as either passive (Locke) or active (Leibnitz).

14. Lockean theories see the mind as reacting to external stimuli, while Leibnitzian theories see the mind as self-propelled. Skinnerian behavior-modification is one outcome of the Lockean tradition of concern with the external, while the phenomenology of Husserl follows from the Leibnitzian tradition of concern for that internal to the mind. (Gordon Allport, <u>Becoming</u>, New Haven: Yale University Press, 1955.) Similarly the anthropologist Paul Radin insisted on the internal character of studies of culture in his statement, "Cultural facts do not speak for themselves, but physical facts do. A pebble is a pebble and a tree is a tree". (Paul Radin, <u>Method and Theory of Ethnology</u> (New York: Basic Books, 1966. Original edition, 1923). Radin in this phrase might well have been echoing Dilthey's earlier statement: "Meaning or value cannot be possessed by something which cannot be understood. A tree can never have meaning". (Wilhelm Dilthey, <u>Pattern and Meaning in History</u>, edited with an Introduction by H. P.

Rickman (New York: Harper and Row, 1962), p. 164.

14. H. V. White, "Translator Preface", in Carlo Antoni, From History to Sociology (Detroit, 1959), p. xi.

15. Dilthey, Pattern and Meaning in History, op. cit., p. 3.

16. Dilthey, The Essence of Philosophy, op. cit., p. 3.

17. G. H. Mead, Mind, Self, and Society (Chicago, 1937).

18. H. P. Rickman, "General Introduction", in Dilthey, Pattern and Meaning in History, p. 18.

19. Ibidem, pp. 41 and 45.

20. Dilthey, Pattern and Meaning in History, op. cit., p. 67.

21. H. N. Tuttle, Wilhelm Dilthey's Philosophy of Historical Understanding: A Critical Analysis (Leiden, E. J. Brill, 1969). Tuttle adds: "This question of the objective validity of historical judgment demands a sustained philosophical inquiry, for the attempt to establish this validity is the key to Dilthey's unique approach to the study of man, and to his important attempt to secure the human studies on an autonomous foundation". (p. 1.)

22. All of the major classical sociologists who contributed to the development of humanistic sociology had extensive backgrounds in the humanities: Max Weber's background in law, economics, history, music, and literature; Florian Znaniecki's background in philosophy and publication of a book of poetry; Sorokin's tremendous historical knowledge and literary scholarship on Tolstoy; and Mannheim's background in the humanities which led to his founding of the sociology of knowledge. Stanislaw Ossowski, himself an outstanding humanist in sociology, in writing about the two types of sociology pointed out that among the factors which makes empirical sociology so popular today is that "one can get knowledge of research methods much faster than one can master a broad humanistic culture". O. Osobliwosciach mamk spolecznych (Warszawa PWN, 1962), p. 200.

23. Quoted in Hodges, op. cit., pp. 24 and 148 respectively.

24. Ibidem, pp. 29 and 146-7 respectively.

25. H. N. Tuttle, Wilhelm Dilthey's Philosophy of Historical Understanding: A Critical Analysis, op. cit., p. 1.

26. H. A. Hodges, Wilhelm Dilthey: An Introduction, p. ix.

27. John Edward Sullivan, Prophets of the West (New York: Holt, Rinehart and Winston, Inc., 1970), p. 122, n. 43.

28. The position assumed by Dilthey resembles that endorsed by Peter Berger and Thomas Luckmann, in their volume on the sociology of knowledge, The Social Construction of Reality (New York: Doubleday, 1966).

29. H. Hodges, op. cit., pp. 146-7.

30. "Historians of the development of sociology frequently complain about the difficulty, obscurity and ambiguity of the concept of 'understanding' when the close study of Dilthey would have done much to minimize these difficulties". H. P. Rickman, op. cit., p. 18.

31. One of the recent contributions to this lengthy debate is a three-chapter discussion in Mokrzycki's Zalozenia Socjologii Humanistycznej (The Assumptions of the Humanistic Sociology), Warszawa PWN, 1971.

32. Windelband, Normen und Naturgesetze (1882).

33. Rickert used the term "cultural sciences" to designate humanities, social sciences, and history.

34. Heinrich Rickert, Science and History: A Critique of Positivist Epistemology, trans. by G. Reisman and edited by Arthur Goddard (Princeton, N.J.: D. Van Nostrand Co., Inc., 1962), p. 23.

35. Ibidem, p. xii.

36. Ibidem, p. 99.

37. Ibidem, p. 23.

CHAPTER VI

TOWARD INTERPRETIVE UNDERSTANDING: MAX WEBER

Kant and Hegel, Marx and Nietzsche, Wundt and Freud made German the language of science in the 19th century. To the development of sociology, the greatest contribution in German was made by Max Weber. The German historicist tradition--particularly as it was manifested in the thought of Wilhelm Dilthey--had a profound influence upon the intellectual milieu in which Max Weber pursued his scholarly career. The scientific ethos of positivism had crept steadily into the German intellectual arena, while the rapidly increasing body of knowledge invited a proliferation of scientific specialities. As the natural sciences gathered together an ever-expanding knowledge of the empirical world, traditional German scholarship, with its roots in Idealistic and Romantic philosophical soil, was called into serious question by Anglo-French positivism.

The influence of the historical debate of the German philosophers regarding the nature of the "human studies" or "cultural sciences" upon the humanistic trend in sociology begins with Max Weber. Although Weber was not always in agreement with the conclusions of Dilthey or the Neo-Kantians, he nevertheless worked on the road to which they opened the gate. Indeed, most historians of sociological theory have treated Max Weber as the real architect of the humanistic approach within sociology.

Although Weber had close personal connections with both Dilthey and Rickert,[1] scholars have generally tended to underestimate the importance of the influence Dilthey exercised over Weber. This is probably largely due to the fact that Weber sided with Windelband and Rickert and against Dilthey and Simmel in the controversy regarding the classification of the sciences.[2] Weber also rejected Dilthey's and Simmel's respective contentions that intuition is a legitimate means of grasping historical knowledge. Instead, Weber placed greater emphasis upon the importance of causal imputation within the methodology of the social sciences. However, Weber's profound excursis on "verstehen" owes a deep and lasting debt to Dilthey and Simmel.[3]

The essential humanistic elements in Weber's sociology were but a continuation of Dilthey's legacy: its translation from philosophical to sociological language. The overwhelming importance of the work of Dilthey and the Neo-Kantians for humanistic sociology resides in the fact that they resisted the positivistic reduction of mind to nature and restored "meaning" as the central focus for historical and/or sociological analysis.

Weber conceptualized sociology as one of the historical sciences. He restored the spatial and temporal dimensions to a position of importance in social analysis. He rejected the view of his intellectual predecessors that one cannot find general laws in history or build theories of historical development. Weber's view of the rationality of human behavior essentially enlarged Rickert's concept of the historical methods in sociology. Weber maintained that in the social sciences we can go beyond the idiographic approach and search for laws. However, laws of the kind possible in the natural sciences where the phenomena under study recur with regularity cannot be constructed in the cultural sciences where such regularities as there are, are merely probabilities. He also emphasized that the discovery of laws is the final goal in the natural sciences, while in the social sciences formulation of social laws only serves to approach the final goal which is "verstehen".[4]

Weber assumed that since social science deals with unique phenomena, causal explanation must refer to each concrete case individually, explaining why a particular outcome resulted and not some other outcome. In Weber's view, the study of unique, concrete cases is the concern of history. Thus, he is as much of an historical relativist as Dilthey although he rejected Dilthey's denial of the possibility of generalization.

Nevertheless, Weber, like Dilthey, was never comfortable with relativism. Indeed, he consistently and sometimes vehemently denied that he was a relativist. Nevertheless, we agree with the judgment of Gerhart Masur that Weber succumbed to the "knife of historical relativism" when he professed a "polytheism" of values.[5] Weber maintained,

> Scientific pleading is meaningless in principle because the various value spheres of the world stand in irreconcilable conflict with each other....If one proceeds from pure experience, one arrives at polytheism...We live as did the ancients when their world was not yet disenchanted of its gods and demons, only we live in a different sense. As Hellenic man at times sacrificed to Aphrodite and at other times to Apollo, and, above

all, as everybody sacrificed to the gods of
his city, so do we still nowadays, only the
bearing of man has been disenchanted and de-
nuded of its mystical but inwardly genuine
plasticity. Fate, and certainly not 'science', holds sway over these gods and their
struggles. One can only understand what the
godhead is for the one order or for the other,
or better, what godhead is in the one or in
the other order.[6]

When the work of Weber's close friend and sometimes collaborator, Ernst Troeltsch, was labelled 'relativistic', the historian of religion responded, "Truth is always polymorph never monomorph; it manifests itself in different forms and kinds, not in different degrees".[7] We suspect that if Weber had directly answered the charge of relativism, he would not have chosen words that differed substantially from the humanistic ethos professed by Troeltsch. But one should remember that the idea of relativism which was a watchword of humanism at that time is a symptom of the threat to the existence of humankind in our time.

Weber found a solution to the problem of how to create a generalizing science (sociology) whose data was unique and irregular in the methodology of the ideal type. The ideal type is an analytic model, not existing in the real world, containing the essential features of the type, which is useful in comparing events and structures actually existing in concrete historical situations. As Albert Salomon points out:

> These constructions are not hypotheses but
> merely aids toward forming hypotheses. They
> provide no copy of the real world, being tech-
> nically constructed concepts, intended merely
> to serve as fixed points of reference for
> measuring the extent of the divergence there-
> from of the individual imputations.[8]

Through the use of ideal types, cross-cultural comparisons are possible and developmental theories feasible. Weber's models of administration which follow from his types of domination, for example, are useful in describing existing administrative bodies and in discovering long-term tendencies toward one model and away from others. As Alfred Schutz has pointed out, the ideal type is not an esoteric procedure, but rather an adoption for scientific use of the basic process of typification in the everyday world. People create types in their minds all the time, Schutz argues. It is a fundamental way in which all people structure and deal with their world.[9] The ideal type of the social scientist, as developed by Weber, differs only in that it is constructed and applied with far more rigor, clarity, and precision.[10]

However, it is worth noting what Mark J. Goodman found, that two basic principles underlying Max Weber's method of ideal type are the following: "...the rejection of conceptual realism (or reification) in favor of the separation of object and construct, and the insistence that value criteria are always present in the selection for study of cultural objects".[11]

In other important ways, Weber's position is quite similar to that of Dilthey. Weber stresses the centrality of meaning to the historian and the social scientist:

> In the context used here (sociology) shall mean that science which aims at the interpretive understanding of social behavior in order to gain an explanation of its causes, its course, and its effects. It will be called human "behavior" only in so far as the person or persons involved engage in some subjectively meaningful action. Such behavior may be mental or external; it may consist in action or omission to act. The term "social behavior" will be reserved for activities whose intent is related by the individuals involved to the conduct of others and is oriented accordingly.[12]

Meaning here is "'subjectively intended meaning' (subjectiv gemeinter Sinn), not objective, metaphysical meaning".[13] Meaning is not simply available to sensory perception, it must be grasped, comprehended, interpretively understood.

Weber recognized the positivistic tradition in sociology insofar as he did not search for social facts but for an understanding of social actions. However, he did not attempt to elaborate a prefabricated method for the objective evaluation of social actions and related social structures. Instead, he elaborated a procedure allowing us to comprehend in as objective a manner as he deemed feasible how the acting persons evaluate, create or destroy social relations and structures.

The German word *verstehen*, used by Dilthey, Simmel and Weber, has become the technical term indicating this narrowed meaning. Its normal translation is understanding, but the more adequate translation of Weber's meaning is interpretive understanding or comprehending. Schutz has clearly demonstrated that *verstehen* is not a matter of "private, uncontrollable, and unverifiable intuition of the observer",[14] but rather a feature of everyday life as well as a method of social science. The human world, natural and cultural, is not private, but rather intersubjective--a point well illustrated by Schutz's discussion of the process of positivistic science:

> ...the postulate of describing and explaining human behavior in terms of controllable sensory observation stops short before the description and explanation of the process by which scientist B controls and verifies the observational findings of scientist A and the conclusions drawn by him. In order to do so, B has to know what A have observed, what the goal of his inquiry is, why he thought the observed fact worthy of being observed, i.e., relevant to the scientific problem at hand, etc. This knowledge is commonly called understanding. The explanation of how such a mutual understanding of human beings might occur is apparently left to the social scientist. But whatever his explanation might be, one thing is sure, namely, that such an intersubjective understanding between scientist B and scientist A occurs neither by scientist B's observation of scientist A's overt behavior, nor by introspection performed by B, nor by identification of B with A.[15]

Verstehen in a culture is the result of learning the intersubjective world, the world held in common with others and in which language and communication are shared. Schutz contends verstehen (interpretive understanding, comprehending) is controllable by others "at least to the same extent to which the private sensory perceptions of an individual are controllable".[16] Verstehen is "subjective because its goal is to find out what the actor 'means' in his action"[17] and not because it is any more private, intuitive, uncontrollable, unverifiable, or value laden than sensory perception.

Verstehen had great significance for further humanistic developments in sociology. It appeared later in Znaniecki's and MacIver's works under the name "imaginative reconstruction" and is akin to what Charles Horton Cooley (who was born the same year as Weber) called "sympathetic introspection". Some sociologists[18] emphasized the operational character of Weber's method of interpretive understanding. Edmund Mokrzycki has recently listed some of the "embarrassing" aspects of the operation of verstehen:

> 1. ...only those mental states of others can be grasped by the Verstehen operation which have in some way become elements of our own inner experience...

> 2. ...its efficient use requires abilities that cannot be fully developed in an ordinary academic training.
>
> 3. ...Verstehen as a procedure is not liable of standardization...
>
> 4. ...the results of such an operation can in a sense be verified intersubjectively, namely by mutual confrontation of results.[19]

It can be doubted whether such a verification, based not on an appropriate criterion, but on the <u>consensus omnium</u>, is satisfactory, and whether it deserves to be called intersubjective. Nevertheless, Mokrzycki acknowledges that,

> If the knowledge of human mental states cannot be acquired otherwise than by means of the Verstehen operation, then, for all the shortcomings of that procedure, we have to accept it as a scientific method, unless we reject the assumption that mental states belong to the subject matter of the social sciences (a subject matter interpreted not necessarily in the way done by representatives of humanistic sociology).[20]

We agree with Mokrzycki that the campaign led by George Lundberg to eliminate the operation of <u>verstehen</u> from the methodology of the social sciences "has failed completely" for no matter how much energy goes into 'operationalizing' or mathematizing terms, human mental states cannot be 'observed'.[21] They must be 'interpreted' by the researcher and expressed through the screen of meaning of the language in which he reports his findings.

Like Dilthey and Simmel, Weber firmly refused to shroud these 'embarrassments' of the data of the social sciences in organismic or physicalist analogies and metaphors.

Weber also resembles Dilthey in his recognition of the relativity of history and the human studies themselves. Neither can be free of values. The culture in which the social scientist lives and participates, and the ultimate values which give his life meaning, structure his conception of reality and form his scientific questions. As Weber stated flatly in his methodological essays, "There is no absolutely 'objective' analysis of culture".[22] Or, as F. H. Blum reiterates Weber, "A social science free from value judgements does not eliminate the problem of values; it makes them part of scientific consideration".[23] Social science is, therefore, based in values. But insofar as it would be still science, Weber insists that it must be value-free in two ways. The values of the scientist should not influence the course of the analysis:

> It is the fate of a cultural epoch which has eaten of the tree of knowledge to be aware that however completely we may investigate history we cannot read its real meaning, and that we must be content therefore to create our own sense of history; that our Weltanschauung can never be the product of progressive knowledge of experience, and that thus the highest ideals and those which move us most deeply, work themselves out permanently only through conflict with rival ideals which are quite as sacred to other individuals as ours are to us.[24]

and secondly, that science cannot find or demonstrate values:

> We know no ideals which can be demonstrated in scientific terms. To be sure, it is only the more arduous a task to draw them from one's own breast in a period of culture which is so subjective. But we have no fool's paradise and no streets of gold to offer, either in this world or the next, either in thought or in action; and it is a stigma of our dignity as men that the peace of our souls shall never be as great as the peace of him who dreams of such a paradise.[25]

These four aspects of Max Weber's thought--that a social act is one which has meaning for the participants in it; <u>verstehen</u>, meaning interpretive understanding or comprehending; the methodology of the ideal type; and the injunction to be value-free--are the essential features of his contribution to the development of humanistic sociology. All stand in fundamental opposition to the positivist program for unified science, and all have been frequently distorted.[26]

In tracing the origins of Weber's humanistic sociology, we cannot ignore the influence of what is today referred to as 'existential humanism'. Although existential humanism is an eclectic amalgam of diverse philosophical positions, William Barrett has convincingly demonstrated that existentialism constitutes a continuity of thought in the western intellectual tradition which grew up in critical response to the ethos of scientific rationalism.[27] While Weber could hardly be regarded as a 'founder' of modern existentialism, Weber's Germany--the Germany of Dilthey, Simmel, Husserl, George, Rilke, Jaspers, Heidegger and the young Lukacs--was the center of the nascent phenomenological movement and Weber's philosophy is informed by the concerns of that movement. With the exception of Dilthey, all of the above tended to regard themselves to some extent as Nietzsche's *epigoni*. Weber himself remarked to one of his students at Munich:

> The honesty of a contemporary scholar, and above all of a contemporary philosopher, can be easily ascertained in terms of his position vis-a-vis Nietzsche and Marx. Those who do not admit that they could not do major parts of their own work without the contributions made by these two men, deceive themselves as well as others. The world in which we live intellectually has been shaped to a large extent by Marx and Nietzsche.[28]

Nietzsche's legacy was but one of the currents of existential or proto-existential thought which stimulated members of Max Weber's intellectual circle. Art historians credit Simmel and Rickert with bringing the vitalism of Henri Bergson to the attention of the German intellectual community--an effort which had an immediate and deep impact in shaping the humanistic ethos of the German expressionist movement and was subsequently absorbed into the 'life philosophies' of Heidegger and Jaspers.[29] While Weber himself ultimately rejected expressionism as escapism--a form of "spiritual narcotic"[30]--he closely followed the activities of the neo-romanticism of Stefan George and his followers.[31] One of George's disciples and a former student of Simmel's, George Lukacs, was an important and highly esteemed visitor to the Weber salon at Heidelberg.[32] Intellectual historians generally attribute the revival of interest in the ideas of Soren Kierkegaard (who was then almost totally forgotten) to the brilliant work Lukacs completed in the sociology of literature during the period before he became active in the Hungarian communist party.[33] In addition, Weber himself had a deep and sustained interest in Russian history and culture.[34] It might be said that the modern existential novel was born in Russia. The works of Gogol, Dostoevsky, Turgenev and Tolstoy held a particular fascination for German intellectuals during the declining years of the Wilhelmic empire. A member of Weber's circle reports the great sociologist developed a special affinity for the works of the brilliant precursor of the modern philosophy of the 'absurd', Fyodor Dostoevsky.[35] Thus Paul Honigsheim reported of his weekly visits to Weber's home, "I don't remember a single Sunday conversation in which the name of Dostoevsky did not occur".[36] We have belabored the documentation of the existential links to Weber's intellectual milieu because American sociologists have tended to ignore or depreciate them. Significantly, Europeans have generally not done so.[37] Recent developments in the sociology of science which have underscored the importance of networks of intellectual apprenticeship and colleagueship in the diffusion of scientific knowledge seem to render the American position untenable.[38] Max Weber was personally acquainted with and in some cases closely associated with nearly all of the most significant figures who shaped the burgeoning German phenomenological movement of his day--in effect, they constituted an important segment of his "personal invisible college".[39]

What bonds of commonality existed between the existentialist tradition and Weber's thought? One common theme is the concern with what Karl Jaspers called the "subject-object cleavage". Rollo May writes, "Existentialism, in short, is the endeavor to understand man by cutting below the cleavage between subject and object which has bedeviled Western thought and science since shortly after the Renaissance".[40] The subject-object dichotomy pertains to the relation between the human subject and objective world: "We always think about particular and definite objects, and there can be no 'object' without a contrasting conscious subject".[41] The subject's knowledge of the external world is particularistic in that it can never approach completeness. By accepting this distinction, 19th-century existentialists found holistic interpretations of reality most untenable.

As we have seen, Weber would agree that knowledge of the external world is at once particularistic and incomplete. He repeatedly stressed the position that sociology is a science "which aims at the interpretive understanding of social behavior".[42] One implication of this statement is that our view of social reality is inevitably pluralistic. Just as Weber had viewed Marx's economic interpretation of the development of capitalism as one of many possible interpretations, he viewed his own work The Protestant Ethic and the Spirit of Capitalism in a similar light. Weber was an important step removed from the naive belief that a total scientific explanation of man and society was forthcoming. This faith in a holistic interpretation of the world arose out of the early 19th-century ethos of scientific rationalism. Weber shared no such vision.[43]

An additional outgrowth of the subject-object cleavage was the assumption that subjective understanding is historically and culturally conditioned. Weber's awareness of this conditional character of subjective knowledge is reflected in his conception of value relevance. This concept arises out of the neo-Kantian conviction that value is the center of human experience--that man imposes meaning of the objective world in accordance with his values. For Weber all scientific endeavors are value-relevant in that the subject's choice of the object to be studied is culturally and historically conditioned. Thus, F. H. Blum writes of Weber, "where human affairs are concerned, there can never be an objectivity in the sense of neutrality--even for a scientist".[44] In short, the cultural, intellectual, and/or historical ambience of the scientific observer influences the nature of the questions he puts to reality.

In addition, the existentialist position regarding the conditional character of human knowledge raises many epistemological difficulties for social scientific methodology. Whereas Jaspers sought to avoid a complete relativism by stressing a cautious use of method, the extreme stress placed upon individualism by Kierkegaard and Nietzsche called any scientific assessments of reality into serious question. And yet, for Weber, the cultural relativism implied in the concept of value relevance does not necessarily lead to scientific anarchy. Values are an integral stone in the foundation of Weber's conception of social science. Through the concept of value relevance, Weber willingly conceded that the subject's selection of research questions was indeed conditional, but at the same time he argued that systematic methods of presenting knowledge in a scientifically valid way could be constructed. Hence, he sought to reconcile the relativistic implications of existentialism's focus upon the subject-object cleavage with scientific rationalism's requirements for exactitude. As we have already seen, the ideal type was one method Weber employed toward securing this end.

Another area of intellectual commonality between existential thinkers and Weber was the preoccupation with individual consciousness, choice, and meaning. Human behavior is viewed as potentially self-directed. Meaning is conferred upon the objective world through choice. Also, in that human social behavior as well as the behavior of those studying it in a systematic fashion is ever-imploded with subjective meaning, the method of verstehen is prerequisite for our understanding of society. Weber shared existentialism's deep reverence for the individual. In his theory of social action, the individual is viewed as the basic unit of sociological analysis. The individual is considered ethically autonomous and free to make responsible choices concerning his or her life and socio-political condition. Science must be wary of encroaching upon the freedom of the individual. The role of science is not to propagandize or to make certitudinous pronouncements, but to present ideas in an ethically neutral fashion.[45] Although Weber envisioned a future society in which the free agent would be bureaucratized and rationalized beyond recognition, through a disenchanted world which would entrap the individual in an "iron cage", Weber never lost faith in the value of ethical responsibility.

Finally, Weber shared existentialism's persistent sensitivity to the predicament of the individual in modern society. Kierkegaard sees the individual as dying a slow death amid the forces of massification. Nietzsche at once denigrates the unthinking, unwilling member of the social "herd" and resurrects the individual in the heroic guise of the "superman". Jaspers recognizes the loneliness and lack of meaning experienced by the individual within the community of masses and stresses the importance of value-related choice. The pathos of Weber's futuristic vision of the "iron cage" parallels the concerns of his existential counterparts. Weber shares the conviction of the existentialists and all the great humanists of the past that the individual serves at once as a focus of analytic concern and a reference point from which a broader understanding of social behavior and the human condition may be derived.

We can summarize the influences of existentialist thought on Weber in this way. In the final analysis, Weber harbored a dual faith in science and the individual. Despite the relativistic implications of human value for the scientific endeavor, he firmly believed in the capability of science to decipher the nature of various aspects of reality through the proper employment of a rigorously defined methodology. The true legitimacy of scientific knowledge, however, lies in its relation to the individual social actor. Science should not attempt to dictate how man should live or construct his reality, but aid him in fulfilling this endeavor in an ethically neutral way. The essential character of Weber's humanistic sociology resides in the uneasy but essential union of a recognition of the validity inherent in the tradition of scientific rationalism and a realization of the freedom and dignity of the individual.

In this brief essay, we cannot explore in any detail the huge biographical literature on Max Weber which has accumulated in recent years.[46] Perhaps no biographer has been more directly concerned with extolling the humanistic facets of Weber's character than Karl Jaspers.[47] For our purposes, it is perhaps sufficient to remind the reader, as Gerth and Mills did, of Max Weber's "humanism, his love for the underdog, his hatred of sham and lies, and his unceasing campaign against racism and anti-Semitic demagoguery".[48] Weber's professorial ethic reflects this humanism:

> The primary task of a useful teacher is to teach his students to recognize 'inconvenient' facts --I mean facts that are inconvenient for their party opinions. And for every party there are facts that are extremely inconvenient, for my own opinion no less than for others. I believe the teacher accomplishes more than a mere intellectual task if he compels his audience to accustom itself to the existence of such facts. I would be so immodest as even to apply the expression 'moral achievement', though perhaps this may sound too grandiose for something that should go without saying.[49]

Jaspers and others have recognized Max Weber's "moral achievement" because the ethic which the great sociologist professed did not "go without saying" in the milieu in which he lived. Jaspers summed up the heroic humanism of Max Weber's character in these words:

> He struggled against the rationalists, because they do not take a critical view of the laws of knowledge, and against the irrationalists, because they fail to recognize the role of knowledge as an irreplaceable means of grasping the truth; against philosophical dishonesty, which for the sake of harmony conceals the abysmal depths with conceptual schematisms; this 'formal garden' style, as he called it, never ceased to arouse his anger. Consequently, Weber was attacked on the ground that freedom from value judgments is supposedly impossible and that science characterized by freedom from value judgments gives no satisfaction. But behind Weber's demands stood a passion for truth, which by pursuing every mode of knowledge with clarity strives the more resolutely toward the point where knowledge is not gained through science, but by acting and producing in the world....He rejected every form of violation of the freedom of conscience.[50]

CHAPTER VI FOOTNOTES

1. Dilthey was a friend of Weber's father and an occasional guest in the home of Max Weber Senior during his son's formative years. Rickert, Weber's contemporary, was a close friend and associate of Weber at Berlin and again in Heidelberg.

2. It should be noted that this debate generated a great deal of antipathy among partisans because its resolution would have a significant impact upon the manner in which the academic departments would be re-organized to accommodate the new discipline of sociology within the German university system during a period when academic appointments were limited and highly coveted.

3. Although we did not devote to Simmel a separate chapter, we agree with Clinton Joyce Jesser also that "Simmel was a humanist in several respects" (Social Theory Revisited, The Dryden Press, Hinsdale, 1975), p. 225.

    We should remember that Simmel, like Dilthey, was primarily a philosopher and that his sociological writings represent only a small portion of his scholarly output. In his philosophy even more than in his sociology, Simmel must be labelled a 'humanist'. Simmel's philosophical approach was deeply influenced by Goethe and Bergson--and Simmel, in turn, influenced the German 'life' philosophers, Heidegger, Jaspers, and Buber. Albert Salomon traces the deep humanist strain in the Simmelian philosophical perspective. Salomon contends that Goethe--surely one of the greatest humanists of all times--occupies a position of supreme importance in Simmel's intellectual orientation. Salomon writes: "Goethe was anti-dogmatic and anti-irrational in his efforts to conceive of the totality of life. He understood the process of nature as dynamic polarity. All phenomena of life have positive and negative, constructive and destructive, aspects of life. Life is complex and dynamic, moving in a variety of polarities. This basic philosophical attitude of Goethe's unites naturalism and spiritualism in a new kind of realism. As such, it has been stimulating to modern efforts to counteract the general trends of positivistic and mechanistic methods and philosophies. In the field of philosophy, George Simmel attempted to find the prototype of his philosophy of life in Goethe's thinking". Salomon maintains that this thesis has been verified by a student of Simmel's, Barker Fairley, in the latter's A Study of Goethe. See In Praise of Enlightenment (Cleveland: World Publishing Co., 1962, p. 174). Elsewhere, Salomon characterized Simmel's "philosophy of life" as "the leitmotif of his thought"--the essential core without which the rest of his work remains largely fragmented and unintelligible. See "German Sociology" in Twentieth Century Sociology, edited by Georges Gurvitch and Wilbert E. Moore (New York: The Philosophical Library, 1945), p. 609. For a thorough exegesis of Simmel's Lebensphilosophie, see Rudolph H. Weingartner, Experience and Culture (Middletown, Conn.: Wesleyon University Press, 1960) and "Georg Simmel" in volume 7 of The Encyclopedia of Philosophy (New York: Macmillan and The Free Press, 1967).

4. From a methodological point of view social sciences are distinguished from natural sciences by the fact that whereas for the latter the formulations of laws on the basis of classified facts is the end goal of knowledge, for the former, by reason of their preoccupation with individual patterns of concatenation, the general laws and norms of causal sequence are merely a means to understanding.

5. Gerhard Masur, Prophets of Yesterday (New York: Macmillan Co., 1961).

6. Max Weber, "Science as a Vocation" in From Max Weber: Essays in Sociology, translated and edited by Hans Gerth and C. Wright Mills (New York: Oxford University Press, 1958), p. 148.

7. Troeltsch quoted by Wilhelm Pauck in Harnack and Troeltsch (New York: Oxford University Press, 1968), p. 90.

8. Albert Salomon, "Max Weber's Methodology", Social Research, 1:2, 1934, p. 161.

9. Alfred Schutz, "Concept and Theory Formation in the Social Sciences", Collected Papers I (The Hague: Martinus Nijhoff, 1967).

10. Unfortunately many social scientists have not been as prudent as Weber in their applications of the ideal type procedure. Consequently, many writers have tended to reify ideal types even though Weber himself punctuated his outline of the methodology of type construction with the following sobering warning: "The maintenance of this distinction in all its rigor often becomes uncommonly difficult in practice due to certain circumstance. In the interest of the concrete demonstration of an ideal type or of an ideal-typical develop-

ment sequence, one seeks to make it clear by the use of concrete illustrative material drawn from empirical-historical reality. The danger of this procedure which in itself is entirely legitimate lies in the fact that historical knowledge here appears as a servant of theory instead of the opposite role. It is a great temptation for the theorist...to mix theory with history and indeed to confuse them with each other....The logical classification of analytical concepts on the one hand and the empirical arrangements of the events thus conceptualized in space, time, and causal relationship, on the other, appear to be so bound up together that there is an almost irresistible temptation to do violence to reality in order to prove the real validity of the construct". Max Weber, *The Methodology of the Social Sciences*, translated and edited by Edward A. Shils and Henry A. Finch (New York: The Free Press, 1949), pp. 102-103.

11. Mark J. Goodman, "Type Methodology and Type Myth: Some Antecedents of Max Weber's Approach", *Sociological Inquiry*, 45 (1), pp. 45-58.

12. Max Weber, *Basic Concepts in Sociology*, translated by H. P. Secher (New York, 1962), p. 29.

13. Salomon, 1934, *op. cit.*, p. 159.

14. Schutz, *op. cit.*, p. 56.

15. *Ibidem*, p. 54. K-O Apel makes a similar point in his "Communication and the Foundations of the Humanities", *Acta Sociologica*, 15:1, 1972, p. 22.

16. Schutz, *op. cit.*, p. 56.

17. *Ibidem*, p. 57.

18. Theodor Abel, "The Operation Called *Verstehen*", in H. Fergl and M. Brodbeck (eds.) *Reading in the Philosophy of Science* (New York, 1953) and Edmund Mokrzycki, "Operation of 'Verstehen'", *The Polish Sociological Bulletin*, No. 2, 1970.

In contrast, Werner Pelz presents a comprehensive review of the uses of "understanding" in social and humanistic sciences in *The Scope of Understanding in Sociology* (London: Routledge and Kegan-Paul, 1974). Pelz argues that these disciplines require "radical reorientation" which "would involve a reappraisal of many scientistic or positivistic assumptions and presumptions, a questioning of much we take for axiomatic and self-evident. Such sociological reorientation may call for a more thorough acknowledgment of our subjectivity and inter-subjectivity as our actuality which constitutes objectivity as merely one of its many objectives. Hence it may suggest conversation rather than argument, dialogue rather than debate, mutual empathy and complementation rather than conjectures and refutations, as the appropriate intercourse between fellow searchers..." (p. xi) Pelz suggests that to some extent even Dilthey and Weber unconsciously adapted the presuppositions of positivism.

19. Mokrzycki, "The Operation Called Verstehen", op. cit., pp. 10-11.

20. Ibidem, p. 11.

21. Ibidem, p. 13.

22. E. Shils and H. Finch, Max Weber on the Methodology of the Social Sciences (Illinois: Free Press of Glencoe, 1949), p. 90.

23. F. H. Blum, "Max Weber's Postulate of 'Freedom' from Value Judgements", in American Journal of Sociology, vol. 50, 1944-45, p. 36.

24. Translated and quoted by Salomon (1934), op. cit., p. 163.

25. Ibidem, p. 164

26. Distortions of Weber seem to result from the attempt to find ways to fit Weber, or at least a part of his thought, into a pre-existing theoretical framework in order to widen or extend its legitimation. Neo-positivist attempts (see for example Theodore Abel, "The Operation Called Verstehen", The American Journal of Sociology, 54 (1948), pp. 211-218) and and Marxist attempts (see for example Irving Zeitlin, Rethinking Sociology, Englewood Cliffs: Prentice-Hall, 1973, pp. 123-36 and 167-70) are relatively transparent. Talcott Parsons' distortions, however, have had the greatest impact because it is largely through Parsons' translations and commentaries that English-speaking sociologists have encountered Weber. In Parsons' translations, key Weberian terms are mistranslated (see R. Aron, Main Currents in Sociological Thought II, Garden City, 1970; R. Bendix, Max Weber: An Intellectual Portrait, Garden City, 1960; R. Dahrendorf, Class and Class Conflict in Industrial Society, Stanford, 1959; and A. Schutz, Collected Papers I, The Hague, 1967, for examples) and the specific is over-generalized and abstracted. Paul Lazarsfeld has pointed out "that the English translation of Weber's Protestant Ethic contains the term 'attitude' about forty times but that in the original Weber used instead a

large variety of nouns". (Bendix, op. cit., p. 272n) The
Weber who emerges from Parsons' distortions is one who fits
nicely into, and legitimates, Parsons' own theoretical
scheme. Compare, for example, the Secher translation quoted
in the text above and the translation of the same passage in
A. M. Henderson and Talcott Parsons, Max Weber: The Theory
of Social and Economic Organization, Glencoe, 1947, pp. 88ff.
Parsons seems not to have transcended his own specific social/
historical location in his dealings with Weber. (See A.
Gouldner, The Coming Crisis of Western Sociology, New York,
1970; D. Foss, "The World View of Talcott Parsons", in M.
Stein and A. Vidich, Sociology on Trial, Englewood Cliffs,
1963; and T. Parsons, "A Short Account of My Intellectual
Development", Alpha Kappa Delta, XXIX:I (Winter 1959). Parsons, son of a minister in the church of the New England
Puritans, clearly embraces ascetic Protestantism (see Parsons'
introduction to The Religion of India, Glencoe, 1958, and the
examples cited by Foss) and does not really comprehend the
larger framework of Weber's analysis. In the present discussion we are concerned with understanding Weber (as opposed
to putting him to some ideological use). Our discussion has,
therefore, been based on Weber's work itself (avoiding where
possible the translations of Parsons and his circle) and in
the discussions of his work by authors thoroughly grounded
in the philosophical tradition which underlies Weber's work
(primarily Albert Salomon and Alfred Schutz, and including
Aron and Bendix). [After the above was prepared, Cohen,
Hazelrigg and Pope's "De-Parsonizing Weber", American Sociological Review, 40:2 (April) 1975 appeared. This article
carefully documents in considerable detail Parsons extensive
and fundamental distortion of Weber.]

27. William Barrett, Irrational Man (New York: Doubleday and Co.,
1962). Barrett follows the development of existential thought
from St. Paul, Tertulian, and Augustine, through Pascal's
protest against an unquestioning scientific rationalism, to
the 19th-century voices of Kierkegaard, Nietzsche and Weber's
young friend Karl Jaspers. Very few attempts have been made
to bridge the gap between the two important approaches to
the study of twentieth-century man and society, sociology and
existentialism. Among the few notable exceptions are: Paul
Pfuetze's Self, Society, Existence (New York: Harper and
Brothers, 1961); Edward A. Tiryakian's Sociologism and Existentialism (Englewood Cliffs: Prentice-Hall, Inc., 1962);
Jean Paul Sartre's Search For A Method (New York: Knopf,
1963); and much of the writing of Karl Mannheim. Tiryakian
directly addresses himself to the task of assessing the
effect of existentialism upon sociological thought. He studies the relationship between the "science" of sociology and
the philosophy of existentialism. His treatment, however,

is incomplete in one important aspect. He does not take stock of the greater philosophical or intellectual implications which existentialism holds for logico-rational thought but focuses upon various existential views of the individual and society. Tiryakian compares a fragmented view of existentialism with an assumedly cohesive view of sociologism. Barrett's work does much to remedy the limitations of Tiryakian's work.

28. Weber quoted in *Masters of Sociological Thought* (New York: Harcourt, Brace Jovanovich, Inc., 1971), p. 250.

29. Bernard S. Myers, *The German Expressionists* (New York: Praeger, 1956), p. 13.

30. Weber quoted by Peter Gay, *Weimar Culture* (New York: Harper and Row, 1968), p. 120.

31. Marianne Weber, *Max Weber: A Biography*, translated and edited by Harry Zohn (New York: John Wiley and Sons, 1975), p. 457.

32. Honigsheim reports that Lukacs and Weber were deeply impressed with each other. Weber once told Honigsheim, "Whenever I have spoken to Lukacs, I have to think about it for days ..." See Honigsheim, *On Max Weber* (New York: The Free Press, 1968), p. 28.

33. *Ibidem*, p. 27.

34. Gerth and Mills report, "The first Russian revolution redirected his [Weber's] scholarly work; he learned Russian, in bed before getting up each morning, in order to follow events in the Russian daily press. Then he chased after the events with his pen in order to pin them down as daily history. In 1906 he published two major essays on Russian, 'The Situation of Bourgeois Democracy in Russia' and 'Russia's Transition to Sham Constitutionalism'". Hans Gerth and C. Wright Mills, "Introduction" to *From Max Weber* (New York: Oxford University Press, 1958), p. 19.

35. One might speculate as to the relation between Ivan Karamazov's declaration that the world is founded upon the absurd and Weber's polytheism of values.

36. Paul Honigsheim, *On Max Weber* (New York: The Free Press, 1968, p. 81.

37. See Salomon, Aron, Jaspers, and Schutz.

38. In their separate researches Diane Crane and Nicholas Mullins have demonstrated the importance of 'invisible colleges' in fostering creativity in both the physical and social sciences. See Crane, *Invisible Colleges* (Chicago: University of Chicago Press, 1972) and Mullins, *Theories and Theory Groups In Contemporary American Sociology* (New York: Harper and Row, 1973). The distinguished Russian scientist, Zhores Medvedev, has pointed out, "the chief means of critical appraisal of any piece of work, the demonstration of its strong and weak points, its methodological inadequacies and its position among other investigations, in the field is, even today, verbal, direct and immediate discussion in a circle of understanding colleagues". See *The Medvedev Papers*, translated by Vera Rich (London: Macmillan, 1971), pp. 133-134; also cited by Mullins, p. 18.

39. Mullins contends every productive scientist has a few trusted assessors often not in the same specialty or even discipline who act as "friendly-critics" of his work. Mullins, *op. cit.*, p. 18. Norman Storer has characterized these trusted assessors as a scientist's personal invisible college. Storer, "Remarks" to a Social Science Research Council Conference on the Social Study of Science (New York: Columbia University, February 1967). Cited by Mullins, p. 18.

Weber's close association with Dilthey, Simmel, and Rickert has been widely commented upon. See for example Gerhard Masur, *Prophets of Yesterday* (New York: Macmillan, 1961); Arthur Mitzman, *The Iron Cage* (New York: Knopf, 1970); and Marianne Weber, *op. cit.* Simmel, Dilthey, Husserl, and Weber were all briefly colleagues at the University of Berlin. Husserl, George, Rilke, and Weber were among Simmel's circle of close personal friends. Heidegger was a student of Husserl's. Both Simmel and George were guests in Weber's Heidelberg home and according to Marianne Weber these visits especially pleased Max Weber. Lukacs and Jaspers were regular members of the Weber salon. Jaspers remained a close associate of Weber's widow after the sociologist's death and championed Max Weber in his writing and lectures as a prototype for a modern existential hero.

40. Rollo May, *Existence* (New York: Simon and Schuster, 1967), p. 11.

41. Edward Tiryakian, *op. cit.*, p. 117

42. Max Weber, cited in J. Freund, *The Sociology of Max Weber* (New York: Vintage Books, 1969), p. 93.

43. Raymond Aron writes, "In Max Weber's eyes, incompleteness is

a fundamental characteristic of modern science. Never would he have envisioned, as Durkheim liked to do, a time when sociology would be fixed and a system of social laws would exist. Nothing is more alien to Weber's way of thinking than the image so dear to Auguste Comte of a science which possesses the essential and has set up a closed and definitive system of fundamental laws. Science as it used to be in times past could imagine itself complete in a certain sense, because it aspired to grasp the principles of reality, the laws of being. Weber's science is by nature in evolution. It has nothing to do with propositions regarding the ultimate meaning of things; it works toward a goal infinitely removed, and it endlessly renews the questions it addresses to matter". Main Currents in Sociological Thought, Volume II (New York: Basic Books, 1967), pp. 183-184.

44. F. H. Blum, op. cit., p. 46.

45. Max Weber, "Science as a Vocation", op. cit.

46. For an excellent summary of the literature published on Weber between 1971 and 1975, see Guenther Roth's Review Essay in Contemporary Sociology, July 1975, pp. 366-373.

47. English readers will find Jaspers' portrait of Weber in Three Essays (New York: Harcourt, Brace and World, 1964). For a discussion of and excerpts from Jaspers' humanistic philosophy, see "Karl Jaspers: A New Humanism", in Adrienne Koch, Philosophy For a Time of Crisis, (New York: E. P. Dutton, 1960).

48. Gerth and Mills, "Introduction: The Man and His Work", From Max Weber, op. cit., p. 43.

49. Weber, "Science as a Vocation", op. cit., p. 147.

50. Jaspers, Three Essays, op. cit., p. 269.

CHAPTER VII

THE HUMANISTIC SOCIOLOGY OF FLORIAN ZNANIECKI

Florian Znaniecki occupies a unique position among the great humanists in sociology for several reasons which are not only related to his substantive contributions but to his personal biography as well. Let us point them out.

First, he belongs to those rare spirits in intellectual history, about whom we can say that they were writing one book during their entire mature life.[1] In his case this "book" consists of many volumes of different titles. It is impressive that from his first sociological co-authorship on the Polish Peasant in Europe and America, he uninterruptedly searched to unify the subject matter and methodology of sociology in the way which led to the system he dared to call "humanistic, inductive sociology".

Second, if one of the necessary characteristics of a humanistic sociologist is a broad educational background (as we mentioned in Chapter I) then Znaniecki's biography shows him to be particularly well qualified by his vast interests and education.[2] Like many other great sociologists of the past, he had no degree in sociology. But he made himself a sociologist. His first publication was a book of poetry.[3] (It is worth mentioning that Dilthey believed that the core of humanism is poetry.) Then, one after another, his philosophical books,[4] articles[5] and reviews[6] began to appear. Reviewing his intellectual development, it is obvious that Znaniecki's philosophical contributions form an introductory part of his life's work. They prepared him to build up a system of humanistic sociology.

Third, he had a particularly broad cultural background and life experience,[7] which is always an important advantage for a humanistically oriented scholar. He was born in 1882 into a Polish gentry family living under Russian rule. Although a Pole to his fingertips, he was also exposed to the influences of Russian language and culture. As a very young man he began to study in Warsaw but soon went to Geneva, Zurich and Paris. His concept of culture as a product of individual creativity has French and Polish roots. Evidence of his admiration for the French culture was his translation into Polish of Bergson's L'Evolution Creatrice. His contact with American culture followed. William Thomas, who offered the young Polish philosopher a co-authorship in the work on the Polish Peasant, introduced Znaniecki into American sociology. However, it seems worth emphasizing that it was not sociology itself, but certain characteristics of Thomas' personality and interests which exercised so decisive an influence on Znaniecki that he was led to make a permanent commitment to sociology. Znaniecki was particularly impressed by Thomas' sensitive understanding of the uniqueness of each human personality. In Thomas, the sociologist, the young Polish philosopher found an attitude toward, and interest in, the problems of culture and personality "close to his own, though the former treated these matters more empirically and sociopsychologically than philosophically".[8]

Fourth, Znaniecki the sociologist, like Durkheim and Simmel, never ceased to be a philosopher. In the period of his collaboration with Thomas, he wrote Cultural Reality,[9] published a year after the appearance of the first two volumes of the Polish Peasant in Europe and America. Although in his later works Znaniecki did not directly address philosophical problems, his sociological works were philosophically well-grounded and his understanding of social phenomena had its roots in his philosophical orientation.

Fifth, Znaniecki served two national sociologies: American and Polish. American readers of sociological literature know about his contributions to and position in American sociology. These were honored by the American Sociological Association which elected him to be its President in 1953.[10] The small volume, On Humanistic Sociology, edited by Robert Bierstedt, offers a good, if too brief, general introduction to some of his ideas along the lines of our concern. In the United States, however, he is much less known as one of the founders of Polish sociology and the organizer of its institutional life. The list of his Polish publications is shorter than that of his American publications. However, his impact on the development of Polish sociology is still evident. In 1920 he took the chair at Poznan University and there organized the Polish Sociological Institute in 1927. In 1930 he founded the Przeglad Socjologiczny (Sociological Review), the first sociological periodical in Poland, which he edited until WWII. The war ended his career as a Polish sociologist, but those of his students in Poland who survived the war have played a highly significant role in the development of sociology in socialist Poland.[11] However, their master's name and ideas were banned from academic life during the Stalinist period and only began to regain some prestige in the 1970's.[12]

Sixth, the last point of Znaniecki's biography which probably has quite a serious influence on his sociological thought, was his experience as the director of the Society for Protection of Emigrants (Towarzystwo Opieki nad Wychodzcami) in Warsaw, 1911-14. It was in this capacity he met William Thomas who visited Poland to collect materials concerning Polish emigrants to the United States. Znaniecki accepted Thomas' offer to help in the study on emigrants. But he still wanted to be a philosopher, even when Thomas offered him a partnership in his great sociological enterprise. Thirty-four years later Znaniecki confessed his feelings at that time, "A year earlier I would have refused /this effort/. As a philosopher trying to develop my own system, I wanted to generalize, not to become absorbed in the study of particular concrete data. What made me change my attitude was /the/ fascinating influence of Thomas".[13]

We have devoted more space to Znaniecki's biographical information than to others not only because in general, "his reputation suffered from the fact that almost half of his books were written in Polish, a language inaccessible to most of his American and English readers",[14] but also because his biography may serve as an example of the influence of life experience and educational background on intellectual ideas. As we said above, Znaniecki wrote "one book" throughout his entire sociological career. But this does not mean that he did not develop his ideas. It means only that he consistently tried in each new volume to improve his main ideas and his general approach. It is very impressive that, in each preface to a new work, Znaniecki tried to relate it to his previous works and criticize his earlier ideas. The prefaces written to his own books could serve as models of scientific modesty and seriousness.

As a young philosopher, in his early Polish works, he dealt with problems of moral values, moral facts, and the forms and principles of moral creativity. These considerations led him to two convictions: first, that values are fundamental and irreducible elements of human experience; and second, that the entire realm of culture is not a refined branch of the natural universe but a product of man himself.

While working with Thomas on the <u>Polish Peasant</u>, he found enough time to prepare a synthesis of his philosophical ideas concerning culture and published it under the title <u>Cultural Reality</u>.[15] A synthesis of his views on the phenomenon of culture as widely separated from that of nature, it was an anti-naturalist manifesto of a young philosopher-becoming-sociologist.

The essential focus of his concern was:

> ...how to reconcile the conceptions of reality as a world of practical values and of thought as empirically creative and yet objectively

valid human activity, which an adequate philosophical treatment of cultural problems seemed to demand, with the naturalistic view of reality prevalent in science, and the idealistic view of thought found not only in systems of philosophical idealism, but in almost all classical logic.[16]

The main effort of Znaniecki's life was to liberate sociology as social science from the "prevalent" naturalistic views. In order to achieve this liberation he devoted much time and energy to presenting and explaining the nature of social phenomena as qualitatively different from natural phenomena. He distinguished four orders of reality: physical, psychological, sociological and ideal. Discussing sociological order, Znaniecki wrote:

...this new extra-psychological reality is as relative to the psychological reality as the latter is to physical reality. It is the specific reality which is common to psychologically differentiated and isolated individuals--common not because composed of self-existing transpsychological things or processes, but because determined by superindividual schemes.[17]

In this early work he acnowledged the influence of Bergson on the one hand and American pragmatism on the other. He was undoubtedly influenced also by the German "Humanistic Revolution in Philosophy", though he did not mention Dilthey. The separation of social phenomena into a separate order of reality was done previously by Ludwig Gumplowicz, then by Durkheim and others. Znaniecki found in these precedents a fundamental rationale for developing a _humanistic_ approach in sociology. His humanism has nothing in common with the naturalistic humanism of ancient Protagoras or the twentieth-century philosopher Schiller. He wrote that modern thought "must maintain against naturalism that man is not a product of the evolution of nature, but that on the contrary, nature, in a large measure at least, is the product of human culture, and if there is anything in nature which preceded man, the way to find it leads through historical and social science, not through biology, geology, astronomy or physics".[18] (Let us remember here that Karl Marx expressed a similar antinaturalistic statement: "The root of man is man", which unfortunately was not bought by his followers, including Engels.)

Znaniecki brought his humanistic attitude and views from philosophy to sociology. It was his great luck that he met William Thomas, about whom he wrote: "never have I known, heard or read about anybody with such a wide, sympathetic interest in the vast diversity of sociocultural patterns and such a genius for understanding the uniqueness of every human personality".[19] Due to the congenial conditions which Thomas, twenty years older, created for his young friend, Znaniecki was able to introduce some of his humanistic ideas into the Polish Peasant--on which he began work as Thomas' assistant but was soon invited to be co-author. Their work opened the first empirical period of American sociology.[20]

It is, however, generally acknowledged today that the most essential part of the Polish Peasant, its "Methodological Note", was mainly Znaniecki's work. Thomas had neither the philosophical training nor methodological interest comparable to that of his assistant. On the other hand, it is obvious that Znaniecki was not yet a matured sociologist able to do this work without Thomas' guidance. Bierstedt's opinion about their cooperation is highly convincing: "Thomas' contribution was a psychological penetration, a comprehensive curiosity, and a rare wisdom; Znaniecki's, a philosophical sophistication, an historical erudition and a talent for systemization".[21]

In general one can say that, while Thomas' basic concept used in this study was that of "attitude", Znaniecki added the concept of "values". Both elements have had fundamental significance in the further development of the humanistic trend in sociology, though, it must be acknowledged, similar ideas appeared independently at the same time or even before in the thought of Max Weber. The most original humanistic element introduced to sociology by their study was the method itself.

In the "Methodological Note", we can find some fundamental humanstic ideas which were later refined, redefined, and developed in Znaniecki's other works. The "Methodological Note" constituted a declaration of the anti-positivist sentiments of its authors. The development of a new methodology presented in the "Note" has been described in dozens of publications. Our aim is to emphasize only the humanistic element inherent in it.

The idea of using personal documents for sociological analysis was humanistic by its very nature. Thomas had collected an immense variety of documents concerning East European immigrants even before he met Znaniecki; the latter developed a systematic method of using them. Although they relied on many types of personal documents (court archives' acts, archives of the immigrants' organizations, etc.), the most ambitious and unprecedented effort was their use of private correspondence. This method had a humanistic character because it constituted a search for human values rooted in the cultural background and shared by the peasant authors --values which enabled them to communicate and act. This approach expresses a sociological conviction that knowledge of values and motives functioning in both individual and group behavior are fundamental for understanding social phenomena.

In the Polish Peasant, a second but related method was the use of an autobiography as a source of information for scientific purposes: an approach which was also explicitly recommended by Dilthey. The theoretical explanation and justification for its use was delivered in the introduction to the 200-page autobiography of a Polish immigrant.[22] The source which until then was used only by historians, appeared to be highly important for the humanistic approach in sociology because Thomas and Znaniecki also focus on the study of the development of human personalities. They assumed that

> the human personality is both a continually producing factor and a continually produced result of social evolution, and this double relation expresses itself in every elementary social fact; there can be for social science no change of reality which is not the common effect of pre-existing social values and individual attitudes acting upon them.[23]

Defending their autobiographical method, they declared "that personal life-records, as complete as possible, constitute the perfect type of sociological material, and that if social science has to use other materials at all it is only because of the practical difficulty of obtaining at the moment a sufficient number of such records to cover the totality of sociological problems, and of the enormous amount of work demanded for an adequate analysis of all personal materials necessary to characterize the life of a social group".[24]

Today this "practical difficulty" is largely diminished due to the use of computer techniques. During the first decades of the century the autobiographical method, although it did not win acceptance in the United States, was successfully developed by Znaniecki in Poland. In 1921 he organized a competition for a "Zyciorys wlasny robotnika" (Autobiography of a Worker). This kind of enterprise was the first in the history of sociology.[25]

Znaniecki developed and improved the method used in The Polish Peasant; where this method was conceived as an "application of the methods of social psychology to an evolving human personality" (p. 1831). In 1924, when he edited and published one of the collected autobiographies,[26] he emphasized in the introduction that he was using the autobiography as a document reflecting the personality of a given author and his relations to his social milieu. Znaniecki treated knowledge concerning these relations as a source for the sociological analysis of attitudes and values created by and accepted in a given social group.[27]

Znaniecki's search for the methodological assumption of the humanistic sciences, as sciences about cultural phenomena, distinguished from and not reducible to any sort of natural phenomena, found its full expression in his Polish work, <u>Wstep do socjologii</u> (An Introduction to Sociology).[28] There he formulated his famous principle called the "humanistic coefficient".

The earliest English formulation of this idea was done in his article, "The Object Matter of Sociology".[29] Arguing that "the sphere of the humanist's investigation is not a world of independent realities", he wrote,

> We use the term "humanistic coefficient" to indicate the fundamental character of cultural phenomena (...) the essential feature that when taken as objects of theoretic reflection, they are already data given to somebody in the course of his experience, or activities performed by some conscious subject as viewed by himself or by others.[30]

The product of any kind of cultural activity, individual or collective, of material or spiritual nature, myth, works of art, legal systems, is understandable for us

> only with reference to some known or hypothetically reconstructed complex of experiences and activities of particular empirical, limited, historically determined conscious individuals or collectivities who produced them or who were, or are now using them.[31]

Several years later Znaniecki tried to make this idea methodologically useful. He elaborated on it in his <u>The Method of Sociology</u>. In a sub-heading titled "The Humanistic Coefficient of Cultural Data" he assumed that:

> ...every cultural system is found by the investigator to exist for certain conscious and active historical subjects i.e., within the sphere of experience and activity of some particular people, individuals and collectivities, living in a certain part of the human world during a certain historical period.[32]

Therefore, he concluded that the data used by any researcher of cultural phenomena are always transferred to the researcher or taken by him from somebody else. We can understand them only so far as we know the meaning and use of the given cultural phenomenon in a given time and place. He wrote:

> This essential character of cultural data we
> call the humanistic coefficient because such
> data, as objects of the student's theoretic
> reflection, already belong to somebody else's
> active experience and are such as this active
> experience makes them.[33]

Znaniecki used the term humanistic coefficient many times in his later works. He further elaborated this concept in Social Actions,[34] where he applied it to the analysis of "Social Actions as Dynamic System"[35] to the explanation of the "distinction between main patterns of actions...",[36] and to his consideration of "Sharing Attitudes".[37] Showing the "objective relativity" of terms like "beautiful", "ugly", "good", and "bad", he argued that their "axiological significance belongs objectively to the value itself as an object taken with its original humanistic coefficient".[38]

Znaniecki had serious difficulties in finding an all-convincing definition of his term. However, it should be said that he did not care about the term itself but only about the notion. He openly expressed this standpoint in the Preface of Social Actions, saying: "...I do not insist upon any of the terms I have chosen and consider nearly all of them as merely provisional, inadequate stop-gaps. In science the term does not matter but /the/ concept /does/".[39]

In Cultural Sciences, written after WWII, Znaniecki used this concept several times again.[40] The best explanation of the meaning of humanistic coefficient for the distinction between natural and social studies is provided in this source. (He called the latter "cultural" to emphasize the cultural relativity of all social phenomena.) The fact that the natural scientist studies "an order among empirical data entirely independent of /the/ conscious human agent" is obvious. Znaniecki's merit was in showing that in his search for an order among empirical data the student of culture has to take them with their humanistic coefficient,

> i.e., as it appears to those human individuals
> who experience it and use it. He can apply
> this coefficient both to data which natural
> scientists include in the physical world - a
> star, a mountain, a plant, an animal--and to
> those which they /naturalists/ exclude from
> it--religious myth, the fictitious plot of
> a novel, an ethical ideal. Furthermore, in
> applying the humanistic coefficient, an inductive student of culture does not accept
> the doctrine that his own active experience
> constitutes the main and the most reliable

source of knowledge about the data which he experiences. The investigators who are developing modern sciences of cultural data do not function as introspective psychologists, but as <u>historians</u>; and while their techniques for gathering evidence differ, depending on how near or how distant the past they investigate, their methodological approach is the same.[41]

For our considerations, there are two significant elements in his claim to use the humanistic coefficient. The first which is particularly evident in the above quotation is the assumption that sociology is closer to history than is generally assumed by positivists and behaviorists. The second element is that this method demonstrates that all social researchers respect the fundamental idea of the sociology of knowledge that our recognition or perception of reality is socially constructed. In elaborating the concept of the humanistic coefficient, he described "scientific theories as cultural products"[42] and compared the concepts of space and time as expressed in human consciousness and in scientific theories.[43] Nevertheless, he himself did not clarify the relation between his concept of sociology and the ideas of the sociology of knowledge.

In general, the significance of the concept of the humanistic coefficient has been both theoretical and methodological. However, it never received a clear definition under his pen. It is more easily demonstrated with negative examples, which Znaniecki himself used very often. For example, without this coefficient, "Islam or the Bank of England will appear as...bewildering chaos of sounds, bodily movements, psychological processes, piles of wood, bricks and mortar, masses of ink-spotted paper..."[44] The same will be true about philosophical systems, foreign languages, religions, etc.

It is interesting that the roots of his humanistic coefficient can be easily found in <u>The Polish Peasant</u>. Its authors maintained that a social personality consisted not only of biological form and temperamental attitudes because these exist in an animal as well as in an infant in human society. A similar situation exists:

> whenever an individual of low level of civilization gets in touch with higher civilized environment, a worlding with a body of specialists, a foreigner with an autochthonic society, etc. In fact human beings for the most part never suspect the existence of innumerable meanings—scientific,

artistic, moral, political, economic--and a
field of social reality whose meanings the
individual does not know, even if he can observe its sensual contents, is as much out of
reach of his practical experience as the other
side of the moon.[45]

Znaniecki's humanistic sociology appeared in both Poland and the United States on ground dominated by the naturalistic theories of positivism, evolutionism, organicism, physicism and psychologism. In both countries his ideas challenged the existing philosophical assumptions of the developing sociologies. In Poland the "analytical philosophy" of Lwow-Warsaw School of Philosophy had a period of great influence on the epistemology and methodology of social sciences. In the United States residues of positivism and evolutionism mixed with native pragmatism provided the dominant perspective. Nevertheless, Znaniecki's ideas were so original and philosophically well founded that, in spite of many negative reactions and the manifest disinterest of some of his contemporaries; he was able to establish a strong sociological school in Poland as well as to become one of the few Europeans who has had a profound influence on American sociology.[46]

Znaniecki's fundamental epistemological concept separating the world of nature from the world of culture was not a new one. It has well-grounded roots in the German "Humanistic Revolution" of the end of the 19th century, described in Chapter V. However, his strong belief in the possibility of creating a nomothetic science of social phenomena inclined him to reject the idea of "understanding" as an essential element of social epistemology. Nevertheless, he, like Max Weber, separated nature from culture, and gave similar sense to the concept of social action. Despite these kinships, Znaniecki did not show an interest in the work of this other giant of the humanistic approach in sociology. He devoted only marginal remarks to Weber, e.g., in Social Actions Weber is mentioned only in the annotated references;[47] in Cultural Sciences Znaniecki refers in one sentence to Weber's concept of "ideal type",[48] in Modern Nationalities and in the Social Role of the Man of Knowledge Weber's name did not even appear in the "Index to names".

Not only the philosophical roots of both authors were common. At approximately the same time they independently formulated two different theories in which social action is the core concept. Nevertheless there are essential differences between their formulations. Max Weber formulated his famous definition of social action in The Theory of Social and Economic Organizations,[49] Znaniecki, in his Polish work, Wstep do Socjologii. Weber assumed that actual social actions are only those which were directly and meaningfully turned to other people. Znaniecki added to this by pointing out that social actions are tied or related to various categories of values, because it is value which inclines people to undertake meaningful actions. Although this idea originally appeared in Wstep do Socjologii, he did not develop it in full extent in this work. Nevertheless, as the elements of sociology he did distinguish social values and social activities.[50] The concept of social actions was later formulated by him in English. Znaniecki saw social action as the basic element of sociological studies, because he assumed that:

> Social actions are the simplest kind of social data: they constitute the background of mores and laws, of personal roles and of group organization; they may be said to be the stuff out of which all the more complex and elaborate social realities are made. Consequently, their study must precede other sociological studies and condition them.[51]

Therefore, in his views on sociology as the study of four social systems, social actions occupy the first place before social relations, social persons and social groups.

Developing this definition further in the next chapter of Social Actions, he wrote:

> Social actions, ..., are actions which have as objects conscious beings, individually or collectively, and which purpose to influence those beings. While thus distinguishing social actions, we have intentionally neglected to define actions in general, relying on the popular understanding of the term.[52]

Although Znaniecki's definition grasped "the essence of that what is social--the active relation of one man to others",[53] it limited the meaning of social actions too much to become popular.

This great humanist, who relentlessly opposed positivism and behaviorism, nevertheless tried to introduce positivistic standards of conceptual precision to sociology. A humanistic sociologist cannot be criticized for his aspiration toward precision. However, it can produce an unwanted by-product. In the case of Znaniecki, his attempt to elaborate a general concept of the subject matter of sociology was affected by this inclination toward precision which unduly narrowed its scope. This tendency characterized the development of his thought. From the position which he accepted together with Thomas in the Polish Peasant where the idea of universal psychological tendencies dominated, through the idea of four social systems ("social actions", "social relations", "social persons" and "social groups") in The Method of Sociology, to his finally elaborated "four logical classes of social systems"[54] ("social relations", "social roles", "social groups" and "societies"), one may observe his great effort to define sociological subject matter as strictly as possible.

To the end of his life Znaniecki assumed that sociology could neither study a culture as an entity, as Sorokin tried to do, nor investigate society as a whole in the manner of Comte and Spencer.[55] Although Znaniecki's views on sociology as a humanistic discipline were not changed, he extended the subject matter of sociology in Cultural Sciences, the last work published during his life. Znaniecki understood that people live in several cultural orders. They are subjects and objects of social actions; however, at the same time they participate in other cultural "orders" and this fact influences their social relations and social roles.[56]

Znaniecki's humanistic approach was not limited to the theoretical consideration of sociological problems. He was a humanist tout a fait. His humanism concerning social problems found the most interesting expression in 1934 when he wrote in Polish on People of Today and the Future Civilization.[57] Znaniecki shared the opinion of many American educators[58] that "the future generations must be capable of consciously directing social evolution if civilization is to avoid tragic catastrophies".[59] This statement, set forth forty-three years ago, is particularly interesting today, although we are rather inclined to use the term "development" instead of "evolution" to avoid a suspicion of something like genetic engineering.

Znaniecki divided chapters of this book into two parts and bluntly said in the preface that only the second part, titled "Luczie terazniejsi" (contemporary people), possessed a scientific character and emphasized that it "is not a part of general theory of the social person, but only an application of it to such questions which can be treated scientifically, i.e., with full objectivity and with the help of the inductive method, which, however, because of their nature cannot be grasped with precision".[60]

In this part he dealt with four types of personalities formed by their: (1) "good breeding", ("well-bred people"), (2) attitude toward work; ("people of work"), (3) attitude toward play ("people of play"), and (4) sub- or super-deviation from that which in a given society is treated as social normality ("deviants").[61] Although this part of Znaniecki's work may still evoke some sociological interest, we will devote even more attention to the first part of this book, despite its actually non-scientific and utopian character. It is this part of his work where he was one of the first among sociologists to take a strong position against the emerging ideology of technocracy.[62] His book is largely a criticism of the developing technological civilization.

The first part, subtitled "Mozliwosci nowej cywilizacji" (Possibilities of a New Civilization), was described by himself as a reflection on how we should rear and educate the youth of the new generation in order to make them capable of achieving the cultural ideals which seem to be necessary for building a new civilization.[63]

We agree with Znaniecki, as he agreed with technocrats, that a new civilization is possible, that in our cultural life there are ongoing processes which can bring about a total transformation of all spheres of culture. However, today we perhaps know better than he did, that this "great future is uncertain". Over forty years ago, he believed that there existed only one alternative:

> ...a new universal civilization will develop, a civilization which will not only save everything that is worthy to be saved from national civilizations, but even will elevate mankind to the level higher than all dreams of utopians; or national civilization will fall apart, it means that...their greatest systems, most valuable patterns will lose all significance for the life of human communities for a span of many generations.[64]

Znaniecki pointed out in the 1930's that there were beginning to appear some germs of a universal civilization, which he emphasized were not identical with "international civilization". He believed that a possibility existed of developing a synthesis of the most valuable elements of national civilizations into one universal civilization. His observation was that the symptoms of decline of the national civilizations are their internal struggles and internal crises. He saw their causes in the "domination of products over producers".[65]

The second part of this alternative was a great warning, set forth five years before WWII, which is even more timely today. We know perfectly well that global catastrophies ominously loom due to uncontrolled demographic growth, pollution, the exhaustion of natural resources, and preparation for atomic confrontations. Therefore, we have to make a great effort to build what Znaniecki called "humanistic civilization with the dominating spiritual culture different from all previous civilizations which were naturalistic with a dominating material culture".[66] He assumed that the future civilization will be characterized by humanism, social harmony and dynamic fluidity. By dynamic fluidity he meant social and cultural mobility, as well as what the architects of "detente" intended to achieve: a flow of information, ideas and people free of political restriction.

Humanism is by its definition nonaggressive, therefore, humanistic attitudes can reduce antagonisms and conflicts and open the way to social harmony. Only in these conditions can independent creativity be dynamic as a normal cultural function of individuals and groups. These conditions did not exist in any previous civilizations, which were culturally stable and static.

Although Znaniecki's vision of humanistic civilization could be called a utopia of the 1930's, today we know better than he knew then, that this utopia must become a reality if we are to avoid a total catastrophy.

Znaniecki pointed out that all conflicts among cultures "have their source not in the nature of cultural systems but in the people who compete for expansion of their systems".[67] He outlined a general pattern of competition between cultural systems and illustrated its applicability to economic and religious systems.

On the basis of anthropological data available in his time, Znaniecki assumed that cultural competition did not exist or was highly limited in "folk-civilizations". It became a dynamic factor in the development of national civilization from ancient to modern times. Unfortunately, in most cases the "spirit of progress" is simultaneously a "spirit of fight". Znaniecki pointed out that the association of those two spirits was maintained by the ideologists of progress from Heraclitus to Nietzsche and Lenin. This view led, however, to the situation in which:

> The conviction that in order to create one thing, something else must be destroyed, and that to incline people to accept one thing they should be persuaded to reject something else, penetrates all active national civilizations.[68]

As far as it concerns cultural goods and values, he rejected this view and argued that it would be justified only if the sum total of cultural achievements were limited and stable. But the growth of spiritual values which form the foundation for any cultural progress has no limits. Cultural systems, he assumed, do not need to compete, and if the expansion of cultural systems of national civilizations usually had a militant character one should explain it by the slow rising of creative and humanistic trends in the old civilizations.

During his historical period when continuity of cultural growth was highly threatened, Znaniecki, great visionary of the future, defended this continuity. His negative attitude toward Marxism and the Russian Revolution was to a large extent rooted in his belief in the significance of continuity for the growth of civilization.

However, he separated the continuity of cultural systems and the "need of new men and new social groups in order to build up a new civilization". And from this viewpoint he criticized all those

> who assume that the new civilization could be built up at once by one continuous action according to this or that plan based on some great system, which would be economic for communists--technological for technocrats, political for fascists and hitlerites, or religious in the case of Catholic or Protestant reformers.[69]

Znaniecki acknowledged that the dream of building a new civilization is very old but argued that its realization has always been hampered by the destruction of old cultural systems, by antagonism, by conformism, and by neglect of the idea of spiritual development of culture. In his own time, Znaniecki saw the greatest enemies of the new civilization in the emphasis on the development of material culture and "physical might of social groups" on the one hand, and in the limiting of creative possibilities by established dogma on the other. He assumed that a new civilization would not be built without a new man. Thus, in order to build a new civilization, we should immediately and on a large scale create new people according to the model of the future man. However, in the meantime, he contended we should also start to form a new cultural system consonant with the vision of the future system. He emphasized that we should not produce "people of a 'transitory' period and a 'temporary' system".[70] Therefore, placing great hope in education, he devoted much of his energy and time to the problems of the sociology of education.[71]

Znaniecki's conviction that a new civilization cannot be created by the old sort of people had an incidental but nevertheless interesting counterpart in the fundamental criticism of the revolutionary intelligentsia by another Polish author--Waclaw Machajski, himself a classical representative of this stratum.[72] They both, despite all philosophical and political differences, reasoned in the same way: the fate of the future civilization depends upon the new type of men. In the case of Znaniecki, the present type of cultural man is unable to give a new content to the new system in the future. In the case of Machajski, the member of the revolutionary intelligentsia will, after revolution, create a social system according to his own views, needs and tastes. Znaniecki did not refer to Machajski's works and probably did not know them. Yet, the parallel is provocative.

For the construction of the humanistic civilization we need people with two dominant virtues: wisdom and goodness. Znaniecki's uncritical optimism and trust in the human spirit reached the apogee when he expressed his belief that:

> There must appear on the global scale a substantial and real collective of all wise and good people accepting the ideal of the new civilization.[73]
>
> A 'wise' man is the one who, accepting various cultural systems and being able to use various criteria of importance, appreciates culture in its entire richness and multiplicity and cares about its duration and development.[74]
>
> A 'good' man treats any human being and community as a basically positive social value.[75]

These people only, Znaniecki believed, could initiate the movement which would lead to the new civilization. Znaniecki's appeal for wise and good people as the element without which the new civilization could not be built is in agreement with all the great religious traditions. This idea has always been opposed by social philosophies which have maintained that a better social system itself could produce better people.

Znaniecki knew that the idea of a universal civilization in which humanistic and spiritual elements dominate over material elements was very old, known even to Stoics. However, "Unlimited, free and objective creativity as a source of cultural fluidity [mobility--AG] just recently began to penetrate the ideals of civilization".[76]

Wise and good individuals who are able to overcome the demands and limits of their own cultural heritage will initiate the building process of the new civilization. "They will be the first source from which the young individuals and groups will derive creative and ethical individualism".[77]

Znaniecki, who in these works appeared to be a romantic and idealistic utopian, believed that these wise and good people would be entirely devoted to the bringing up and educating of the young generation. He expected that later there would develop within the new society a stratum consisting of people more creative and ethical than the contemporaries. They will know much better than we know today how to influence and manage the society. Thus, this stratum without struggle for power

> will dominate the old society, and deliver its own aspirations and social organization to all children and youth of the world; as a result, in the next generation the entire mankind will creatively participate in the new civilization.[78]

It is difficult to believe that this fantastic dream was put down only forty-three years ago by an outstanding sociologist, able to think and write realistically on other problems. But perhaps the fault is on our side. We are skeptical, if not cynical. Our views on the relation between intellectual leaders and youth are corrupted by the events of wars, the experience of totalitarian states, and the youth-oriented cultural and political revolutions, caused by the corrosion of the materialistic and pleasure-oriented generation of parents and teachers. In contrast, Znaniecki was a product of the two most idealistic societies of his time: The Polish intelligentsia which heroically rebuilt its nation's state after 123 years of foreign domination; and those American intellectual circles which were best represented by the idealism of Woodrow Wilson, the President and historian who helped to build independent states for all nations between the Baltic and Adriatic Seas. Thus, Znaniecki's view of the possibilities for the peaceful transformation of the old civilization into a future humanistic civilization was much different than is our own. Nevertheless, we have to acknowledge that his vision presented a case of utopian optimism. Jan Szczepanski, a pre-war student of Znaniecki, accurately called this book a "manifesto of humanistic attitude"[79] and reminded his readers that similar enthusiastic optimism was expressed many times prior to Znaniecki by the founders of utopian socialism.[80]

In the second part of Znaniecki's work, one can also find elements of high interest from the viewpoint of contemporary humanistic sociology.[81] However, for better understanding of his main ideas, let us mention first the historical circumstances in which his humanistic manifesto was born.

Znaniecki wrote this book as a call to his contemporaries about the need for developing new people who would be able to deal with the dramatic and unavoidable transformations which have been taking place within the existing civilization and may lead it either to catastrophe or to a new civilization. However, not only technological progress and ideology were regarded as a threat for a future humanistic civilization. On both the eastern and western boundaries of his own country (he wrote this book while living and teaching in Poland) two new socio-political systems were growing. Both of them promised, not only to their own people but to the entire world to bring about the fundamental transformation of the civilization. One of them promised a paradise for the world proletariat in the name of Soviet Communism. The second pledged to build a "thousand-year-long" domination of the German Herrenvolk and to liberate mankind from the "inferior races".

In 1934 Znaniecki understood, better than his contemporary western colleagues could, what was beyond the great slogans of Fascism and Communism. And, although he did not discuss these systems at all, his book is one of the most interesting answers to the propositions which pretended to model a new man.

Architects of the totalitarian states began to produce a new generation of heroes for the future world conquest. They wanted them to be obedient, disciplined and fanatic. Fascist and Nazi concepts of man differed in many points from that of Communists, but they also contained some very essential similarities.

Behind the political embodiment of the violent hero of the twentieth century stand authors of the nineteenth century and the very beginning of the twentieth century, like Marx, Nietzsche, Wagner, Sorel and Pareto. They, however, did not realize how soon and in what manner perversions of their ideas would be transmitted into grim political realities. Seeds of violence sown by these prophets grew up in two opposite camps.

In 1909 Mussolini, reviewing Sorel's Reflexions sur la violence, expressed his hope that the struggle of proletariat against bourgeoisie "will generate new energies, new moral values, new men who will be close to ancient heroes".[82] Soon after, he confessed that for him violence had moral value.

At the very beginning of the twentieth century, Lenin successfully propagated the idea of the party based on conspiratory and military patterns and wrote: "We never rejected terror on principle, nor can we ever do so. Terror is a form of military oppression that may be usefully applied..."[83] Before the Russian Revolution the virtues wanted and needed for the Communist Party member as a builder of the future civilization were: class-consciousness, activism and courage. After the Revolution, however, at the top of the hierarchy of virtues appeared obedience. What happened to the nation and party itself which was built upon these virtues during the next three decades [1924 (death of Lenin) to 1953 (death of Stalin)] is today common knowledge, even in the West.

This was east of the country where Znaniecki dreamed about a future man of wisdom and goodness. But less than one hundred

108

miles west of the old city of Poznan where he taught his humanistic ideas, the leader of the German nation preached:

> We must distrust the intelligence and the conscience and must place our trust in our instincts....Providence has ordained that I should be the greatest liberator of humanity. I am freeing men from the restraints of an intelligence that has taken charge; from the dirty and degrading self-mortifications of a chimera called conscience and morality, and from the demands of a freedom and personal independence which only a very few can bear.[84]

In this context of historical events the simplicity of Znaniecki's utopian program can be better understood and justified as the desperate call of a humanist.

The concept of four social personalities developed in the second part of his book is related to both his theory of "social persons" and theory of "social groups" presented in his Method of Sociology. The individual plays several social roles, in each of which he appears as a particular social person. "The entire cultural person" is an amalgam of all his roles. He is "composed of all activities and all experiences of a person participating in cultural systems which exist objectively in a given civilization".[85]

Znaniecki was well aware of a number of social personalities which can compose one "cultural person". However, he focused on only three groups of personalities typical for his time, and on two types of deviants: subnormal and supernormal. His analysis tended to show how all these types of personality had been formed and determined by their social circles (what we today call "reference groups").

The first type is "well-bred people", whose education and cultural behavior was so totally controlled by elders during their entire childhood and youth that it programmed their thinking, mores and manners forever. Znaniecki did not expect these people to make a significant contribution to society, not because of their good manners and education, but because overcontrol by the elders had limited their independent thinking and initiative.

The second personality type is "people of work", who had a short period of education and a limited period for leisure and play but started to work so early that the influence of the duty of work basically determined their mentality. This type is not limited to the working classes. At the time of the democratic workshop of labor, Znaniecki rejected the idealization of work.

He wrote that if a thinker or democratic activist would independently analyze

> what is happening to this most valuable material of civilization, which is human individuality, he will understand that the liberation of the human masses from the oppression of economic or political tyrants is only part of a much larger task which is to liberate them from the pressure of work.[86]

By the term "pressure of work", Znaniecki understood the internal compulsion of the work ethic.

The third type is "people of play". These are people who, despite educational control and later or earlier pressure of work, had a period of uncontrolled play with their peers that was longer than in the case of the other types. He assumed that social influence of peer groups on an individual is more durable than that of older groups.

> Characteristic for all circles of play is that the emphasis is put on social function, and neither on the physico-psychic self as in educational circles nor on social status as in working circles.[87]

According to the character of play in which people participated in their youth, Znaniecki found them later divided into three sub-types: societal pleasure seekers, people who play political games, and fighters active in group struggles.[88]

Besides the three basic types, Znaniecki described people whose deviations from norms accepted by society pushed them to the bottom of society as subnormal people or raised them over society as supernormal deviants. The subnormal deviant has been studied for a long time in the framework of criminology and psychopathology. Therefore, Znaniecki focused more attention on the supernormal deviant. He tried to show that deviation from the social normality (assuming that normality is an average adaptation to group demands) could also have a supernormal character and that the product of this deviation is moral, spiritual or intellectual greatness. He assumed that "sub" and "super" are modifiers of "norm" rather than references to intellectual capacity.

The concept of personality types which Znaniecki used in his last Polish book helped him to postulate programs of the future civilization, and this was deeply humanistic. Znaniecki dreamed about socio-cultural conditions which would encourage the development of

> people of creative dynamism and independence, without revolting against established order and without breaking norms which tied them with their social environment...

He had in mind

> people for whom independence in relations with their social circles [reference groups] would be from the very beginning normal and this independence would be rooted in the structure of the circle in which they grow and live.[89]

Closing our considerations on the humanistic sociology of Florian Znaniecki, we should emphasize that the essence of his views remained the same to the end of his life, although in his last work on <u>Cultural Sciences</u> he partially changed his terminology. From the viewpoint of the student of humanistic sociology, his unfinished system might be summarized in this way: humanism is an ontological concept in which man, being the basic category and the greatest value in himself, is at the same time the only creator of social values, which in turn form the foundation of social reality. The humanistic character of this reality caused its separation from the universal nature into an independent realm governed by its own laws. "The world of culture is a world of values; and values are primary data of human experience irreducible to any natural categories".[90] This view formulated before he began his collaboration with William Thomas, survived as the main point of Znaniecki's sociological creed throughout all his works. And although he died dissatisfied because his attempted explanation of causal interaction between values and attitudes --in his own opinion--"did not work so well as was expected"[91]-- the problems raised by him and the light which his analysis has thrown on those problems make Znaniecki one of the greatest sociologists in the humanistic tradition.

CHAPTER VII FOOTNOTES

1. Helena Znaniecki-Lopata expressed similar views in "Florian Znaniecki: The Creative Evolution of a Sociologist". Paper given at the Conference on "Florian Znaniecki and his Role in Sociology" organized by the Sociological Institute of the Adam Mickiewicz University and the Poznan branch of the Polish Sociological Society, Poznan, Poland, Dec. 15-16, 1972: "He consistently sought to clarify and organize the subject matter of sociology and to outline the methodology with which it should proceed in the analysis of its data. All his published works, spanning almost 50 years (1909-1958), focused upon the same themes".

2. As in any well-to-do noble family of his time, he received his first education at the hands of private tutors. Besides subjects common to any good grammar school, his curriculum also included Greek, Latin, French, German and Russian. At the gymnasium (secondary school where students took six to ten compulsory courses each year from the first to the eighth grade), Znaniecki began to write poetry and studied literature. See: Florian Znaniecki On Humanistic Sociology, Selected Papers, edited and with an introduction by Robert Bierstedt (Chicago: The University of Chicago Press, 1969), p. 1.

3. Florian Znaniecki, Cheops: Poemat Fantastyczny (Cheops: A Poem of Fantasy) J. Fiszer publisher, Warszawa 1903, p. 84.

4. (1) Zagadnienie wartosci w filozofii, (Problems of Values in Philosophy) pp. IV and 115, Wydawnictwo 'Przegladu Filozoficznego', Warszawa 1910.

   (2) Humanizm i poznanie, p. 231, the same publisher, Warszawa 1912.

   (3) Translated into Polish and edited: Henry Bergson, Ewolucja tworcza (Creative Evolution) pp. X and 310, Gebethner i Wolff, Warszawa 1913.

   (4) Edited Zasada ekonomii myslenia, jej historia i krytyka (Principle of the Economy of Thinking, its History and Criticism) by Joachim Metallmann, Warszawa 1914.

   (5) Cultural Reality, pp. XV and 359, University of Chicago

Press, Chicago 1919.

(6) <u>Upadek cywilizacji zachodniej, szkic z pogranicza filozofii kultury i socjologii</u> (The Decline of Western Civilization, A Sketch from the Border of the Philosophy of Culture and Sociology), pp. IX, 111, Poznan 1921.

5. (1) "Etyka filozoficzna i nauka o wartosciach moralnych" <u>Przeglad Filozoficzny</u> XII, 12, 1909.

    (2) "O definicji faktu moralnego", <u>Przeglad Filozoficzny</u>, XIII, 1910.

    (3) "Mysl i rzeczywistosc", <u>Przeglad Filozoficzny</u>, XIV/2, 1911.

    (4) "Elementy rzeczywistosci praktycznej", <u>Przeglad Filozoficzny</u>, XV/2, 1912.

    (5) "Znaczenie swiata i czlowieka", <u>Swiat i Czlowiek</u>, IV, 1913.

    (6) "Formy i zasady tworczosci moralnej", <u>Przeglad Filozoficzny</u>, XVII, 1914.

    (7) "Zasada wzglednosci jako podstawa filozofii", <u>Przeglad Filozoficzny</u>, XVII, 1914.

    (8) "Tresc, przedstawienie i przedmiot", <u>Przeglad Filozoficzny</u>, XVIII, 1915.

    (9) "The Principle of Relativity and Philosophical Absolutism", <u>The Philosophical Review</u>, vol XXIV, 1915.

    (10) "Prad socjologiczny w filozofii nowoczesnej", in a Memory Book for Prof. W. Heinrich, Krakow 1927.

    (11) "Zadania syntezy filozoficznej", <u>Przeglad Filozoficzny</u>, XXX/2, 1927.

6. He published only a few reviews of philosophical works. However, he also found time and energy to write articles on some social problems.

7. As a young student in Warsaw "he belonged to an underground group that was in rebellion against the Russian authorities; the students lectured to one another on forbidden subjects--namely, books that had been written by Polish authors", Bierstedt, <u>op. cit.</u>, p. 1.

When expelled from studies in Warsaw, he began to study abroad. "His Wanderjahren included a brief period in the French Foreign Legion--although a man less military inclined than Znaniecki can hardly be imagined--from which he was discharged with a shoulder wound, and also a period during which he served as editor of a French literary magazine". Bierstedt, op. cit., p. 1.

8. Comp: Jozef Chalasinski, "Florian Znaniecki - socjolog polski i amerykanski", p. 26, in Florian Znaniecki i jego rola w socjologii, a collection edited by Andrzej Kwilecki (Poznan: The University of Adam Mickiewicz Press).

9. In the period 1900-1920 his Cultural Reality was one of only three philosophical works published by the University of Chicago Press. (The two others were Studies in Logical Theory by Dewey and Pragmatism and its Critics by Moore.) Pointed out by Chalasinski, op. cit., p. 26.

10. "Znaniecki has been for many years a leading sociologist in both Europe and the United States, and although he stood for some time in the shadow of W. I. Thomas, his collaborator on The Polish Peasant in Europe and America, his mature and penetrating insight have won him independent recognition". P. Valien and B. Valien, "General Sociological Theories of Current Reference" in Howard Becker and Alvin Boskoff, eds., Modern Sociological Theory in Continuity and Change (New York: Dryden Press, 1957).

11. Jozef Chalasinski, Tadeusz Szczurkiewicz, Jan Szczepanski, W. Okinski, Waclaw Krynski, Jerzy Piotrowski, and Antonina Kloskowska.

12. A Special Session on "Florian Znaniecki and His Role in Sociology" was organized by the Institute of Sociology of the Poznan University and the Poznan Section of the Polish Sociological Society. The papers delivered at this Session on December 15-16, 1972, were published under the title of the Session in 1975.

13. Znaniecki, "William I. Thomas as a Collaborator", Sociology and Social Research, vol. 32, 1948, p. 766.

14. Bierstedt, op. cit., p. 5.

15. Znaniecki, Cultural Reality (Chicago, 1919).

16. Op. cit., p. 22.

17. Op. cit., p. 284.

18. Op. cit., pp. 21-22.

19. Znaniecki, "William I. Thomas as a Collaborator", op. cit., p. 766.

20. See: Chalasinski, op. cit., p. 27.

21. Bierstedt, op. cit., p. 11.

22. Thomas and Znaniecki, in the introduction to Part IV "Life-Record of an Immigrant", The Polish Peasant in Europe and America (New York: Dover Publications, Inc., 1958), vol. 2nd, pp. 1831-1914.

23. Op. cit., p. 1831.

24. Op. cit., pp. 1832-33.

25. See: Zygmunt Dulczewski, "Florian Znaniecki jako Tworca metody autobiograficznej w socjologii", in Florian Znaniecki i jego rola..., op. cit., pp. 75-88.

26. W. Berkan, Zyciorys wlasny (edited by Znaniecki) Poznan 1924.

27. See: Dulczewski, op. cit., p. 79.

28. Znaniecki, Wstep do Sociologii, Poznan, 1922, p. 467.

29. Znaniecki, "The Object Matter of Sociology", American Journal of Sociology, vol. 32, 1927, pp. 529-584.

30. Op. cit., p. 536.

31. Ibidem.

32. Znaniecki, The Method of Sociology (New York: Farrar & Rinehart, 1934), pp. 36-37.

33. Op. cit., p. 37.

34. Znaniecki, Social Actions (New York: Farrar & Rinehart, Inc., 1936).

35. Op. cit., Chapter III, Subtitle 2, p. 71.

36. Op. cit., p. 618.

37. Op. cit., Subtitle 3, p. 532.

38. Ibidem.

39. Op. cit., p. XIII.

40. Znaniecki, Cultural Sciences (Urbana: University of Illinois Press, 1963) [first edition 1952].

41. Op. cit., p. 132-133.

42. Op. cit., p. 172.

43. Op. cit., p. 138.

44. Znaniecki, The Method of Sociology, op. cit., p. 38.

45. Thomas and Znaniecki, The Polish Peasant, op. cit., p. 1850.

46. "Becker estimates that the most lasting influences in American sociology have been those of Toennies, Pareto, Durkheim, Max Weber, Znaniecki, and Wiese". Preston Valien and Bonita Valien, op. cit., p. 81.

47. Znaniecki, Social Actions, op. cit., pp. 673, 713 and 714.

48. Znaniecki wrote: "We borrow the term 'ideal type' from Max Weber, though we disagree with his theory that the most important ideal type from the point of view of cultural history, especially modern history, is that of rational actions in the teleological sense". Cultural Sciences (Urbana: University of Illinois Press, 1952), p. 205.

49. "Action is social insofar as, by virtue of the subjective meaning attached to it by the acting individual (or individuals), it takes account of the behavior of others and is thereby oriented in its course". Max Weber, The Theory of Social and Economic Organization (New York: Oxford University Press, 1947), p. 88.

50. Wstep do Socjologii is a book difficult to find in the United States. Although it was this sociological work which twenty-five years ago turned me from economics to sociology, I cannot trust only my memory and, therefore, have to use in this matter the best possible source of information, an article by one of my own most respected teachers of sociology Professor Pawel Rybicki, "Znanieckiego Wstep do socjologii odczytany po latach piedziesieciu" (Znaniecki's Wstep do Sociologii reread after fifty years) in Florian Znaniecki i jego rola w socjologii, op. cit., pp. 35-45 [A.G.].

51. Znaniecki, Social Actions [first published in 1936 by the Polish Sociological Institute, Poznan, Poland] (New York: Russell & Russell, 1967), p. 2.

52. Ibidem, p. 65.

53. P. Rybicki, op. cit., p. 39.

54. H. Znaniecki-Lopata, op. cit., quoted from F. Znaniecki Presidential Address to the ASA in 1954.

55. Comp. Rybicki, op. cit., p. 41.

56. Znaniecki, Cultural Sciences (Urbana: University of Illinois Press, 1952), chapter 14.

57. Znaniecki, Ludzie terazniejsi a cywilizacja przyszlosci [first edition 1934] PWN-Publisher: Warsaw 1974. This book was a by-product of his second invitation to America in 1931, by a team of American sociologists from Columbia University, to participate in collective research on the educational system in the States. The aim of this research project was to find whether the existing educational system in this country developed in young men the capabilities of adoption to the fast changes characteristic of modern civilization. It is interesting that Znaniecki used in this project his previously developed "autobiographical method". With the help of several American scholars and the "willing cooperation of students" from his seminars, he "investigated about 700 biographies and almost 60 group and educational institutions" (quotations from the preface written by himself to Ludzie terazniejsi a cywilizacja..., pp. 3-4.

58. "Dewey, Kilpatrick, Russell, Bagley, Rugg, Counts, Bruner, Newlon, Raup, Watson, Snedden and others". Op. cit., p. 5.

59. Ibidem.

60. Op. cit., p. 6.

61. Exact translation of the chapter titles he used are: (I) "Well-bred People", (II) "People of Play", (III) "People of Work", (IV) "Deviants".

62. Znaniecki's criticism was turned against Howard Scott, W. W. Parrish and others. Before Znaniecki but the same year Parrish published An Outline of Technocracy (New York, 1933).

63. Znaniecki, Ludzie terazniejsi..., pp. 5-6.

64. Op. cit., p. 22.

65. Ibidem.

66. Ibidem.

67. Op. cit., p. 48.

68. Op. cit., pp. 51-52.

69. Op. cit., p. 96.

70. Op. cit., p. 98.

71. Znaniecki, Socjologia wychowania (The Sociology of Education), 2 volumes, published by the Ministry of Education of Poland: Warsaw 1930.

72. Waclaw Machajski (1866-1926) a Polish revolutionist and intellectual who totally joined the international movement and wrote only in Russian. His main thesis is expounded in Umstviennyi Rabochyi (Intellectual Worker), published under the pseudonym A. Wolski, and in Bankrostvo Socyalizma (Bankruptcy of Socialism). Writing about Machajski in English is Max Nomad, Aspect of Revolt - Saga of Waclaw Machajski (New York: Bookman Associates, 1959) and in Polish, Zygmunt Zaremba, Slowa o Waclawie Machajskim, Paris 1967.

73. Znaniecki, Ludzie terazniejsi..., p. 356.

74. Op. cit., p. 351.

75. Op. cit., p. 352.

76. Op. cit., p. 355.

77. Op. cit., p. 382.

78. Ibidem.

79. Jan Szczepanski, "Introduction" to Znaniecki's Ludzie Terazniejsi..., p. XXXI.

80. Op. cit., p. XXII.

81. Although there is no place for an entire review of the book, we are taking the opportunity of giveing the American reader a basic outline of Znaniecki's views because his book on contemporary people and the civilization of the future is unavailable in English.

82. Words from Mussolini's review of Sorel's Reflexions sur la violence quoted by Laura Fermi, Mussolini (Chicago, 1961), p. 77.

83. Lenin, Iskra, May 1901, Collected Works, Vol. IV, Part I,

Where to Begin.

84. Herman Raushing, The Voice of Destruction (New York: G. P. Putnam's Sons, 1940), pp. 222-23 and 225. (Quotations from Hitler's statements.)

85. Znaniecki, Ludzie terazniejsi..., p. 101.

86. Op. cit., p. 201.

87. Op. cit., p. 264.

88. Op. cit., p. 271-274.

89. Op. cit., p. 346.

90. Znaniecki, Cultural Sciences, p. 238.

91. Ibidem.

CHAPTER VIII

LOVE HAS A POWER OF ITS OWN: PITIRIM SOROKIN

"Sorokin Lives!" These words served as a slogan of solidarity for the members of the Sociology Liberation Movement who staged a minor "insurrection" against the sociological establishment at the 1968 convention of the American Sociological Association. Sorokin, who once had been regarded as something of a pariah in certain leftist circles, won the enthusiasm of the maverick sociologists by virtue of his deathbed denouncement of the American participation in the Vietnam War.[1] While a humanistic sociology is not likely to inspire any coups, we, too, believe the spirit of P. A. Sorokin Lives!

He filled his canvasses with bold strokes in an age when timid lines were considered prudent. The versatile mind of this Titian could not be contained by the categories of middle-range theories or the conventions of academic departmentalization. The scope and depth of his thought remains unparalleled in American sociology and includes such diverse areas as criminology, rural sociology, sociology of revolution, philosophy of history, philosophy of science, methodology, law, comparative studies, sexual behavior, marriage and family, ethics, sociology of religion, epistemology, and ontology. Sorokin's work has been translated into over fifteen languages.[2]

It is worthy to be mentioned how another great humanist, the late Arnold Toynbee, saw Sorokin's contribution against the background of contemporary world problems.

> The blinkers that have been inserted between the so-called disciplines into which the study of human affairs has been arbitrarily partitioned are as much against the interests of mankind as any political iron curtain is. In the Atomic Age that has now overtaken us, it is a good deed to provoke people, if one cannot entice them, to cross these perverse man-made barriers. If the trans-frontier traffic

becomes brisk enough, the barriers will gradually be worn down, and to get rid of them is one of the present vital interests of the human race. In the Atomic Age, as we know, the choice confronting us is "one world or none". Sorokin has overridden the conventional barriers between the "disciplines". He has taken human affairs as a whole, and has studied them from any promising angle by any promising method. Perhaps this is the greatest of his many services to mankind's common cause.[3]

His early commitment to humanistic scholarship is evident in the volume, Leo Tolstoi as a Philosopher.[4] The humanistically oriented sociologist will find it interesting that at about the same time, Max Weber also planned to write a book on Tolstoi.[5] The parallel interest in Tolstoi of these two great sociologists is especially provocative in light of Tolstoi's devastating criticisms of the sociology of Comte and Spencer which he regarded as founded upon the fundamental error of organicism which fails to give adequate recognition to the essential human quality--consciousness. Tolstoi regarded positivism as an essentially evaluative perspective which has two aspects, the philosophical and the political. Sometime before 1887, he wrote, "Only the first part was adopted by the learned world--that part which justified, on new premises, the existent evil of human societies; but the second part, treating of the moral obligations of altruism, arising from the recognition of mankind as an organism, was regarded as not only of no importance but as trivial and unscientific".[6]

For the purposes of this exposition, we will concentrate on the humanistic character of Sorokin's sociology as manifested in five dimensions of his thought: (1) the demonstration that philosophical issues are inescapably relevant for social science; (2) the combination of sociological analysis with a concern for human suffering; (3) his studies of altruism and the application of sociology to discover and create solutions to human problems; (4) his methodological position which posits centrality of "meaning"; and (5) his belief in the possibility of indeterminate action.

Sorokin's work offers much to the student concerned with understanding the ongoing relevance of philosophy for the social sciences. The methodological implications of philosophy for social scientists should almost go without question. For example, in his analysis of legal order in capitalist societies Quinney argues that because of the positivist's "naive acquaintance with epistemological and ontological concerns...what is ignored in the approach to explanation is an examination of the philosophical assumptions by which the observer operates".[7] Merleau-Ponty succinctly states the sociologist's predicament: "the sociologist philosophizes every time he is required to not only record but comprehend the facts".[8] Yet, Kimmel critically asserts, "American and English philosophy, with almost exclusive emphasis upon naturalistic empiricism or positivism, fails to come to grips with the problems facing modern man at a level which is genuinely problematic because it fails to call into question its own metaphysical presuppositions".[9] With the proliferation of the positivist ethos, growing methodological empiricism, and development of "scientific" sociology, how much farther removed from its metaphysical roots has been the dominant flow of American sociology?

Fortunately, voices of criticism are becoming louder and louder. Let us quote George Psathas who emphasized that "American trained social scientists need to read and study extensively in philosophy in order to discover the roots of their own discipline. The ground or origin of any system of thought, such as science, is to be found in philosophical quests and not in social scientific analyses (i.e., the sociology of sociology does not reveal the epistemic and ontological groundings of the discipline itself, what is taken to be knowledge or truth, and what means are to be used to arrive at such knowledge). At the same time, the philosophical quest does not in itself necessarily lead to an understanding of how the results of philosophical investigations can produce a more informed or even modified social science".[10]

The fact is that philosophical issues have been ignored by the majority of American sociologists. The pretheoretical suppositions, paradigmatic orientations, or to use Gouldner's terms "domain assumptions" with which American sociologists inevitably approach the workbench have gone largely unacknowledged. Graduate students, budding young statistical experts, specialists in various "career-oriented" areas of investigation often share the same superficial views of philosophy: philosophy was something studied as an undergraduate; major philosophical issues were somehow settled during the early part of the 20th century; or, while philosophical questions possess some import for social science, they have little relevance to the everyday "doing" of sociology. With an almost religious fervor for empiricistic exactitude, the "modern" researcher isolates some small problematic aspect of social reality, formulates hypotheses, constructs a research design, locates an "acceptable" sample, gathers and analyzes the "data", and writes up his or her conclusion(s). The entire research process can be conceived of and carried out with little or no consideration of the epistemological underpinnings of the process itself. If American sociologists tolerate philosophy in the abstract, it has little life. That is, it has little to do with the activities of the sociologists themselves. The gap between sociological practice and philosophical reflection remains large and, in part, has contributed to a growing fragmentation within the discipline. Playing upon Weber's imagery, our work has become encased in one small compartment within the great "iron cage". We move closer to becoming "specialists without spirit, sensualists without soul".[11] As long as sociologists continue to ignore the transcendent implications and foundations of their concrete actions and problems they run the risk of falling prey to Nietzsche's forboding: "Ich habe meine Grunde vergessen"--I have forgotten my roots.

Sorokin heeds Nietzsche's warning well. Philosophical considerations are central to the man and his thought. To those who would argue the irrelevancy of philosophy for social science, he replies:

> As to the revolt against 'armchair philosophy' in sociology, here again a sociologist can reject a specific brand of philosophy as a wrong philosophy but no sociologist can dismiss philosophy qua philosophy from sociology and sociological research. The very nature of psychological, cultural and value-problems cannot be properly defined and analyzed without some philosophical--epistemological, ontological, and phenomenological--presuppositions.[12]

As Joseph Ford observes, "Sorokin's catholicity of interests leads him to treat almost every branch of philosophy. Metaphysics, epistemology, ethics, and the philosophies of history are central concerns".[13] He faces many crucial philosophical issues in the magnus opus Social and Cultural Dynamics. Two of these issues will be discussed presently.

First, in the tradition of Heraclitus, Lucretius, or Asclepius, Sorokin conceives reality as a neverending process of "being in becoming". A static equilibrium or material inertia are alien to his conception of the human ontological condition. Change is inherent in the nature of reality itself. These ontological suppositions are the philosophical foundations upon which his dynamic principle of social change--the Principle of Immanence--rests. Consistent with Aristotelian metaphysics, Sorokin argues that change is imminent to the object itself--be it an amoeba, flower, individual, or socio-cultural system. For Sorokin, reality and social reality is a "many-sided and multifaceted thing". It can be approached, therefore, from various theoretical positions. These can be very different and even conflicting, but nevertheless, they may be equally "true".

Secondly, through the construction of ideal types, Sorokin identifies three main culture mentalities: ideational, sensate, and idealistic. Whereas the first is concerned with the super-empirical and dwells upon metaphysical or spiritual phenomena, the second is primarily oriented around the empirical or material aspects of reality. The third represents a mixture of the idealistic and sensate culture mentalities. Within his theory of social change, the last 2500 years of western history have witnessed a rhythmically re-occurring fluctuation of these three cultural modalities. What concerns us here, however, is that Sorokin arrived at the formulation of these concepts through a "sociologico-phenomenological interpretation" of socio-cultural phenomena. This method allows the sociologist to interpret the internal aspect of a culture *both* through the more widely accepted causal-functional method as well as a logical method. From an essentially phenomenological perspective, the observer can logically derive the central integrating or conflicting principles within a given cultural system. Put simply, Sorokin argues that we need not demonstrate the relationships between various cultural elements in a strictly causal fashion as many rigid empiricists contend. Instead, he maintains these relationships may be derived logically.[14]

These exemplifications of the ontological and phenomenological basis of Sorokin's theory of social change illustrate the centrality of philosophy to his work. His philosophical roots, however, go beyond the theoretical.

Kierkegaard asserted, "Truth exists only in so far as the individual produces it in action". Much of Sorokin's later work implies the necessity of action. Consider these remarks by Natanson:

> It is unnecessary to dramatize the importance of philosophy and its relevance for the social sciences. The student who remains fragmented in his disciplinary cell avoids the touch of reality; the sense of security he gains is achieved at the expense of his fundamental education. The moral and pedagogic dimension of the social sciences is illuminated by existential commitment.[15]

Humanism is an affair of both head and heart, of intellect and compassion. Sorokin combines scholarship with a benevolent and active concern for individual welfare and the betterment of humankind. Few thinkers have called such exacting and compassionate attention to the massive social and cultural crisis of our time. He writes:

> ...every important aspect of the life, organization, and the culture of Western society is included in the crisis. Its body and mind

are sick and there is hardly a spot on its
body which is not sore, nor any nervous fiber
which functions smoothly. We are seemingly
between two epochs: the dying Sensate culture of our magnificent yesterday and the
coming Ideational culture of the creative
tomorrow.[16]

Much of Sorokin's work may be regarded as an etiology of human suffering.[17] His empathy for the human casualties of political, economic, and social upheaval was born of personal knowledge.
Having been imprisoned three times under the Tsarist regime and
three times under the Soviet regime and once condemned to death,
Sorokin was only too well aware of the magnitude of disruptive
and dehumanizing forces impinging upon the human organism.[18]
World war, massive military destruction, famine, ideological fa-
naticism, economic hardship, and other "earmarks" of the 20th
century were all too familiar to him. Sorokin believed it is not
enough for social scientific investigations to merely describe
human social ills. They must attempt to eliminate them. He criticized those who prescribed "remedies" for social ills without
first analyzing the causal forces involved. Sociology was the
tool Sorokin employed to carve out an understanding of 20th century social problems. Hence, Sorokin's sociology is not sociology for sociology's sake but a discipline with a hierarchy of
priorities which are relevant for bettering the human condition.
While the methods and perspective are social scientific, the aims
and ethos of the work are humanistic.

A third humanistic thread in Sorokin's sociology is his later
work concerning love done at the Harvard Research Center in Altruistic Integration and Creativity. The human experience of love
remains a relative stranger within the empiricistic corridors of
dominant sociological concerns. Despite innumerable behavioral
manifestations of love in everyday life--parental self-sacrifice,
a tender embrace, religious dedication, altruistic selflessness,
charity--the notion of love retains an almost ethereal quality.
For expert illumination of the nature of love, we usually turn to
either poets or sages and seldom to social scientists. If love
has been a slippery phenomenon to define for specifically-oriented
and positivisitically-inclined sociologists, it is still more
difficult to "operationalize". Current methods fall short of
elucidating the complexity of this phenomenon.

Sorokin conceived of love as an integrating force in social
life.[19] Love has a power of its own. If social scientists could
develop further understanding of the character and social impact
of altruism, then this knowledge could be utilized to solve many
human social problems. Sorokin's humanistic concern for a health-
ful and life-affirming society is here most evident, as it is in

the work of many humanistic psychologists and psychoanalysts.[20] He considered the growth of love and altruistic behavior essential for the construction of a new cultural era for humankind. The understanding and inculcation of altruism could stem the apocalyptic tide of the 20th century's decadent sensate culture.[21] Joseph Matter states Sorokin's humanistic optimism, "If humanity mobilized all its widsom, knowledge, beauty, and especially the all-giving and all-forgiving love or reverence for life, and it a strenuous and sustaining effort of this kind is made by everyone--an effort deriving its strength from that love and reverence for life--then the crisis will certainly be ended and a most magnificent new era of human history ushered in".[22] It is significant that Sorokin could conceive of a world altruism. The specialized intellectual focus and detached skepticism characteristic of most contemporary students of society almost precludes the entertainment of such a thought. Indeed, Albert Camus remarked, cynicism is the only way of avoiding mockery in the twentieth century.[23] With a growing recognition of international interdependency, the possible emergence of a global community, and growing ecological consciousness, Sorokin's optimism is not necessarily so platitudinous or utopian as it may seem. In this century, we have experienced the horrors of human destructiveness on a previously unimagined scale; but we have only just begun to see the dawning possibility of a world culture. We must continually remind ourselves of the elementary sociological precept formulated by W. I. Thomas, refined by Robert K. Merton, and reaffirmed by contemporary phenomenological sociologists: "shared assumptions about reality become taken-for-granted and, like a self-fulfilling prophecy, create 'objective' situations which exert constraint upon us".[24] If we assume the inevitability of world destruction, we contribute to it.[25] Lewis Mumford reminds us:

> Almost any achievement of man, from the stone ax of neolothic times to the planing machine of the twentieth century may well be characterized as the attainment of the impossible by means of the inadequate. Every goal seems to be demonstrably attained.[26]

Sorokin considers humankind capable of fashioning a path out of 20th-century crisis and he believes sociological analysis can help lead the way. In order to further the development of altruism, he offers various suggestions and strategies all predicated upon sound sociological evidence and argument. These include: (a) meditation and other techniques of ego-transcending; (b) weakening interpersonal or intergroup hatred; (c) heroic example; (d) rational persuasion; (e) bridging the gap between intellect and emotions, nurturing both simultaneously; (f) encourage friendship and good will; (g) promote collective activity; (h) prayer; (i) examination of conscience; (j) altruization of children within the family; and (k) enhancing social scientific understanding of the causes and effects of altruism within social life.[27]

Sorokin's studies of altruism also nicely illustrate his methodological flexibility and introduce a fourth characteristic of his humanistic sociology. He was too serious an epistemologist to indulge in methodological purism. Sorokin recognized love's "transempirical part" and outlined its religious and ontological dimensions within cultural reality.[28] Though reckoning with love's transempirical dimensions, he also sets about the task of formulating more specific definitions of the concept and suggests methods by which it can be measured. Consistent with his overall sociological work, he affirms the utility and scientific worth of more rigorously empirical modes of sociological investigations, but also recognizes their inherent limitations to explain all aspects of social reality and human experience. Sorokin's disdain is for a "crude" or "narrow-minded" brand of empiricism which denies or ignores the existence of socio-cultural phenomenon which are not amenable to systematic measurement or fit into accepted theoretical schemes.[29] Just as Dilthey and Weber struggled against the intrusion of the all-encompassing pretensions of Anglo-French positivism on the European front, Sorokin, several decades later, combatted the scientistic excesses of American sociology. Like Dilthey and Weber, Sorokin held that essential differences exist between natural and social scientific modes of investigation. We have already alluded to the methodological quarrel between the historicists and positivists. The entire controversy seems to emerge from two different views of human nature: the naturalistic and the humanistic. Sorokin's methodological assumptions, and concomitantly, his view of man in society, fall within the humanistic tradition. Due to man's innate capacity to create meanings in the world, to create culture out of matter and spirit, he cannot be studied in the same manner as atoms or galactic movements. Sorokin's Polemic against a naturalistic view of man and its methodological offsprings--neo-positivist empiricism or "Lilliputian fact-finding"--appears sporadically throughout his works. For example, he writes, "the peculiar nature of the socio-cultural 'causality' is fundamentally different from that of the causality of the natural phenomena"; and, "the meaningful components of socio-cultural phenomena make them fundamentally different from physio-chemical and biological phenomena and call for a logico-meaningful method profoundly different from the pure causal or pure probabilistic method of the natural sciences".[30] Or gain, with critical reference to mechanistic-naturalistic sociologies, he states:

> When one approaches mechanically the study of the relationships between most of the socio-cultural phenomena, and takes, for example, the relationship between the movement of quantitative nudity in pictures and of nominalism,

> treating them just as two variables, one can hardly find any relationship; one can hardly even guess that in some way they may be interdependent. Still less possible is it to find through such a mechanical procedure, any relationship of interdependence between thousands of phenomena--meanings, vehicles, human agents that make our supersystems, and thousands of processes of which the life of the supersystem is made up. No inductive method in its mechanical application, no statistical correlation technique can even be applied to such a task.[31]

One of the most outstanding defenses of the humanistic standpoint in sociology against a simplified empiricism and various statistical approaches appeared in Sorokin's later work, <u>Fads and Foibles</u> in <u>Modern Sociology</u>. Here he launched an offensive against the abuses of statistics in chapters entitled "Cult of Numerology" and "Quantafrenia" as well as pointing to the neglect of knowledge of the history of sociology itself, which resulted in the "Discovery Complex" among many contemporary authors he sarcastically called "New Columbuses".[32]

In the early 1950's Sorokin accused Parsons of plagiarizing his work and circulated copies of this change to all members of the American Sociological Association.

The humanistic ethos of Sorokin's sociology is further reflected in his critical posture toward the "fashionable cult" of behavioristically-derived psychological images of man. He writes:

> ...the ritualistic procedures of this cult: with mechanical tests...and statistical operations...always delivering to us 'objective, quantitatively-precise knowledge' of all the mysteries of the human soul and mind...'mathematical models of robots', and pseudo-experimental studies of mechanical man and his 'mindless mind', 'emotionless emotions', 'will-less will'...all 'the invariant variations' of man's behavior and psychological processes...the unhesitating extension upon man of conditioned reflexes or the mechanisms of learning observed in rats, mice, dogs, rabbits, or other animals...the still more mechanistic interpretation of man's psychology and behavior by the principles of cybernetics, with its 'feed back' and extension of control and communication in the machine upon man...[33]

Sorokin's overall image of humanity reaches beyond the theoretical and methodological parameters of an S-R model. With its often underlying philosophical and spiritual dimensions, Sorokin's sociology pays due deference to the almost overwhelming complexity of human social behavior. Contrposed to behaviorism, Sorokin's <u>homo sociologicus</u> is more closely associated to that of the existential psychoanalystic school in breadth and depth. As Rollo May writes:

> Existential psychothereapy is the movement which, although standing on one side on the scientific analysis owed chiefly to the genius of Freud, also brings back into the picture the understanding of man on the deeper and broader level--man as the being who is human. It is based on the assumption that it is possible to have a science of man which does not fragmentize man and destroy his humanity at the same moment as it studies him. It unites science and ontology.[34]

Sorokin's criticism of behaviorism also reveals the central place of meaning in his sociology. Tacitly contained within Sorokin's works is the recognition that, due to the subjective character of human activity, the universe of elements within a given culture are imploded with meaning. The ideational, sensate, and idealistic cultural types are in essence massive unities of particular subjective conceptions of reality or expansive systems of meanings. Here Weber's ideal type method and operation of <u>verstehen</u> are utilized to the utmost. Like Dilthey and Weber before him, meaning is the central focus for Sorokin's historical and sociological analyses. Behaviorist psychology's efforts to reduce human behavior to stimulus-response phenomena ignores or cannot begin to understand the "inner experience" which attends social action. Sorokin writes:

> Further inadequacy of the strictly behaviorist description of human actions and psychology is shown in that it cannot grasp at all what is styled the 'meaning' of either overt actions or subjective psychical processes, or that of symbolic social phenomena like science, religion, ideology, church, school, and so on. 'Meaning' is generally indescribable in the terminology of strict behaviorism...[35]

The final motif of Sorokin's humanistic sociology that we will consider is his position that, in varying circumstances and to relative degrees, human freedom does exist. The massive power of the historico-sociocultural process to shape human destinies is readily apparent for him. Yet, he does not regard man as a passive victim. Sorokin explicitly recognizes indeterminate action. In his scheme, human beings have some input into shaping the course of individual and historical events.

Sorokin maintains there is "no exit" from the cosmic flux of "being in becoming". Socioculturally, too, humanity cannot simply disengage itself by some supreme act of will from the recurrent patterns or "superrhythmic" transformation from, for example, a dying sensate phase to budding ideational phase. There are forces larger than the individual. On a macro-sociocultural level, however, Sorokin states that "so far as the future of the system is determined mainly not be external agents, but by the system itself (in keeping with the Principle of Immanent Change), such a determinism is indeterministic or free, as flowing spontaneously, in accordance with its nature, from the system itself".[36] In like manner, he views the behavior of individuals acting and thinking within the recurrent rhythms of sociocultural change. Othmar Anderle points out that Sorokin believes the individual can consciously act within the context of historical processes:

> It would then be nonsensical to cling most mightily, with one hand, to the dwindling sensate values and to resist, with the other, the germinating ideational tendencies. Rather, it would make sense to do the opposite, for in the former case, one would swim against the current and be destined to suffer shipwreck. In the latter case, by swimming with the current, one's success would be assured.[37]

In arguing the merits of a humanistic sociology, we believe we are swimming with the current. Sorokin also thought sociology would move in this direction. In his 1965 Presidential Address to the American Sociological Association entitled "Sociology of Yesterday, Today and Tomorrow", he contended:

> Today's predominantly analytical and fact-finding sociology is at a cross-roads. If it chooses to stay for an indefinitely long time in that state, it condemns itself to the sterile state of knowing more and more about less and less; if it chooses the way of growth, it must pass eventually into the phase of synthesizing, generalizing, and integrating sociology.[38]

Sorokin's quarrel was not with fact-finding activities *per se*. Rather, he cited the thesis elaborated by Spencer, Tarde, Bernard, Whitehead, Berr, Joel, and himself that there is "a recurrent alteration of analytical, fact-finding periods and generalizing or synthesizing periods in the history of science and philosophical thought.[39] He regarded the period 1920 to 1965 as primarily preoccupied with fact-finding whereas the early period in sociology's history (1875-1920) was more productive in formulating comprehensive sociological synthesis and discovering large-scale uniformities and trends. He argued that the potential of the present analytic phase has been realized and pointed out that:

> ...stagnant periods in the development of science...show a long-conservative adherence to the prevalent, established, routine patterns of thought, style, or activity. The longer such patterns persist, the more frequently repeated and practiced, the more hackneyed, sterile, and uncreative the respective sciences become.[40]

Sorokin believed that the present age of "Alexandrians" is drawing to a close. Lenin regarded Sorokin as a weathervane.[41] In this regard, we concur with the revolutionary leader. Sorokin himself acknowledged that he had been remarkably successful in the thorny art of social forecasting:

> ...sociology will choose the road of creative growth and will eventually enter its new period of great syntheses. I hope that in this conjectural prognosis I may be as lucky as in my previous prognostications of the wars, revolutions, liberation in man of 'the worst of the beasts, dictatorships, and other changes in sociocultural life, which I did at the end of the 1920's and reiterated in considerable detail in my *Dynamics*. Despite severe criticism of my 'forecastings' almost all of them have come to pass. I hope that my guess of 'the shape of sociology to come' will also be confirmed by its objective development in the future.[42]

In our concluding remarks, we will turn our attention from Sorokin the seer to Sorokin the professional sociologist. Sorokin seems to have taken seriously Carl Becker's dictum: the purpose of the scholar is to think otherwise. For Sorokin has been described as "a gadfly" as well as "a trail blazer"--a combination that is not likely to make one popular.[43] A former student describes him in these words:

> In an age of spreading conformity, Sorokin was one of the exceptions who continued to exemplify the best tradition of the indepen-

> dent scholar. A man of extraordinarily wide
> interests and long views, he remained rela-
> tively unmoved by passing political tempests,
> just as he had been generally unaffected by
> most of the short-term enthusiasms in social
> science.[44]

Genius has never fitted easily into the mythos of social science and, with few exceptions, academic social science has not treated its geniuses kindly--witness the careers of Tonnies, Simmel, Michels, Veblen, Thomas, Willard Waller and Ernest Becker. Unquestionably Sorokin compounded his own situation for he was not overburdened with modesty. Self-effacement and dissembling were alien to his character. Reading his autobiographical account of his career, A Long Journey, one realizes that Sorokin regarded his monumental works as monumental works. In criticizing the works of others, he was unsparing and occasionally unfair.[45] His gift for language combined with an old world ironic imagination turned his pen into a rapier. It sometimes cut deeply. Sages are seldom tolerant of fools masquerading as sages. The "New Columbuses" of sociology who are afflicted with serious cases of "amnesia" and "discoverer's complexes" concerning the history and achievements of their own fields never ceased to inflame his caustic wit.[46] If his style was too flamboyant, the timid men had their silent revenge. For Sorokin was not awarded the esteem within the profession which he so richly deserved. He was not elected president of the A.S.A. until sixteen years after his junior colleague and long-time adversary, Talcott Parsons, and even this was accomplished only through a write-in campaign organized in the hinterlands. Today, one hears the newest Columbuses crediting Parsons with introducing American sociologists to Max Weber. In his classic, Contemporary Sociological Theories (1928) which was the authoritative source on theory until the 1950's, Sorokin presented an extensive exposition of Weberian sociology.[47] While we are indebted to Parsons for assuming the tedious task of translating a substantial part of the Weberian legacy into English, Parsons himself admits that he never heard of Weber before he went to Heidelberg in the mid-twenties.[48] Sorokin also alienated himself from his contemporaries on other grounds. He refused to profess the catechism of value-free sociology. His student, Arthur Davis, gives a lucid account of Sorokin's position on this issue:

> ...Sorokin has usually--with now and then a
> lapse--addressed himself to the basic problems
> of the age without being sidetracked by the
> current cult of 'objectivity'. According to
> the latter view, which seems to prevail among
> sociologists of some leading North American
> universities, a social scientist should re-
> ligiously avoid making value judgments in his

> scientific work--as if this were really possible! May not such antisepsis in science invite sterility rather than progress?
>
> Writers who do not adhere to the canon of objectivity are likely to be looked upon by orthodox social scientists as 'philosophers' rather than 'scientists'--and in this context, 'philosopher' is hardly a complimentary term. The orthodox are inclined somewhat to look askance at these deviant characters, among whom are commonly included Sorokin, Toynbee, the Marxians, Charles Beard, Veblen, and others. A distinguished list of sinners, indeed!
>
> The great social thinkers of all times have dealt with the leading social and ethical issues of their day. In so doing they have necessarily made value judgments. Perhaps facing up to the leading ethical questions of the day is by itself not a sufficient condition of greatness--one must come up with some relevant answers, too. But it is surely a necessary condition of greatness.[49]

In this sense Sorokin fulfilled the necessary conditions for greatness.

There was an element of his personality, however, which throws a shadow on his greatness. He suffered from a serious lack of modesty which is so essential in the self-criticism process. He eventually concluded that "between Hegel and Sorokin, there is nothing".[50] In later years, he referred to himself in the third person. We know of a case when, upon signing a copy of a book for a student, he was queried why he did not provide first initials before his last name. Sorokin replied, "Would Aristotle have set down initials before his last name?"[51]

With the possible exception of his failure to observe the rather staid conventions of the Anglo-Saxon traditions of academic discourse (a transgression which we can forgive an itinerant church painter from northern Russia who acquired a formidable education without the usual bourgeois comforts); we can truly say of Sorokin that he was (to abuse Weber's metaphor) a generalist with spirit and a specialist with heart--yes, Sorokin lives!

CHAPTER VIII FOOTNOTES

1. For Sorokin's own account of his early difficulties with the American left, see *A Long Journey* (New Haven: College and University Press, 1963). For an account of the 1968 A.S.A. convention as viewed by a partisan participant, see Martin Nicolaus, "The Professional Organization of Sociology: A View from Below" in *Radical Sociology* edited by J. David Colfax and Jack L. Roach (New York: Basic Books, 1971).

2. Sorokin has earned an impressive reputation in the history and development of sociological thought. For an assessment of the breadth of his importance for sociology, see Edward A. Tiryakian, ed., *Sociological Theory, Values and Sociocultural Change* (New York: Harper & Row, 1967); Carle Zimmerman, *Sorokin, the World's Greatest Sociologist* (Saskatoon: University of Saskatchewan, 1968); and Philip J. Allen, ed., *Pitirim A. Sorokin In Review* (Durham, N.C.: Duke University Press, 1963).

3. Arnold J. Toynbee, "Sorokin's Philosophy of History" in Allen, ed., *Pitirim A. Sorokin In Review*, op. cit., pp. 93-94.

4. Originally published in Russian.

5. For an account of Weber's affinity for Tolstoi, see Guenther Roth, "Max Weber's Generational Rebellion and Maturation" in *Scholarship and Partisanship: Essays on Max Weber* by Reinhard Bendix and Roth (Berkeley: University of California Press, 1971).

6. For a full and fascinating discussion of Tolstoi's opinion of sociology (including many more quotations) see Don Martindale, "The Roles of Humanism and Scientism in the Evolution of Sociology" in George K. Zollschan and Walter Hirsch (eds.), *Exploration In Social Change* (Boston: Houghton Mifflin Co., 1964), pp. 473-474.

7. Richard Quinney, *Critique of Legal Order* (1974), p. 3.

8. Maurice Merleau-Ponty, "The Philosopher and Sociology" in *Signs* (Northwestern University Press, 1964), p. 101.

9. Jean Wiles and William Kimmel, *The Search for Being* (New

York: Noonday Press, 1969), p. 9.

10. George Psathas, Phenomenological Sociology (New York: John Wiley and Sons, 1973), p. 7.

11. Max Weber, The Protestant Ethic and the Spirit of Capitalism (New York: Charles Scribner's Sons, 1958), p. 182.

12. P. A. Sorokin, "A Quest for an Integral System of Sociology", in Memoire du XIX Congress International de Sociologie (Mexico, B.F., 1960).

13. Joseph B. Ford, "Sorokin As Philosopher", in Phillip J. Allen, Pitirim A. Sorokin In Review (Durham, N.C.: Duke University Press, 1963), pp. 39-66.

14. Sorokin's phenomenological position is also evident in his formulation of the four types of cultural integration: (1) special or mechanical adjacency; (2) indirect association through some external factor; (3) causal or functional integration; (4) logico-meaningful integration. For discussion see P. A. Sorokin, Social and Cultural Dynamics (New York: American Book Company, 1937), vol. I, Chapter I.

15. Maurice Natanson, Philosophy of the Social Sciences (New York: Random House, 1963), p. 26.

16. P. A. Sorokin, Social and Cultural Dynamics (New York: American Book Company, 1937), p. 535.

17. The concern for human welfare was never far from Weber's work. Consider his early studies of the East Elbian question, his reformist zeal, and active efforts to win the cause of women's rights. The scope and depth of Weber's sorrow and concern for the "disenchantment of reality" is reflected in his work on bureaucracy. Fromm also combines humanistic fervor with analytic insight. See especially Erich Fromm, The Anatomy of Human Destructiveness (New York: Holt, Rinehart and Winston, 1973). Also, Barrington Moore, Jr. has examined the causes of human suffering. See Reflections on the Causes of Human Misery (Boston: Beacon Press, 1972).

18. For a biographical account, see Sorokin, Leaves From a Russian Diary (Boston: Beacon Press, 1950).

19. P. A. Sorokin, Explorations in Altruistic Love and Behavior (Boston: Beacon Press, 1950).

20. Fromm speaks of "dialectic humanism" in The Heart of Man (New York: Harper and Row, 1964). See also his The Art of

Loving (New York: Harper & Row, 1962). See Rollo May, *Love and Will* (New York: Dell Publishing Company, 1969). For a sociologico-phenomenological consideration of the meaning of love, see William A. Sadler, *Existence and Love* (New York: Charles Scribner's Sons, 1969).

21. P. A. Sorokin, *Social Philosophies of an Age of Crisis* (Boston: Beacon Press, 1951).

22. Joseph Allen Matter, *Love, Altruism and World Crisis: The Challenge of Pitirim Sorokin* (Totowa, New Jersey: Littlefield, Adams and Company, 1975), p. 2.

23. Albert Camus, *The Rebel* (New York: Vintage, 1959).

24. David Silverman, "Methodology and Meaning", in Paul Filmer, Michael Phillipson, David Silverman, and David Walsh, *New Directions in Sociological Theory* (Cambridge, Mass.: The M.I.T. Press, 1972), p. 192.

25. For an actual account of how official expectations of violence generated violence during the September 1971 Attica prison rebellion, see Tom Wicker's *A Time To Die* (New York: Ballantine Books, 1975).

26. Lewis Mumford, *Findings and Keepings: Analects For an Autobiography* (New York: Harcourt Brace Jovanovich, 1975), p. 28.

27. The reader may glean an overall grasp of Sorokin's sociological effort by examining the following works: *The Reconstruction of Humanity* (Boston: Beacon Press, 1948); *The Ways and Power of Love* (Boston: Beacon Press, 1954); *Forms and Techniques of Altruistic and Spiritual Growth* (Boston: Beacon Press, 1954). For discussion, see J. A. Matter, *op. cit.*

28. P. A. Sorokin, *Explorations in Altruistic Love and Behavior*, *op. cit.*, pp. 3-15.

29. Sorokin's paradigmatic openness and methodological flexibility are also reflected by the fact that he includes two articles dealing with parapsychology in the anthology on altruistic love. See Sorokin, *ibidem*: J. B. Rhine, "Parapsychology and the Study of Altruism", pp. 165-180; and S. David Kuhn, "Extrasensory Perception and Friendly Interpersonal Relations", pp. 181-187.

30. P. A. Sorokin, *Social and Cultural Dynamics*, *op. cit.*, and Volume IV, pp. vii-viii, cf. 4 n. 1. Near the end of his

life, Sorokin even came to regard the statistical method with increasing skepticism and explained his extensive use of this tool which had been borrowed from the natural sciences as a concession to the Sensate culture in which he worked.

31. Ibidem, vol. iv, p. 433.

32. Pitirim Sorokin, Fads and Foibles in Modern Sociology and Related Sciences (Chicago: Henry Regnery Company, 1956).

33. Ibidem, p. 135.

34. Rollo May, Ernest Angel, and Henri I. Ellenberger, Existence: A New Dimension in Psychiatry and Psychology (New York: Simon and Schuster, 1958), p. 36.

35. P. A. Sorokin, Contemporary Sociological Theories (New York: Harper and Row, 1964), paperback edition, pp. 623-624.

36. P. A. Sorokin, Social and Cultural Dynamics, op. cit., vol. IV, p. 619.

37. Othmar F. Anderle, "Sorokin and Cultural Morphology", in Phillip J. Allen, op. cit., p. 103.

38. P. A. Sorokin, "Sociology of Yesterday, Today and Tomorrow", Presidential Address delivered at the annual meeting of the American Sociological Association in Chicago, September 1965, published in the American Sociological Review (December 1965, Vol. 30, No. 6), p. 837.

39. Ibidem, p. 833. This notion closely parallels the currently popular conceptualizations of the history of science inspired by the Kuhnian thesis.

40. Ibidem, p. 838.

41. Nicolaus, "The Professional Organization of Sociology...", op. cit., p. 57.

42. Sorokin, "Sociology of Yesterday...", op. cit., p. 843.

43. Edward Tiryakian, "Preface" to Sociological Theory, Values and Sociocultural Change, op. cit., p. X.

44. Arthur K. Davis, "Lessons from Sorokin", in Sociological Theory, Values and Siciolcultural Change, op. cit., p. 6.

45. A notable example is his assessment of Simmel in the 1928 volume--an assessment that was reversed in Sociological

Theories of Today (1966).

46. Sorokin, Fads and Foibles..., op. cit., pp. 3-20.

47. We do not wish to imply that American sociologists were not familiar with Weber before Sorokin's 1928 volume. Max Weber was not exactly a minor figure in German academic circles. During the Weimar era, students from thoughout the world were attracted to Germany just as they had been in the pre-World War I period. Political scientists in America were reading Weber in the twenties. Robert MacIver was an early master of Weberian theory. We "New Columbuses" should remember that forty years ago American scholars were not as linguistically handicapped as they are today--at the very minimum, a Ph.D. had at least a reading knowledge of French or German.

48. Talcott Parsons, "On Building Social Systems Theory: A Personal History", Daedalus (Fall, 1970).

49. Davis, "Lessons from Sorokin", op. cit., pp. 5-6.

50. This information is owed to the kindness of Dr. E. Merle Adams who was Sorokin's assistant at Harvard in 1949.

51. This story was related by Dr. Elwin Powell based on his personal contact with Sorokin. Dr. Powell assumed, however, that Sorokin's over-exaggerated pride and conceit was partially a playful ruse.

CHAPTER IX

SOCIOLOGICAL CULTURE: KARL MANNHEIM

The great Symbolist poet, Rainer Maria Rilke, once advised students of man that they must be devoted above all to the ques-tions themselves--the lonely ventures into the unknown.[1] The questions posed by Karl Mannheim probe deeply into the structure of twentieth-century thought and existence. In Mannheim's work, some of the most important currents of modern intellectual history intersect and are cogently synthesized. Mannheimian sociology is a creative amalgam of German historicism, the Marxian theory of ideology, and Weberian macrosociology.[2]

Karl Mannheim was born in Budapest in 1893 of Jewish parents.[3] After graduating from the humanistic gymnasium in that city he left Horthy's Hungary for good. He studied at Berlin, Budapest, Paris, and Freiburg, before being habilitated as a Privatdozent at Heidelberg in 1926. Mannheim's teachers included Georg Lukacs, Bela Zalai, Emil Lask, Heinrich Rickert, and Edmund Husserl. In 1929 he was named to a professorship at Frankfurt. He had the distinction of being among the first (along with Paul Tillich, Hugo Sinzheimer, and Max Horkheimer) to be dismissed from that institution by the Nazis in 1933.[4] By this time Mannheim had attained international recognition and therefore received an appointment as a lecturer in sociology at the London School of Economics. In 1941 he moved to the University of London and became a professor of education in 1946. Shortly before his death in 1947, he was nominated as director of UNESCO but his failing health prevented him from accepting that position.

His intellectual and geographical migrations allow David Martin to say: "A few men can have been better prepared for the study of the social roots of culture or more open to the notion that truth is what works in context, and that what you 'know' depends on where and who you are in time and space".[5]

Throughout his life, Mannheim enjoyed the privilege of stimulating intellectual companionship. At Frankfurt, Mannheim belonged to a discussion group known as the Kranzchen--its members included Tillich, Leo Lowenthal, Friedrich Pollock, Kurt Riezler, Adolph Lowe and Karl Menniecke.[6] In these early years of his development, Mannheim presented himself as a metaphysical idealist.[7]

In England he participated in a distinguished intellectual circle known as the Moot--its members included Joseph Oldham, Alec Vidler, T. S. Eliot, J. Middleton Murry, and other eminent literary and academic figures, civil servants, and theologians. Some authors assume that through his association with the Moot, Mannheim became sensitized to the possible role which religious belief might play in the reconstruction of society.[8] Nevertheless, we are inclined also to accept David Martin's opinion that Mannheim "walked the intellectual margins fascinated and fascinating, but not belonging".[9]

Mannheim came of age intellectually in a time when central Europe was extraordinarily favorable to the development of scholarly talents, when "Vienna Circle" radiated with its ideas of neopositivism, when "Lwow-Warsaw School of logic" exercised a powerful influence on local philosophy, and when the intellectual standards of German universities justified Mannheim's characterization of the climate in Weimar Republic as "a new Periclean Age".[10]

At the time of his arrival at Heidelberg, it was the most prestigious center for sociological studies within the German university system and the city itself was something of an intellectual magnet for gifted social theorists, philosophers, and literary figures. Leading personalities of the period included Rickert, Alfred Weber, Marianne Weber, Lukacs, Karl Jaspers, Emil Lederer, and such members of the Stefan George Circle as Friedrich Gundolf and Ernst Kantorowicz. However, it was the influence of the recently deceased Max Weber that dominated the intellectual life of Heidelberg during the twenties.[11] And even the erosion of years did not dissipate Mannheim's strong admiration for Weber. In 1937 he wrote the following in response to an inquiry regarding the books that he considered most important and of greatest influence in the development of his own intellectual perspective:

> There is [sic] a large number of sociological books, some of them very valuable; but if one wants to have the greatness of the achievement in this field fused in a single person, then one can only point to Max Weber....As an introduction one should read his two lectures, 'Politics as a Vocation'...and 'Science as a Vocation'....The technique of analysis and the moral position will impress the reader and effectively assist him in his own search.

> Then one should turn to Weber's great work, Economy and Society...and to the collected essays on the sociology of religion...No easy reading; but he who has worked through it will see the world with new eyes and understand history in a new sense. Marx's great achievement--formulating the social process as a theoretical problem--is here transformed into detailed concrete research, all the while avoiding the suggestion of a political attitude by means of science. Unfortunately, Max Weber's work does not extend into the most recent period. What one can obtain from him is the equipment for understanding society; the application to our problems one must make oneself.[12]

Karl Mannheim used that equipment well.

Mannheim's intellectual activities fall within four distinct stages as suggested by Gunther Remmling in his monograph on Mannheim's Sociology.[13]

From 1918 to 1932 his main interests were philosophy and sociology of knowledge. In this period Mannheim accepted "an absolute historicism as the basis of the interpretation of socio-cultural reality".[14] From 1933 to 1938 he turned to the sociology of planning. During WWII he focused on the sociology of religion, of values and that of education. The last phase of his sociological interest was devoted to the political sociology and sociology of power (1945-1947).

During the early period, he came to terms with the legacy of German idealism by outlining the most important ideas of his sociology of knowledge. However, in 1933 Mannheim's intellectual commitment was redirected by the historical moment--as Kurt Wolff puts it, the specter of totalitarianism led Mannheim "to devote himself ever more singlemindedly to thinking about the salvation of society, lest the spirit itself perish".[15]

Mannheim is often referred to as the founder of the sociology of knowledge. Actually Max Scheler was the first to use the phrase, "sociology of knowledge", but Mannheim developed most significantly the sub-discipline which carries this name.[16] Marx and Dilthey are usually described as the intellectual precursors of this sub-discipline. Whereas Marx had demonstrated the class bias of ideological thought and Dilthey outlined the cutting edge of "the knife of historical relativism",[17] Mannheim carried the dialogue to its logical conclusion by arguing that not merely the content but also the very structure of thought is existentially conditioned. He contended, "there are modes of thought which cannot be adequately understood as long as their origins are obscured"[18] because "it is impossible to conceive of absolute truth existing independently of the values and position of the subject and unrelated to the social context".[19] Mannheim's early studies in this area bear a marked affinity to those of Lukacs. Like his teacher, Mannheim based his early conceptions of the social genesis of "cultural objectifications" upon a historical approach to art forms.[20] Lukacs' influence is also important as an indicator of the early input of the Marxist component in Mannheim's approach to the interpretation of weltanschauung.[21] We agree with Shils that Mannheim borrows the concept of weltanschauung itself from Wilhelm Dilthey and Eduard Spranger.[22]

Like Dilthey and Weber, Mannheim was critical of the naive philosophical presuppositions of positivism. Positivism assumes 'knowledge' can be adequately explained empirically only through the special sciences. Positivists therefore claim they can dispense with metaphysics and ontology. But, Mannheim points out, "a doctrine which hypostatizes certain paradigmatic methods, and the reality spheres corresponding to them, as 'absolutely' valid, thereby becomes a metaphysic itself--albeit a particularly limited one".[23] Nevertheless, Mannheim regards the positivistic commitment to empiricism as a genuine contribution to social science. In sum, he maintains, "that substantively positivism has performed the essential turn toward a way of thinking adequate to the contemporary situation; systematically and methodologically, however, it did not rise above a relatively primitive level, since, among other things, it did not realize that its 'this-worldly' orientation, too, involves a metaphysic".[24]

Mannheim regards his own work as an attempt to provide contemporary society with a program which would permit the application of organized intelligence to social affairs. According to Frankel, Mannheim contends that the mode of detached thinking found in mathematics or physics "lacks the vitality, flexibility, and commitment to values which thinking must have if it is to make any practical difference in the world".[25] Mannheim would abandon the value-free mystique of sociology in favor of what he refers to as "the Third Way", a type of planning which is not totalitarian but is under the control of the community in which the main forms of freedom are not abolished".[26] He maintains that this type of sociology must take an active interest in the sphere of values.

His consideration of values as well as that of social planning were too innovative to be easily accepted in sociological communities of his own time. Victorious democracies continued their existence on the outworn principles of laissez-fairism (though slightly modified), and with the idea of cultural and ethical relativism leading to the blind alley of "total suspicion".[27]

Mannheim's mind was for years occupied with the two greatest problems which he realized are in our era decisive for the future of the human race: social values and social planning.

The fall of the Weimar Republic turned Mannheim to analyze the self-destroying mechanism of liberal democratic society. He then wrote in German a book on Man and Society in an Age of Reconstruction.[28] Its dedication says: "to my Masters and Pupils in Germany" because it was published when he went into exile. Although Mannheim was at that time a well-known sociologist, the works which lifted him to the rank of the greatest humanist in sociology were above all his two last and least academic. They are Man and Society and Diagnosis of Our Time.

The first of them has a peculiar history because its first version, written and published in German, was addressed to people who "had experienced in their own lives the tremendous changes of an age of transformation".[29] However, five years later this book "revised and considerably enlarged" was published in England during the Battle of Britain. In its new version it attempted to deliver, in the name of those people who survived and escaped from Hitler's Germany, a message "to a world which has only hearsay knowledge of such changes and is still wrapped in an illusion of traditional stability".[30] Mannheim regarded sociology as modern man's guidepost for averting disaster and a means of reconstructing society as well as the individual,[31] and assigned sociology a supreme role in the process of planning. The new sociology envisioned by Mannheim was premised upon the belief that knowledge of the most important developments in psychology, psychotherapy, anthropology, and history, must be integrated. Because sociology is the most general and most basic social science, he believed it could best accomplish the task of the 'integration of knowledge'. In Mannheim's scheme, sociology is not the splendiferous queen of the Comtean hierarchy but rather a kind of a central clearinghouse for the integration and processing of the products of the special sciences. The planning process requires such a clearinghouse as a means of effecting a union between theory and praxis.

Mannheim embraced the idea of social planning only reluctantly. He regarded democratic planning as a defense against totalitarianism:

> At the stage we have just reached, it seems to be greater slavery to be able to do as we like in an unjust or badly organized society, than to accept the claims of planning in a healthy society which we ourselves have chosen. The

>realization that fair and democratic planning does not involve the surrender of our freedom is the mainspring of those arguments which show that an unplanned capitalistic society is not the basis of the highest form of liberty.[32]

But the question, 'Who plans the planner?' deeply disturbs Mannheim: "The longer I reflect on this question, the more it haunts me".[33] Nevertheless, he posits the conviction that society "must be guided by groups who proceed on the basis of a decisive political will and of corresponding psychological and sociological knowledge and do not leave the most important steps to desperadoes, military agitators, and radio managers".[34]

Kurt Wolff, who was a student of Mannheim's at Frankfurt, contends that within Mannheim's scheme "sociological culture" is the modern functional equivalent of classical or humanistic culture.[35] Mannheim maintains that "Sociology is the adequate life orientation of man industrial society", whereas the old humanistic culture increasingly serves merely as a shrine for the storage of cultural relics. Mannheim contends there is a "sharp conflict and competition" between the cultural ideals of humanism and democracy.[36] He characterizes the humanistic ideal as "today critically menaced if not already doomed" and warns:

>If the humanistic ideal is about to be discarded by our culture, it is not because of the inadequacy of its ultimate aspirations but because it cannot provide enrichment of life for broader masses. Because of the conditions of mass existence, the humanistic ideal in its present form cannot be meaningful for the average man. Nevertheless, it is our opinion that <u>this ideal contains elements indispensable for a full and rich life, and cultural ideals of a more universal appeal should make use of these elements in changed form</u>.[37]

Mannheim lists five "limitations" of historical humanism:

>(a) Its confusion of its own elite sector with 'the' world itself....
>(b) Its lack of contact with the stark realities of life....
>(c) Its purely aesthetic relationship to things....
>(d) Its neglect of the personal, biographical, and contingent element in literary or artistic creation.

(e) Its antipathy towards the dynamic and unexpected.[38]

A casual reader might dismiss Mannheim's conception of a "sociological culture" as a byzantine flourish--as some strange aberration which only a professorial mind could produce. Yet, a more temperate approach to Mannheim's ideal would reveal that it is not without formidable antecedents. The germ of this notion can be found in the lectures which Max Weber delivered in Munich near the end of his life. In these lectures which we know under the titles "Science as a Vocation" and "Politics as a Vocation", Weber described science (which for him at that point in his life meant sociology) as a calling which requires the kind of passionate commitment that religion had demanded in an earlier historical period.[39] He regarded science as a discipline for those "destined to live in a godless and prophetless time". Weber's sociological science retained none of the illusions--none of the naive optimism--which buoyed its French and English counterparts. Rather, he described science as a mere "means" of "meeting the demands of the day"[40]--a day which holds no warm promises or high resolves: in Weber's famous words, "Not summer's bloom lies ahead of us, but rather a polar night of icy darkness and hardness..."[41] A member of the Weber Circle, Paul Honigsheim, described the regime of science under which Weber labored:

> Max Weber suffered under science; with Simmel, he understood clearly that the structure which we call 'science' presents a parallel to the naturalistic-capitalist form of life, and further, that in all the world there has never been anything analogous to it; it was a form of the 'God-distant' age in which we are condemned to live.[42]

In the philosophical writings of Weber's disciple and Mannheim's contemporary, Karl Jaspers wrote that Weber's notion of 'commitment' to science is transformed into a kind of existential heroism. A critic of Weber recently described the role Jaspers played in mythologizing Max Weber by ascribing to Weber's personality "that existentialist moralism which had such great effect among German students in the 1920s and again after the Second World War".[43]

Karl Mannheim saw this "existential moralism" as a basic requirement for the survival of freedom in a totalitarian world. The greatest expression of this view is his last work, <u>Diagnosis of Our Time</u>.

While Mannheim contended that the intellectual strata must fulfill a special role in the planned society:

> ...the fate of the world of thought is in the
> care of a socially unattached, or barely attach-
> ed, stratum whose class affinities and status in
> society cannot be precisely defined; a stratum
> which does not find the aims it pursues within
> itself but in the interests of strata with a
> more definite place in the social order....If
> ...there were no such stratum...it might easily
> happen that all spiritual content would dis-
> appear from our increasingly capitalistic so-
> ciety and leave nothing but naked interests.[44]

he attempted to circumvent the elitism of historical humanism through a strong and lasting commitment to mass education:

> We have to educate people to live in a world
> which presents, and will in the future present,
> situations which cannot be anticipated.[45]

> ...our society is in a state of dissolution
> [and] cannot hope to recover unless the mil-
> lions realise that by finding new responses
> to their own particular situation they are
> not only working for themselves but contrib-
> uting to a general reorganisation...[46]

Mannheim attacked intellectual hubris since it fosters contempt for the masses. Similarly, he argued against the prevailing intellectual snobbery which viewed 'popularization' with contempt. Instead, Mannheim endorsed the idea of "creative dissemination":

> The future of culture depends not only on our
> ability to guarantee the conditions of survival
> for original thinkers at higher levels, but
> also on our inventiveness in finding new forms
> for the dissemination of the substance of cul-
> ture without diluting it.[47]

> Those who succeed in the great venture of being
> genuine on the lower levels of communication
> contribute at least as much to the preservation
> of culture as those who keep existing fires
> burning in small selected circles.[48]

It might be noted here that Mannheim's "popularizers" bear little resemblance to many of those individuals who have become known in academic parlance as 'academic entrepreneurs'--the instant authors and glamorous but glib media sensationalists.[49] Similarly, the "New Mandarins" described by Noam Chomsky bear no resemblance to Mannheim's intellectual strata since the mandarins are anything but socially unattached.[50] Mannheim himself spoke of intellectuals who abandon their claim to membership in the intellectual strata by becoming "muskateers of free enterprise".[51] It should also be mentioned that he did not understand the difference between the 'intelligentsia' and the 'intellectuals', as presently defined and, although his analyses of these groups' social role and position belong to the most interesting, they have the same weakness as most of the western publications, i.e., they do not distinguish between the social stratum of the intelligentsia and the category of intellectuals. Of course, at this time this distinction was not yet clearly visible either in Germany nor in England.[52]

Humanistic sociologists can benefit from Mannheim's attempt to deflate intellectual arrogance because those who would combat demagoguery and confront such pressing world problems as the ecological crisis and overpopulation are dependent upon 'popularization' of their ideas.

In spite of all his efforts to overcome the elitism of the old humanistic ideal, Mannheim's notion that the socially unattached intellectual can serve as an arbiter of perspectivism has drawn a critical response in the most divergent ideological quarters. Even such a sympathetic reader as C. Wright Mills places Mannheim's intellectual strata within the tradition of the philosopher-king and remarks sardonically, "Were the 'philosopher' king, I should be tempted to leave his kingdom" but Mills also ponders the question, "when kings are without any 'philosophy', are they not incapable of responsible rule?"[53]

In the most inhuman time of WWII, and probably because of the explosion of racial and ideological hatred on a scale unknown in human history until then, Mannheim rediscovered the Christian idea of universal love as the basis for the neighborly relations for the world at large. He responded to Cooley's view that the commandment "Love your neighbor" is the paradox of Christianity as far as it is taken as a love to the whole mankind. Mannheim assumed that this commandment "should not be taken literally but should be translated according to the conditions of a great society.... The equal rights of citizens in a democracy are abstract equivalents of the concrete primary virtues of sympathy and brotherhood".[54]

From the viewpoint of our search for what is most essential to contemporary problems of humanistic sociology we shall focus mainly on his views originating in the second period. There is nothing more essential for our survival than the defense of human values in the rudimentary conflict of our times: conflict between freedom and necessity of planning. Mannheim's views on values and religion, although developed later, should be taken as a continua-

147

tion of his thinking on the future of human development.

To the chapter VII of his <u>Diagnosis of Our Time</u>, written "For a group of friends, Christian thinkers", as he indicated in a footnote, Mannheim raised the question about Christianity: "Will it associate itself with the Classes or with Ruling Universities?"[55] Mannheim touched this problem twenty years before the Vatican Council II gave the answer. And this answer has much in common with Mannheim's analysis of "Christianity in the Age of Planning".[56]

Mannheim is the first humanist in sociology who realized that the unavoidably rising new world based on planning will need spiritual integration. Nevertheless the idea to revitalize Christianity to achieve social goals has a long tradition in sociological thought. From Saint-Simon to Mannheim, many great, religiously indifferent authors turned finally to the fundamental problem: how to pour the new wine into the old bottles? The greatness of Christianity as a moral and social order appealed to their imagination. However, there is an essential difference between the turn to religion of Saint-Simon, August Comte, or Benjamin Kidd and Emile Durkheim on the one side and Mannheim on the other. The former needed religion as an instrument of social control in societies of flowering liberalism. The latter writing had appeal at the time when communism and fascism tried "to develop and superimpose a pseudo-religious integration in order to create a psychological and sociological background for planning".[57] And when on the other side of the ideological barricade social life was characterized in the "moral crisis" and by the chaos which "revealed that not only economic laissez-fairism produced structural maladjustment, e.g. mass unemployment, but that nearly every other sphere of social life has a chaos of its own".[58] Mannheim was right in attributing failures of the West (in its effort to build a Great Society) to the lack of the "methods of value adjustment, value assimilation, value reconciliation and value standardization which were always active in small communities,..."[59]

Saint-Simon and Comte also wanted to get societies out of chaos, but for them it was primarily an economic and ideological chaos, and their aim was imposition of an order for the improvement of productivity. Mannheim called for getting out of chaos in order to save freedom. He realized that

> with the advent of Great Society the habit of letting things take their own course does not represent the principle of real freedom, but simply surrenders the cultural inheritance to a few capitalist concerns, which reflect only too often the lowest denominator of democratic culture,...

Therefore, he continued to argue that

> Freedom can only be achieved if its conditions are organized according to the democratically agreed wishes of the community. But the latter can prevail only if the community has a vision of aims to be achieved and a knowledge of the means by which they can be achieved....This guidance can only be given if the integration of the community goes much deeper than is the case at this moment when the forces of disintegration have done their best to undermine tacit consensus and to overemphasize differences existing in our midst.[60]

This was written in 1943 when due to the events of WWII the set of Greco-Christian values spiritually mobilized millions of people to defend the threatened democracies and their promises. What would he say today about our disintegration and its result: losses of the democracies in their undeclared campaigns of WW III?

Mannheim's suggestions for his Christian friends are interesting today for many reasons. The religious ferment in many Christian churches today, as well as renovation of Catholicism, moved churches closer to the people and put greater emphasis on the "social gospel" than the transcendental element of religious life. But this is not the way Mannheim saw social salvation. He called for an "entirely new enthusiasm which lends significance to every individual's life and every activity in it".[61] Having personally observed the birth of the secular religion of race in Germany and deeply understanding the pseudo-religious character of Soviet communism, Mannheim warned his contemporaries that: "genuine religious experiences will emerge, or pseudo-religious movements will be produced as a substitute...."[62] In opposition to the idea of "Social Gospel", Mannheim believed that:

> ...complete penetration of life by religion will only occur if those who represent Christian tradition are once more able to go back to the genuine sources of religious experience and do not think that the habitual and institutional forms of religion suffice for the reconstruction of man and society.[63]

This point needs some explanation. We are inclined to think about religion more as an institution than an experience. We are living in a world so deeply secularized and our sociological tradition is so overwhelmingly anti- or a-religious that the majority of contemporary readers treat Mannheim's views on the significance of religion as a conservative element in the sociological thought of a great defender of freedom.

It is not so. Mannheim's understanding of religion as fundamental human experience led him to the conclusion that no humane and humanistic social system can be built if the religious element of social existence is not respected.[64] Although he spent all of his life in Protestant countries, he found Catholicism more suitable to coincide with social transformation of our time than other Christian denominations because Catholicism is closer to the "needs of social order beyond individualism"[65] than Protestantism. He found also that Catholicism gave "courage to associate religious experience, wherever possible, with strict rationality and responsible thought".[66] Therefore, he saw in it "a great counterpoise to the worldliness of unbridled irrationality of modern movements".[67]

Mannheim appreciated Thomism which, being a kind of early sociology, enabled its followers to "deal with social institutions in terms of functions".[68] But his appreciation of Thomism did not make him blind to the danger of reapplication of thoughts from agricultural, preindustrial and preindividualist epochs to the societies of the post-liberal era.

On the other hand, he expected that the traditions of Protestantism, its emphasis on individual freedom, "will always be the great antithesis to the coming form of authoritarianism, centralization and organization from above".[69] Mannheim strongly emphasized that the role of religion which he saw in the future should not lead to a religious totalitarianism. For him the core values of Christianity are delivering the moral framework for the Planning for Freedom. But for their realization structural changes have to take place, because "one cannot be a good Christian in a society where the basic rules are against the spirit of Christianity".[70]

It would be a great mistake to treat Mannheim's view on religion as a separate issue, because it creates an integral part of his sociological analysis of social existence in general and his contribution to the construction of a more human future. He assumed that even a cooperation of sociology and theology has been possible since the "extreme Rationalism had run its course and the axiomatic limitations of the different types of rational analysis in human affairs became apparent to those who used them".[71] On the other hand, fundamental Christian ideas were given in the form of parables able to be applied to any new historical context. Therefore, he was convinced that in the very complexity of our civilization men of religion and social scientists will have to "join in the work for reinterpretation".[72]

Many statements of Mannheim acquire greater importance today than they had in his own time. His views on the role of religion, his critical analysis of the idea of Progress and his ideal Planning for Freedom are radiating today against the background of the dark clouds looming over the societies of affluence, cheap optimism, and dehumanizing effects of busybody mass culture.

His reflections on totalitarianism are continued today by many western political thinkers. It is very surprising, however, to find that this theme is neglected by sociologists who are often giving priority to the good relations with communist authorities over attempts to analyze the greatest and growing danger of our time: totalitarian deprivation of subjugated people.[73]

In American sociology, Mannheim's work has never received the serious and sustained discipline-wide hearing that it deserves. Several factors account for this failing: (1) although Mannheim's work is distinguished by its conceptual clarity and skillful elaboration, it often assumes a level of philosophical sophistication that methods-oriented sociologists seldom possess or require; (2) the strong influence of Marxian notions within the Mannheimian system has met ideological resistance within the American sociological establishment; on the other hand, despite the McCarthyism of the 1950's, the influence of vulgar Marxism, as well as naive views of the social achievements of Soviet communism so common in American universities (at least until Khrushchev's "secret speech" and the messages of Russian dissidents), resulted in Mannheim's ideas being subjected to a great deal of irresponsible criticism; and (3) due to the disruption of his career, no stable group of disciplines emerged from his students to carry on his ideas. Only one of his books, <u>Ideology and Utopia</u>, has been widely circulated in America and there is some question as to how faithful a rendition of Mannheim's ideas the English translation of this book presents.[74] Also, in Germany, Mannheim's ideas were rejected by Horkheimer and Adorno and therefore had virtually no impact upon the Frankfurt School of Sociology.[75]

Mannheim's legacy has been fully appreciated only in England where he founded the International Library of Sociology and Social Reconstruction which greatly contributed to the diffusion of sociological ideas and eventually led to the acceptance of sociology as an academically respectable discipline.[76]

Mannheim's "sociological culture" remains a utopian ideal. In the West, the "radio managers" **have** relinquished their control over the promulgation of social values to the television producers who faithfully serve the interests of their corporate sponsors. And everywhere, "desperados" and "military agitators" contrive the eclipse of human freedom.

Mannheim's humanism lies in his belief in man even in the conditions of the mass society. This belief allows him to avoid pessimism in looking into the future. He neither shares the pessimistic views of Ortega y Gasset nor those of C. Wright Mills. Mannheim made the first great effort to show that the essential elements of liberalism do not need to be last in the new type of society which is planning its future.

The main message of Mannheim's work is that sociology should play a key role in human efforts to build up a new society within which socioeconomic planning will not limit individual freedom and justice. This aim was known to all socialists of the past. But since the communists began to abuse the old idea, any independently thinking person looking on their practices and results was shocked. Therefore, probably for this reason, Mannheim avoided the term "socialism".

His attempt to show the way to build a new society without physically destroying the old is a great humanistic contribution of sociology to the socio-political thought of our time. The influence of his ideas was, however, limited, although some authors claim that they formed the foundation of the now floundering postwar economic and social order of Great Britain. He has also many silent enthusiasts in the People's Republics of Eastern Europe where some intellectuals would like to preserve the essential elements of liberalism in the frames of a socialist system.

CHAPTER IX FOOTNOTES

1. Abraham Maslow quotes Rilke in support of his own contention that "The assault troops of science are certainly more necessary to science than its military policement" or, put more prosaically, creative thinkers not technicians are responsible for the advance of science. The Psychology of Science (New York: Harper and Row, 1966), p. 14.

2. Edward Shils explicates Mannheim's sociology in terms of these three categories. If they point to the three strongest currents in Mannheimian thought, they nevertheless do not exhaust all the influences which play important roles in the synthesis presented by Mannheim's subtle and learned mind. For Shils' discussion, see "Karl Mannheim" in International Encyclopedia of the Social Sciences, ed. David L. Shils (New York: The Macmillan Co. and The Free Press, 1968).

3. Biographical data is from Kurt Wolff's excellent "Introduction" to the collection of Mannheim's writings which he recently edited. From Karl Mannheim (New York: Oxford University Press, 1971). This volume is an excellent comprehensive introduction to Mannheim's work--the authors of this section has relied heavily upon Wolff's interpretation of Mannheim's position wherever it seemd to be in question.

4. Martin Jay, The Dialectical Imagination (Boston: Little, Brown and Company, 1973).

5. David Martin, "Remembering Karl Mannheim".

6. Ibidem.

7. See Mannheim, "Seele and Kulture", in Wissenssoziologie: Auswahl aus dam Werk (Berlin: Hermann Luchterhand Verlog 1964).

8. For a brief introduction to Mannheim's views in this area, the reader might consult Mannheim's discussion of "Religious Integration in a Dynamic Society" in Freedom, Power and Democratic Planning (New York: Oxford University Press, 1950), pp. 285-289. This facet of Mannheim's thought is discussed by Wolff and Shils. H. A. Hodges presents his version of the influence of the Moot on Mannheim in "Lukacs on Irrationalism" in George Lukacs, ed. G.H.R. Parkinson (New York: Random

House, 1970).

9. David Martin, op. cit.

10. Peter Gay, Weimar Culture (New York: Harper and Row, 1968), p. xiv. Gay reports that Mannheim made this comment in a conversation with Hannah Arendt.

11. Shils, "Karl Mannheim", p. 557.

12. Karl Mannheim, Response to a newspaper pool in 1937, extensively quoted by Wolff in his "Introduction" to From Karl Mannheim, pp. cv-cvi.

13. Gunther Remmling, The Sociology of Karl Mannheim (London: Routledge and Kegan-Paul, 1975), p. 9.

14. Ibidem.

15. Wolff, "Introduction", p. lxi.

16. For an account of Scheler's influence on Mannheim, see Gunther W. Remmling, Road to Suspicion (New York: Appleton-Century-Crofts, 1967), pp. 32-39.

17. Dilthey spoke of "The knife of historical relativism...which has cut to pieces all metaphysics and religion...." "Selected Passages" in H. A. Hodges, Wilhelm Dilthey: An Introduction (New York: Howard Fertig, 1969), p. 154.

18. Karl Mannheim, Ideology and Utopia, trans. by Louis Wirth and Edward Shils (New York: Harcourt, Brace, 1936), p. 2.

19. Mannheim quoted by Stanley Taylor, Conceptions of Institutions and the Theory of Knowledge (New York: Bookman Associates, 1956), p. 74.

20. Lukacs, in turn, was strongly influenced in his own early work (especially Soul and Form and Theory of the Novel) by his teacher, Georg Simmel. Wolff, who is undoubtedly the foremost American expert on Simmel, notes the unacknowledged and probably unconscious presence of Simmel's ideas in parts of Mannheim's exposition.

21. Wolff, "Introduction", pp. xvi-xviii.

22. Shils points directly to the input of Dilthey and Spranger in Mannheim's development of his sociology of knowledge. "Karl Mannheim", op. cit., p. 557.

23. Mannheim extensively quoted by Wolff, "Introduction", p. xxxiv. "The Problems of the Sociology of Knowledge" (1925), p. 150.

24. Ibidem, p. xxxiv.

25. Charles Frankel, The Case for Modern Man (Boston: Beacon Press, 1960), p. 122.

26. Mannheim, Diagnosis of Our Time, Wartime Essays of a Sociologist (London: Routledge and Kegan-Paul, Ltd., 1950) [first edition, 1943], p. 71.

27. Gunther Remmling in his Road to Suspicion, titled chapter 14 "Karl Marx: Exponent of Total Suspicion" (New York: Appleton-Century-Crofts, 1967).

28. Mannheim, Man and Society in an Age of Reconstruction [First English edition, London, 1940]. All following citations are from an edition of a Harvest Book (New York: Harcourt, Brace and World, Inc., no date).

29. Ibidem, p. 3.

30. Ibidem.

31. Mannheim devoted a good deal of energy at this point in his life to formulating his ideas on developing a curriculum for sociological education as well as a curriculum for adult education in social science.

32. Mannheim in Wolff, "Introduction", p. cii. Man and Society, p. 377.

33. Ibidem, pp. xciv-c. Man and Society, p. 74.

34. Ibidem, p. cviii. On the Diagnosis of Our Time, p. 120

35. Wolff, "Introduction", p. lxxx.

36. Karl Mannheim, Essays on the Sociology of Culture (London: Kegan-Paul, 1962), p. 230.

37. Ibidem.

38. Ibidem, pp. 232-234.

39. Recall Mannheim's emphasis on the moral stance of this essay in his response to the newspaper poll cited above.

40. Max Weber, "Science as a Vocation", in From Max Weber,

trans. by Hans Gerth and C. Wright Mills (New York: Oxford University Press, 1958), p. 156.

41. Max Weber, "Politics as a Vocation", in *From Max Weber*, p. 128.

42. Paul Honigsheim, *On Max Weber* (New York: The Free Press, 1968), p. 131.

43. Martin Green, *The Von Richtofen Sisters* (New York: Basic Books, 1974), p. 172.

44. Mannheim in Wolff, "Introduction", p. xliv. "Conversative Thought", p. 128.

45. *Ibidem*, pp. cxii-cxiii. "Adult Education and the Social Sciences" (1938), p. 27.

46. *Ibidem*, p. cxiii. "Adult Education and the Social Sciences", pp. 27-28.

47. *Ibidem*, p. cxxiv.

48. *Ibidem*. "Mass Education and Group Analysis", p. 10

49. This statement may perhaps only reflect this author's indoctrination into the academic cult of snobbery.

50. Noam Chomsky, *American Power and the New Mandarins* (New York: Pantheon, 1969).

51. Mannheim in Wolff, "Introduction", p. xc. "The Problems of Intelligentsia", p. 170.

52. Aleksander Gella, "An Introduction to the Sociology of the Intelligentsia", in A. Gella (ed.) *The Intelligentsia and the Intellectuals* (London and Beverly Hills, Calif.: SAGE-Publications, 1976).

53. C. Wright Mills, *The Sociological Imagination* (New York: Grove Press, 1959), p. 180.

54. Mannheim, *Diagnosis...*, p. 18

55. *Ibidem*, p. 100

56. *Ibidem*.

57. *Ibidem*, p. 102

58. *Ibidem*, p. 104.

59. Ibidem.

60. Ibidem, p. 105.

61. Ibidem, p. 106.

62. Ibidem.

63. Ibidem.

64. The concept of humanism presented by his friend, T. S. Eliot, was not without an influence on Mannheim's thought. Eliot in his polemics with Irving Babbitt writes: "If you find examples of humanism which is anti-religious, or at least in opposition to the religious faith of the place and time, then such humanism is purely destructive, for it has never found anything to replace what it has destroyed". T. S. Eliot, "Humanism of Irving Babbitt", in Selected Essays 1917-1932.

65. Mannheim, Diagnosis..., p. 106

66. Ibidem, p. 107

67. Ibidem.

68. Ibidem.

69. Ibidem, pp. 107-108.

70. Ibidem, p. 114.

71. Ibidem, p. 117.

72. Ibidem, p. 120.

73. Recently published in Zurich was a deep analysis of the Soviet system and its society by Alexander Zinoviev, one of the greatest Soviet logicians, and not yet available in English: Svetloe Budyschey (Bright Future), Zurich 1975.

74. Wolff points out that in the Wirth and Shils translation, "relatively idiosyncratic German" is replaced by "relatively standardized English, thus presenting us with a book of a character quite different from the original". Wolff contends that it is doubtful that a more faithful rendition would have been as popular. "Introduction", pp. lvi-lxii. This writer regards Wirth and Shils' translation as a fine example of "creative dissemination".

75. Thus for instance, Adorno sarcastically dismissed Mannheim's

"reverence for the intelligentsia as 'free-floating' by asserting the answer is to be found not in the reactionary postulate of its 'rootedness in Being' but rather in the reminder that the very intelligentsia that pretends to float freely is fundamentally rooted in the very being that must be changed and which it merely pretends to criticize". Adorno quoted by Jay, <u>The Dialectical Imagination</u>, pp. 291-292.

76. Wolff, "Introduction".

PART THREE: SOCIETAL PROBLEMS

CHAPTER X

SOME REFLECTIONS ON TECHNO-SCIENTIFIC OPTIMISM

We stand at the dawn of a technocentric epoch. Various degrees of technology have always existed, from the stone axe to space satellites. However, at no time in history has technology exerted such an overwhelming influence upon institutional processes and collective life. Robert Nisbet writes, "Modern technology has its own characteristic structures, its built-in drives, its moral codes, its dedicated servants (as hierarchically ordered and motivated as any to be found in church or state), even its own mystique".[1] While the threat of nuclear holocaust, the depletion of energy resources, and pollution have led some critics to prophesize apocalyptic doom, others foresee the emergence of a technocratic social order free from excessive toil, starvation, and disease. Will technological development spell an end to societal ills or contribute to their proliferation?

The very conception of a cybernetic society grows out of a 17th-century revolution in western thought which conceives of nature as matter in motion within a vast world-machine. Coupled with Bacon's emphasis upon the utility of knowledge, the Cartesian vision fostered the development of science and vast technological innovation. Armed with scientific method and growing technological expertise, humanity attempted to forge a "better life" by discerning the laws of the world-machine and set their energies and ingenuity to the task of dominating nature. Today, the promise of technological and scientific potential holds an even more central place in shaping our perceptions of societal problems and policies designed to secure their eradication. Much sociological practice is predicated upon the assumption that human behavior and social processes are governed by discoverable laws. Knowledge of these laws furnishes the groundwork for prediction; prediction, in turn, will lead to a "better life" free from turmoil, starvation, violence, and misery.

Mounting evidence suggests, however, that techno-scientific and sociological domination of nature and society has not been fully forthcoming. The ubiquity and severity of current societal problems, both systemic and interpersonal, has raised serious questions regarding the survival and utility of ever-expanding techno-scientific and social scientific knowledge.

Visitors to developing nations or major American cities are all too familiar with the marked contrasts between affluence and poverty, the unwashed and washed masses, and the secure and the frightened. Pollution, racial strife, sexism, suicide and homocide, inadequate health care, mental illness, loneliness and despair appear as open sores upon the otherwise sleek and promising face of technocratic society. While technologically we can do so much more and scientifically we know so much more, serious societal problems persist. And yet, in spite of the persistence of human misery, we remain steadfastly committed to techno-scientific remedies for social ills. We direct our energies and faith in technical rather than human agents of social change. A few examples highlight the contrasts between promises of technological deliverance and the persistence of societal problems.

Communications technology is presently poised for unprecedented acceleration. Developing innovations such as the transistor, integrated circuits, computers, cable and microwave technology, videophones, communications satellites, and ultramicrofiche have the potential to vastly transform social, political, and economic life. While the threat of centralization of communications technology exists, so too do possibilities for decentalization. The former may open the door of unsurpassed surveillance of public life, the regulation of political and economic life, and censorship of knowledge; the latter represents a key to increased democratic pluralism, the instantaneous retrieval and coordination of knowledge, and an educated and socially-aware populace. The following excerpts from a report prepared by the Rand Corporation amply reflect both the potential social impact and policy implications being wrought by the developing communications revolution.

> Where and how communication satellites, cable transmission systems, computers, videophones, ultramicrofiche, and various other devices will eventually fit into more comprehensive communication systems will not simply be a function of technical capabilities and cost considerations but also of public policy and of entrepreneurial and consumer pressures and choice. Once made, some of these choices may be difficult to reverse because of investments undertaken and the consequent vested interests created....

> Mass literacy was needed for the development of societies such as the United States, but perhaps a world divided between a small elite and a mul-

titude of relatively ignorant workers is again
in the making. On the one hand, chances for a
genuinely literate society would appear to be
improved by the developing communication systems. But the effects that an increasingly
complex technology will have on requirements
for and standards of individual performance
are not self-evident. With improved audiovisual
communications and automated correction systems,
literacy may become less important for many activities. An optimistic view is that any additional sophisticated service available in the
society is a gain for the individual. A pessimistic view considers the possibility that
society might evolve into a situation with users
on one side and system designers, producers, and
manipulators on the other side...

As population increases, the 'choreography'
needed to coordinate a given level of freedom
of choice seems to increase exponentially. This
means that as population grows, the information
and communication requirements for maintaining
a given level of freedom (for most acceptable
definitions of freedom) may increase as rapidly
as or perhaps more rapidly than improvements in
communication technology. Without modern communication technology, it would no longer be
feasible to contemplate the success of political systems involving a large amount of decen-
tralized free choice. As computer networks and
'time-sharing for the masses' grow, it will be
possible to organize political districts on
other than geographical lines. It may be possible to have an even more pluralistic society
than we do now, with each individual participating in many roles and associations.[2]

Six years after this report was penned, its pessimistic implications have become a more evident part of our reality. In
order to understand the actual threat imposed by a centralized control of the mass media by one establishmentarian interest group, no
matter which group, one should remember that some forty years ago,
having only radios and megaphones at his disposal, Hitler was able
to subjugate and indoctrinate eighty million people almost entirely.
Twenty-four years after the Nuremberg trial, Albert Speer, who called himself an "apolitical technocrat", confessed: "The more technological the world becomes, the greater is the danger". He delivered many highly interesting insights into the technocratic structure of power used by Hitler.[3]

Let us consider health care. The 19th-century progress of science raised great hopes in the areas of medicine and health care. However, in the latter part of the 20th century, the richest country in the world has not solved its own problems related to health care services and delivery. Summing up the situation in the United States, William Ryan wrote in 1972,

> The majority of Americans are in rather good shape, yet in our technologically advanced, science-worshipping, pill-swallowing nation, about one-fifth of the population suffers from blatant medical neglect....Our infant mortality rate is also a national disgrace. Although it has declined somewhat in recent years--from 29.2 per thousand in 1950 to 23.4 in 1966--it gives every sign of leveling off, and some fear that it might begin to rise again. Relative to other nations, our infant mortality rate does not look good and, in comparison, our performance on this score is rapidly worsening. At one time, the United States ranked sixth among all the nations of the world in this crucial measure of effective health care....Today, out of a total of fifty-seven nations, we stand only fifteenth.[4]

It is our position that our technological optimism and commitment to science should be reassessed in relation to sociological approaches to societal problems. We wish to underscore the fact that we are not calling for a utopian retreat into a pretechnosocial past. Nor is it averred that science is responsible for social ills. What is being suggested here is that further technological and scientific developments according to presently existing patterns will not be enough to solve human social problems. It is argued that excessive techno-scientific optimism confounds our understanding of societal problems and efforts to effectively eliminate them.[5] How, then, has the proliferation of technology and science come to interfere with sociology's efforts to explain and offer solutions to societal problems?

Kenneth Boulding regards the explosion of human knowledge and rapidly accelerating changes in the techno-social environment as great of an historical transition as that of the agricultural revolution which triggered the origins of civilization itself.[6] Just as modern technology has been an outgrowth of burgeoning scientific knowledge, so also are many current societal problems grounded in existing techno-social realities. Moreover, scientific and technical developments were at once predicated upon and served to stimulate changes in man's conception of himself and his relation to the universe. An expanding techno-scientific firmament gave birth to a new image of man. Jack Douglas contends that a profound transition in western man's self-awareness has taken place in which the "medieval absolutist metaphysics of man" has been progressively replaced by secularized derivations of the natural scientific paradigm, thereby giving birth to the "absolutist metaphysics of positivistic social science".[7] Thus, western man's perceptions of himself, of his accomplishments and societal problems, has been progressively filtered through the vision of technoscientific rationalism. Our self-images, assessments of existing realities, and hopes for the future were forged within a new weltanschauung. The ethos of progress, our optimism, and perceptions of current problems became inextricably linked to a faith in science and technology. However, this faith lacks sanctification which could be delivered only by theology. Hence, we can observe an interesting marriage of science and technology with theology wedded enthusiastically by some theologians. John L. Reed, one of the most cogent critics of technocracy, turns our attention to a noteworthy example of the unification of science and theology. In his opinion, it was Pierre Teilhard de Chardin who largely contributed to this process. "Probably no other thinker", writes Reed, "has come as close to enshrining science, progress, and power as the technocratic trinity".[8]

In response to the ever-apparent inconsistency between technological optimism and existing societal problems, many authors are critical of technocratic social tendencies which have increased indifference to human needs and aspirations. Lewis Mumford speaks of the growth of centralized complexes of power, "irrational factors present in our machine-oriented technology", and concomitant mechanistic weltanschauung, with the same analytic acumen and humanistic concern as that which prompted Sorokin to pen The Crisis of Our Age. Mumford sees the techno-social power complex becoming increasingly dissociated from human culture and insulated within an "isolated subsystem centered not on the support and intensification of life but on the expansion of power and personal aggrandizement".[9]

In modern society, we are faced with a growing centralization of political and corporate power and dominance of technocratic priorities and values. The gap between technocratic and humanistic conceptions of man grows wider. Individually, we risk enslavement to technique. Man's inner life, his ethics, aesthetics, spiritual and emotional needs become increasingly displaced by the demands of techno-social realities. The sensitive and the poetic each day become more dispossessed of social relevance. Erich Fromm observes:

> A specter is stalking in our midst whom only a few see with clarity....It is a new specter: a completely mechanized society, devoted to maxi-

> mal material output and consumption, directed
> by computers; and in this social process, man
> himself is being transformed into a part of the
> total machine, well fed and entertained, yet
> passive, unalive, and with little feeling.[10]

Collectively, we may face even greater peril before the specter of techno-social trends. It is not enough that we have already seriously damaged the environment so as to induce widespread disease and jeopardize human life itself, but efforts to redress the ecological situation have been met with resistance from corporate and governmental officials alike. "Economic exigencies" hold precedence over organismic welfare; technical and humanistic values clash. Ecologists and consumer advocates like Ralph Nader are portrayed as "thorns in the side" of big business, ruminating "idealists" or "do-gooders". In addition, the threat of nuclear destruction has become a permanent fixture in the international arena. Overpopulation and mass starvation have ironically invested new "truth" in Malthus' ecologico-economic prophecies. As Marion Levy observes, the increased interdependency and centralization of modern society enhance the probability that "the implications of any error in our planning will spread catastrophically to all parts of the world", resulting in "death by stupidity".[11] Levy also warns against tendencies toward excessive authoritarianism which potentially inhere in modernized society. Increased institutional interdependency, a growing reliance upon highly technological systems to coordinate production and delivery of energy, food, and services entail further specialization and centralization. Increased centralization, in turn, invites more totalitarian modes of political and social organization. Human freedom and basic democratic values stand in jeopardy. Concerned about the potential directions of social change, Loren Eiseley, a noted biologist, extols his fellow scientists to rethink their faith in science and technology:

> Even now in the enthusiasm for new discoveries,
> reported public interviews with scientists tend
> to run increasingly toward a future replete
> with more inventions, stores of energy, babies
> in bottles, deadlier weapons. Relatively few
> have spoken of values, ethics, art, religion--
> all those intangible aspects of life which set
> the tone of a civilization and determine, in
> the end, whether it will be cruel or humane;
> whether, in other words, the modern world, so
> far as its interior spiritual life is concerned, will be stainless steel like its exterior,
> or display the rich fabric of genuine human
> experience.[12]

How are humanism and technological aims and ideals to be wed?

By what means can rapid technical advancement and scientific developments be made to serve humanity rather than threatening its very existence? How might we mete out some measure of creativity, emotional fulfillment, and freedom from ever-impinging technocratic realities? These questions beg no simple answers. Possible solutions are as many-sided as the factors which have given rise to present dilemmas. A retreat into the past is not in question. Scientific and technological developments are indispensably related to the present and future functioning of modern societies. By recognizing the inseparable and dynamic link between objective social conditions and human subjectivity, however, the humanistic sociological perspective can discern and explicate the potentially destructive implications of an overcommitment to the natural scientific paradigm and an uncritical technological optimism. Paradigmatic exclusivity beckons a rejection of alternatives, a solidification of interests, and incomprehension of limitations. Humanistic sociologists are especially atuned to the interplay between technology and values. Early in the industrialization process, technology was employed by various institutions to obtain rationally conceived ends. As the industrial revolution progressed, however, technology became a more autonomous force in the social process. One result was the emergence of the ethos of "technology for its own sake".[13] Values became subsumed within and subservient to technological priorities. In an essay examining the relationship between technology and values, Boulding observes,

> ...there has been a constant interplay between changing technologies and changing values, both of these being an integral part of the larger process of change in what Teilhard de Chardin calls the "noosphere" or the totality of images of the world in the minds of the living. The interaction between values and technologies is so complex that it is quite impossible to say which precedes the other. It is a hen and egg problem in n dimensions.[14]

The effects on society of the increasing application of technique to all aspects of human life is extensively analyzed and documented in Jacques Ellul's *The Technological Society*. For Ellul, technique is "the Totality of methods rationally arrived at and having absolute efficiency (for a given state of development) in every field of human activity". Techniques (rational, efficient methods) which originally were a means to a human end, become not only an end in themselves, but the supreme and only value. Ellul writes,

> 'Everything which is technique is necessarily used as soon as it is available without regard to good and evil....' Technique is nec-

essarily totalitarian; there can only be one <u>best</u> way. Other ways are less efficient and therefore not rational. Planning is the technical method in modern society. The plan cannot allow individual decisions which run counter to it. For the plan to be implemented, coercion must be available. Technique operates and expands in all spheres of full development. 'No matter how liberal the state, it is obliged by the mere fact of technical advance to extend its powers in every way....' 'True technique will know how to maintain the illusion of liberty, choice, and individuality; but these will be integrated into the mathematical reality merely as appearance.' 'Technique... pursues no end, professed or unprofessed. It evolves in a purely causal way: The combination of preceding elements furnishes the new technical elements. There is no purpose or plan that is being progressively realized. There is not even a tendency toward human ends. We are dealing with a phenomenon blind to the future, in a domain of integral causality. Hence, to pose arbitrarily some goal or other, to propose a direction for technique, is to deny technique and divest it of its character and its strength.[15]

Presently, we explore how humanistic sociology might find its way toward discerning the interactions between science and technology and present attempts to understand and grapple with societal problems.

If societal problems and the inability to solve them are intrinsically related to an overcommitment to science and technology, then the need for humanistic sociological alternatives is pressing. The renewed relevance of the humanistic perspective is heralded by Mumford who writes, "Salvation lies, not in the pragmatic adaptation of the human personality to the machine, but in the readaptation of the machine, itself a product of life's needs for order and organization, to the human personality".[16]

American sociologists grow more aware of the many potential pitfalls of neo-positivisitic approaches. Too often, one loses sight of the inherent humanity of the individuals under study amid the calculated mazes of mechanistic theory and technical terminology. If symbolic interactionists, ethnomethodologists, and other phenomenologically-derived thinkers have reminded us of the subjective integrity of those we study, so also have they refocused attention upon the inexorable humanity of the observer. Sociology is by its very nature an endeavor of humanity to understand itself: an existential act. While individually we may study "others", collectively, we study ourselves. Humanistic sociology places the problems of humanity at the center of its intellectual inquiry and aims at the relevance of sociological knowledge for the human condition. So conceived, in accordance with O'Neill's "wild sociology", humanistic sociology is an act of love.[17]

The humanistic sociological perspective is grounded in a belief in the continuity of culture and the transformability of cultural systems. Its paradigmatic underpinnings imply an adherence to an image of man which recognizes the liberating potential of consciousness, human creativity, the importance of power of human values in social life, and man's ontological vocation to develop his potentialities. Human actors are both products and producers of culture. Consciousness emerges out of society and creatively transforms it. To indulge in an Aristotelian metaphysical allusion, "humanness" consists of the inductive manipulation of symbols and the interpretation and creation of socio-cultural reality. The acknowledgement of consciousness, the interpretability of world, and dialectical interplay between objective conditions and subjective existence are central to humanistic sociological thought.

In what is termed a "transformational view" of societal problems, researchers at the Center for Study of Social Policy write,

>...the nature and severity of contemporary societal problems are perceived to be a reflection of the currently dominant paradigm --a paradigm that was admirably suited to the transition from a low-technology to a high-technology state, but is ill-suited for the further transition to a planetary society that can regulate itself humanely. In this view, the very intractibility of these problems, the dismal ends to which continued pursuit of the goals that produced these problems appear to lead, and the current level of social and intellectual upheaval all signal the incipient breakdown of the present paradigm. Little hope is seen for rectifying both present and anticipated societal problems unless there is a pervasive reordering of operative values which in turn is believed possible only if there is an expanded awareness of human possibilities. Thus the emergence of a new dominant paradigm more appropriate to our time is anticipated.[18]

That human action is animated by ideas as well as molded by conditions is an integral dimension of the transformational view. Our consciousness of current difficulties, our point of view, "makes a drastic difference in the nature of plans and actions that are implied".[19] Policy is generated both by expediency and perspective, by conditions as well as paradigmatic orientations. With regard to human efforts to resolve societal problems, therefore, the dynamic effects of "self-fulfilling" and "self-negating" prophesies must be considered. In the spirit of Vico, humanistic sociology distinguishes between human history and natural history; the former being partly informed by consciousness and creative action while the latter is not.[20]

The implications of the humanistic sociological perspective for our present immersement in the dominant metaphysics of techno-scientific rationalism have been developed throughout this work. Here, the general relevance of humanistic sociology for contemporary societal problems can be elaborated upon.

Humanistic sociology constitutes an additional approach to the analysis of societal problems and policy formation. In the tradition of the sociology of knowledge, the relation between an overcommitment to science and technology and our perceptions of contemporary societal problems must be further explored. We must be wary of a paradigmatic "hardening of the arteries". The complexity and irretrievably human consequences of societal problems mandates a diversity of perspectives, styles of inquiry, and policies. In addition, such an investigation should not be predicated upon antagonism. The pressing character of political, economic, organizational, ecological, and psychological problems demands cooperative interchange rather than defensive embattlement. A catholicity of vision and openness to differing modes of knowledge indicative of humanistic sociologists would produce new assessments of our problems as well as providing a wider intellectual context in which sorely needed synthesis might be furthered.

The donning of a humanistic sociological perspective would also serve to stimulate the growth of a moral and social concern as well as a critical self-consciousness among sociologists. Adherence to singularly "scientific" methods and perspectives might become more questionable. The processual link between sociological knowledge and society at large may be better understood. In his discussion of tension between social relevance and scientific sociology, James McKee writes,

> ...that our sociological consciousness has been deficient in failing to appreciate how much of what happens to sociology as it changes and develops is part and parcel of what is happening to the larger world into which we are inextric-

ably interwoven. What has happened to us, what is happening to us, and what will happen to us, is part of a broader experience and change that is happening to the world. We can neither understand nor control our own development except as we become intensely conscious and critical of this basic process.[21]

Such a critical self-consciousness might serve to make sociological practitioners more responsive to impending societal problems and induce a degree of social and moral responsibility, thus minimizing the often ill social effects of academic and scientific specialization. Increased self-consciousness would aid in the revitalization of the discipline. This call for a more critical awareness is not uniquely limited to humanistic sociologists. As a study of the Bulletin of the Atomic Scientists soon reveals, many natural scientists have been concerned about the impact of their ideas and discoveries upon society. Some scientists readily confess little understanding of the emotional structure of people and, as Glenn Seaborg writes, "if we in science could effect one 'human breakthrough'--if we could somehow convince our fellowmen that we now live in an age when fear, mistrust, and blind passions based on and regenerated by past ignorance and error must give way to a new level of understanding and reason among men".[22]

Humanistic sociology would also refurbish sociological interest in the role of values in society and their relation to societal problems. Nowhere is our immersion in values more irksomely profound than in relation to societal problems. Questions concerning defense expenditures, social welfare programs, population control, productivity and unemployment, the distribution of health care services, or which mouths to feed are inevitably value-laden. All the forebearers of humanistic sociology, in one fashion or another, confronted the issue of values. Many who pay deference to the vision of scientism or blindly hold that further technological innovations will provide a sole panacea for present societal ills believe, in essence, that, if enough knowledge is gathered, quantified, and dutifully represented in formulae or graphical schemes, then somehow and at some time the "truth" will be ascertained or effective solutions will be forthcoming.

For those who partake fully in the manna of scientific and technological optimism, the truth is perceived as external. Such a vision ignores the significance of human values in man's attempt to understand man, just as it erodes the credulity of self-willed and politically viable social action. In a sense perfectly continuous with the German idealistic philosophical tradition, for Dilthey, Weber, Znaniecki, Mannheim, and Sorokin, value is intrinsic to human experience. Human action is inevitably social and mind imposes its order or havoc upon the world.

Humanistic sociology will further our understanding of current methodological issues and their implications for society. Though Alvin Gouldner's presidential address, "Anti-Minotaur: The Myth of Value-Free Sociology", did much to undermine the arbitrary ethos of objectivity and rigid quantification within sociology, nevertheless, the professional mythos continues to be permeated by a devotion to the icons of the cybernetic age.[23] Have statistical and technical preoccupations distracted the profession from the study of social problems? Have we become more fascinated with Perfecting the instruments of social research rather than applying existing methods to the study of relevant social issues and dynamics? The "noncommitment" and "noninvolvement" engendered by the objectivisitic ethos in American sociology, at personal and social levels, has contributed to the growing irrelevance of sociological thought. The highly specialized character of much sociological knowledge has fragmented the discipline and severed sociology's link with society proper. By reviewing the development of American "scientific" sociology we can discern a growing disjunction between sociological studies and a concern for societal problems. American sociologists of the 1920's and 1930's were socially responsible and social problems-oriented more so than their recent counterparts. William Carleton observes,

> ...American intellectuals of the 1940's and 1950's, instead of making the comprehensive approach, too often retreated into minitiae, intensive specialization, overconcern for methodology,...an avoidance of commitment, or a renunciation of all values except a faith in scientific techniques; or fell back on abstractionism, dialectic, and a new scholasticism in search of absolutes, eternal verities, and a monistic tradition.[24]

The notion of "scientific validity" must be continuously reappraised and understood with reference to the subjectivity of the scientific observer and changing socio-cultural contexts. The humanistic sociological perspective provides an avenue along which more rigorously methodological questions and conclusions can be linked to their social-historical origins and effects. Valid knowledge might then be conceived to possess two aspects: the satisfaction of certain standards of logico-empirical exactitude; and possessing practical implications for societal problems. Of final methodological importance, humanistic sociology provides a framework in which the sociologist may analyze societal problems and formulate possible solutions independent or in conjunction with the specifications of current methodological models. Dilthey's method of "interpretive reconstruction", Weber's method of "verstehen", Znaniecki's "humanistic coefficient", or Sorokin's "logico-meaningful" method take the sociological observer beyond the parameters of a strictly empiricist methodology. Toynbee, for example, regarded Sorokin's methodological eclecticism, his holistic perspective and utilization of a great variety of methods of study, as his greatest service to mankind.[25] Summarizing Weber's methodological contributions, Peter Berger writes,

> Weber's position is expressed most eloquently in the two essays 'Science as a Vocation' and 'Politics as a Vocation'...[He] stated his positions on the 'value-freeness' of the social scientists and on the moral responsibility of the political actor. The two positions make the best sense when looked at together. For the social scientist Weber insisted on one overriding obligation--that of looking at social reality with objectivity, without injecting his own values or taking into account his personal hopes or fears. For the political actor Weber insisted on the most painstaking moral responsibility, and especially the knowledge of being responsible for the consequences, intended and unintended, of his own actions. The two positions are stated with equal passion. It is in this double passion that Weber's greatness lies. Both in his thought and in his life he tried to bear without flinching the enormous tension between detachment and engagement. And he had contempt for those who sought relief from this tension, be it by denying that moral options are real or by absolutely espousing one single option--the psychological escape routes of, respectively, the positivist and the doctrinaire ideologist.[26]

Developing a humanistic sociological awareness may sensitize sociologists to more deep-seated problems facing techno-social man--problems of loneliness, anomie, alienation, a failing reverence for life, emotional impotence, mental anguish and confusion, powerlessness, fear of violence, and preoccupation with death.[27] Humanistic sociology provides a gateway to understanding the problems of the inner man, their personal and social contours, origins, and effects. It is here that the limitations of scientific sociological method and vision become more apparent. How, for example, are we to assess the impact of technocratic trends or social policies upon human freedom? Can individual freedom be adequately operationalized with a degree of conceptual objectivity remaining intact? Perhaps one unintended consequence of our adherence to the creed of value-free sociology has been to exacerbate the development of the larger technological and social forces already impinging upon human freedom. By ignoring personal and social issues such as the diminution of human freedom and dignity in the name of "objectivity", sociologists have, in effect, contributed to their demise. Humanistic sociology's emphasis upon the inner-meaning of social action, its inherent preoccupation with the symbolic side of social life, and its probing confrontation with human values can enhance our ability to constructively and consciously confront the problems of man in technological society.

CHAPTER X FOOTNOTES

1. Robert Nisbet, "The Impact of Technology on Ethical Decision-Making", in Jack D. Douglas, The Technological Threat (Englewood Cliffs, New Jersey, 1971), p. 41.

2. Herbert Coldhamer, ed., The Social Effects of Communications Technology (Santa Monica, California: Rand Corporation, 1970), pp. 1, 25, and 23, respectively.

3. Albert Speer, Inside the Third Reich (New York: Macmillan, 1970), p. 520.

4. William Ryan, Blaming the Victim, revised edition (New York: Vintage Books, 1976), pp. 161-162.

5. An additional example, despite the often-cited liberating potential of technological developments for women and mounting social scientific evidence of trends toward sexual equality, the gap between male and female wages remains wide. Government statistics show that, while the year-round full-time earnings of women workers in 1957 were 67 percent of those of men, the proportion dropped to 58 percent by 1966 and remained there through 1968. See: Underutilization of Women Workers, Women's Bureau, U. S. Department of Labor (Washington, D.C.: U. S. Government Printing Office, 1971), pp. 4-5.

6. Kenneth Boulding, The Meaning of the Twentieth Century (New York: Harper and Row, 1965).

7. Jack D. Douglas, "The Impact of the Social Sciences", in Jack D. Douglas, ed., The Impact of Sociology (New York: Appleton-Century-Crofts, 1970), pp. 250-280.

8. John L. Reed, The Newest Whore of Babylon: The Emergence of Technocracy (Boston: Branden Press Publishers, 1970), p. 53. Searching for the relations between religion and technocracy, Reed moved back to the beginning of the fifth century to show the influence of the heresy of Pelagius on Bacon, assuming that he 'transformed the Pelagian concept that man could fashion his own spiritual destiny into the modern technocratic doctrine that man can satisfy all his needs and wants by achieving mastery over nature through the medium of natural science' (p. 35).

9. Lewis Mumford, The Pentagon of Power (New York: Harcourt Brace Jovanovich, 1970), p. 245.

10. Erich Fromm, The Revolution of Hope (New York: Harper and Row, 1968), p. 1. Others have voiced similar forebodings of the future. See Jurgen Habermas, Toward a Rational Society (Boston: Beacon Press, 1971), pp. 81-122. Schwartz questions the belief that more technology can create solutions for the side-effects of previous technology. Eugene S. Schwartz, Overskill: The Decline of Technology in Modern Civilization (Chicago: Quadrangle Books, 1971).

11. Marion Levy, Jr., Modernization: Latecomers and Survivors (New York: Basic Books, 1972), p. 72.

12. Eiseley's remarks quoted in Herbert J. Muller, The Children of Frankenstein: A Primer on Modern Technology and Human Values (Bloomington and London: University of Indiana Press, 1970), pp. 135-136. Muller's brilliant work presents a systematic analysis of present and future developments in the social and natural sciences in modern technological society.

13. For a brief discussion, see Jack D. Douglas, ed., pp. 1-4, 37-38.

14. Kenneth E. Boulding, "The Emerging Superculture", in Kurt Baier and Nicholas Rescher, eds., Values and the Future: The Impact of Technological Change on American Values (New York: Free Press, 1969), p. 345.

15. Jacques Ellul, The Technological Society (New York: Vintage Books, 1967), pp. XXI, 99, 125, 181, 228, 139, and 97, respectively.

16. Lewis Mumford, Art and Technics (New York: Columbia University Press, 1952), p. 14.

17. John O'Neill entreats the profession to join a celebration of humanity and create a "human community". His work merits scrutiny by humanistic sociologists. See Making Sense Together: An Introduction to Wild Sociology (New York: Harper and Row, 1974).

18. O. W. Markley, D. A. Curry and D. L. Rink, Contemporary Societal Problems, Educational Policy Research Center (Menlo Park, California: Stanford Research Institute, June/1971), p. 24. The present chapter owes much to the formulations of these authors. With an eye toward both synthesis and the future, they outline the intricate relations between paradigmatic orientations, images of man, and approaches to under-

standing and acting upon societal problems. Of further relevance and value, see O. W. Markley, program director, et al., Changing Images of Man (Policy Research Report 4), Center for the Study of Social Policy (Menlo Park, California: Stanford Research Institute, 1974).

19. Ibidem, p. 27.

20. See Veljko Korac, "In Search of Human Society", in Erich Fromm, ed., Socialist Humanism: An International Symposium (New York: Doubleday and Company, 1965), pp. 1-15.

21. James B. McKee, "Some Observations on the Self-Consciousness of Sociologists", in Larry T. Reynolds and Janice M. Reynolds, eds., The Sociology of Sociology (New York: David McKay Corporation, 1970), pp. 98-113.

22. Seaborg's remarks appeared in the January 1968 issue of the Bulletin of the Atomic Scientists and are quoted by Herbert J. Muller, op. cit., p. 386.

23. Alvin Gouldner, "Anti-Minotaur: The Myth of Value-Free Sociology", Social Problems (Winter, 1962), Vol. 9, No. 3, pp. 189-213.

24. William G. Carleton, Technology and Humanism (Vanderbilt Press, 1970), pp. 235-236.

25. For a discussion see C. C. Zimmerman, "Some Sociological Theories of Pitirim Alexandrovich Sorokin", National Taiwan University Journal of Sociology, Vol. 5, April 1969, pp. 37-47.

26. Peter Berger, Pyramids of Sacrifice: Political Ethics and Social Change (New York: Basic Books, 1974), pp. 224; parentheses are the author's.

27. Of related significance, see: (1) Margaret Mary Wood, Paths of Loneliness (New York: Columbia University Press, 1953); (2) Peter L. Berger, Brigitte Berger and Hansfried Deller, The Homeless Mind: Modernization and Consciousness (New York: Random House, 1973); (3) Erich Fromm, The Sane Society (New York: Fawcett World Library, 1955); (4) Elizabeth Hall and Paul Cameron, "Our Failing Reverence for Life", in Psychology Today (April, 1976), pp. 104-113; (5) Rollo May, Love and Will (New York: W. W. Norton and Company, 1969); (6) George Gerbner and Larry Ross, "The Scary World of TV's Heavy Viewer", in Psychology Today, op. cit., pp. 41-45; and (7) Elisabeth Kubler-Ross, On Death and Dying (New York: Macmillan Publishing Company, 1969).

CHAPTER XI

EDUCATION IN THE TECHNO-INDUSTRIAL COMPLEX:

HUMANISM OR TECHNICISM?

If the humanistic and scientific perspectives have been the poles for the development of sociological thought, they have also informed American educational thought and practice. Humanist and scientist, cultivated generalist and technical expert, have stood at loggerheads on seemingly irreconcilable grounds. In the field of education, like that of sociology, the issues between the two forces have been both intellectual and social.

American education has been enmeshed within larger social, political and economic realities. In general, educational philosophies and policies have been fashioned in consonance with the interests of the techno-industrial complex. A survey of educational change in America reveals the growing influence of bureaucratic and corporate aims and values. Nineteenth-century education grew more responsive to the burgeoning needs of industrial society and "the men who ran the schools differed little in their attitudes and outlook from the men who ran the businesses".[1] With a satirical vengeance, Veblen was one of the first to explore the multi-pronged infusion of business functionaries and entrepreneural practices into American higher education.[2] During the 19th century, the administrative helm was passed from stiff-collared and spiritually-minded clergy to starch-shirted and efficiency-minded businessmen. Thus Joel Spring points out, "Since 1900 the power of schooling has tended to be in the hands of businessmen, political leaders, and professional educators who have been instrumental in the development of the corporate state".[3]

Educational socialization has been designed to meet and facilitate the demands of larger corporate, scientific, and technological trends. Due to a growing emphasis upon technical problem solving, the acquisition of instrumental skills, efficiency, productivity and organization, the human-centered and diversifying ethos of the liberal arts tradition was put on the defensive. The distinction between "general education and specialized education, between education and training, between liberal and vocational, and between the humanistic and technological or technical" became ever more apparent.[4] Humanists were made wary by a sense of impending obsolescence and human tragedy. While the pragmatic idealism of Dewey sought to bridge the gap between an alienating technological apparatus and the indivudal by creating a sense of community through the educational process, the encroachment of corporate and technical priorities upon the educational arena accelerated.[5] Specialized training programs, vocational counseling, an increasing emphasis upon scientific research, professionalization, and channeling students toward various technical careers and services reveals the responsiveness of educational institutions to the requirements of the technocracy. International and national political developments and recent recessionary crises within the capitalist economy have prompted further "restructuring" and "reallocation of resources" within educational institutions toward greater complementarity with techno-industrial objectives. "Employability" and "technical applicability" have entered the vocabulary of administrators and academic planners. Scientific management and systems theory have become guiding contexts for administrative decision-making.

A new generation of educators emphasizing "self-realization" are attempting to reshape the educational process to meet the needs of individuals--needs which go beyond employability, paycheck, and expertise. The satisfaction of individual needs for self-expression, creativity, and a sense of belonging, as well as furthering self-understanding, social and historical consciousness, aesthetic sensitivity, and autonomous decision-making abilities are pointed out by the new generation of educators as the goals of humanistic education. Some teachers, in the name of these aims, are promoting the free-school movement, face-to-face interaction between students and teachers, and the institutional implementation of the open classroom concept. By these methods and concepts, they hope to make changes in the real world--to make an individual and collective impact upon shaping people's lives and society proper in humane directions. These experimental and yet not always fully responsible teaching enterprises constitute a reaction against the subversion of an educational system under the auspices of a growing technocracy, replete with computerized instruction and monitoring of student and faculty movements and ideologies. Recent trends have instilled chilling portent into Orwell's vision of future society. Jacques Ellul pointed out the historical roots of the failures of contemporary education in France:

> The Napoleonic conception that the Lycees must furnish administrators with social needs and tendencies, has become world-wide in its extent. According to this conception, education

> no longer has a humanist end or any value in
> itself; it has only one gaol, to create tech-
> nicians.[6]

However, Ellul's assessment of educational development suffers from an ahistorical bias. One has to remember that the Lycee gave 19th-century France the lustre of intellects and contributed to the period which Frenchmen call la belle epoch. The ideas and system of education which worked positively in the 19th century became a cause of a mass student revolt in May 1968 and a more recent protest in April 1976. The massive Paris demonstration opposed government reforms "aimed at bringing university courses in line with France's economic needs (and to) alter courses of study to equip students better for jobs after graduation from universities".[7] Like Ellul, Fromm argues that the machine-like function of contemporary educational institutions has been determined by the organizational needs of modern industrial society. He writes:

> The concentration of capital led to the for-
> mation of giant corporations managed by hier-
> archically organized bureaucracies. Large
> conglomerations of worker and clerks work to-
> gether, each individual a part of a vast or-
> ganized production machine, which in order
> to run at all, must run smoothly and without
> interruption. The individual worker becomes
> merely a cog in this machine.[8]

The image of the individual as a "cog" in an educational machine is antithetical to the values underpinning humanistic education. Some humanistic values defended in educational theories and practices, are represented by A. S. Neill.[9] Contrary to the Hobbesian heritage, he is convinced of the inherent goodness of the child and defines the primary aim of education in the naturalistic tradition as finding happiness in work and life. Education, according to Neill, should be oriented around the psychic needs and abilities of the child and should stimulate both emotional and intellectual development. Finally, individual freedom must be guarded against the infringements of overt or covert authoritarianism. The emphasis upon freedom, personal and intellectual growth is reiterated by Carl Rogers who writes:

> A way must be found to develop, within the
> educational system as a whole, and in each
> component, a climate conducive to personal
> growth, a climate in which innovation is not
> frightening, in which the creative capacities
> of administrators, teachers, and students are
> nourished rather than stifled.[10]

What is the relevance of humanistic sociology for current crises in education? The school is the major institution of socialization in this century. While the impact of sociology cannot approach that of education in breadth and social effect, a humanistic sociological perspective can do much to illuminate the problems facing educators, the relationships between the educational process and wider society, and the implications of present policies for future human wlefare.

First, humanistic sociology facilitates an understanding of educational practices and policies within a social and cultural context. The growing failure of education to integrate humanistic and technological dimensions is critical for the future of a humane society. As Judith Wechsler states, "The problem is how to develop an awareness and knowledge of the role of science in culture and civilization without sacrificing a high degree of technical education".[11] Continued specialization presents a threat to the continuity of culture and our ability to conceive and create more holistic models of the future. The broad foundations of western education have been seriously narrowed. Individual expertise is dearly purchased with broader socio-educational fragmentation. A growing incomprehension of social and political problems and issues has eroded the probability of socially and morally informed democratic action. As Burton Clark points out, "The efforts to bring liberal education to the expert constitute a social response to the strain, an attempt to avoid a barbarism of men acute in technical judgment but myopic in social affairs, politics, and cultural understanding".[12] A restatement and recommitment to humanistic principles and priorities in education would check potentially dangerous trends toward the technical specialization of knowledge and political authoritarianism.

Secondly, a humanistic sociological perspective takes us several steps closer to explicating the relation between education and societal problems. On one hand, insofar as education generates <u>unbridled</u> development of technological values, it can be viewed as part of the problem rather than a solution. On the other hand, as John Rich ably argues, humanistically-oriented analyses and policies are necessary to effectively grapple with societal problems such as the lack of international world government, pollution, overpopulation, over-urbanization, neglect of domestic problems for foreign wars, the inability to develop a new political philosophy for our age, and inadequate planning.[13] Problems such as the disposal of radioactive wastes or escalating fusion research are not purely technical endeavors but <u>social</u> issues.[14] Humanistic sociology would enable us to better assess the human costs of blindly following the dictates of the technological imperative--"whatever can be done must be done". Education must equip individuals with both a technical and social consciousness of the implications of their actions and ideas. Don

Price continues, "The scientist who first comprehends the connections between his professional specialty and a broader humane learning is in the best position to help first his fellow scientist and next his fellow citizens understand the problems they must solve in making science a force for freedom".[15]

Thirdly, due to its affinities with the sociology of knowledge, humanistic sociology can explore the consequences and liabilities of education's progressive immersement in a purely techno-scientific paradigm. In September 1959 scholars, educators, and scientists gathered at Woods Hole to discuss the improvement of education in science.[16] In part, cold war tensions and Russia's launching of sputnik prompted the reappraisal of American science curriculums. A fundamental conclusion of this conference was that educational processes should seek to shape learning with a primary emphasis upon the "structure of knowledge". Individual intellectual development should occur in accordance with the existing structure of scientific knowledge and methods. The Woods Hole conference triggered an immediate reaction from humanistic educators who argued that the learning process should be oriented around considerations of individual needs and social welfare rather than in supplication to a given system of knowledge. The humanistic approach in sociology provides a medium through which the implied values and societal effects of a singular commitment to a techno-scientific paradigm can be explored. Glenys Unruh maintains, "If curriculum development is to be responsive to the needs of individuals and predictable alternative futures, an adequate theory must be based on humanistic values and American democratic ideals, while using materialism as the support system for human service".[17]

Finally, in view of urgent societal problems, a humanistic perspective would broaden the analytical basis of the sociology of education. Research students and our understanding of the educational process, its social determinants and effects, would be better informed by historical knowledge. A knowledge of larger socio-historical trends would also lead to more accurate appraisals of future educational developments and policy needs. In consonance with John Reed's motives for his speculative work on the emergence of technocracy, our awareness of what could happen rather than what will happen in the future would be considerably enhanced.[18] Most centrally, however, humanistic sociology's concern with consciousness and meaning in social life, its commitment to the preservation of freedom and betterment of the human condition, its thinking-feeling-deciding model of man, would help guard society against the dehumanizing effects of technology on our social life. Over fifty years ago, Max Weber observed:

> Behind all the present discussions of the
> foundations of the educational system, the

> struggle of the 'specialist type of man'
> against the older type of 'cultivated man'
> is hidden at some decisive point. This
> fight is determined by the irresistibly ex-
> panding bureaucratization of all public and
> private relations of authority and by the
> ever-increasing importance of expert and
> specialized knowledge. This fight intrudes
> into all intimate cultural questions.[19]

Since his time, this fight has devastated the cause of the 'cultivated man' and brought further victory to the 'specialized type of man'. However, it was only a <u>Pyrrhic victory</u>. The 'specialized type of man' appears to be an obedient instrument in the hands of modern tyrants and unconsciously helps to build an inhuman totalitarian state. Therefore, he is a potential threat for the survival of democracies which are still above ground only in the smaller part of our globe. Our dilemma is that we urgently need technological expertise in order to avoid mass starvation and poverty; but if this expertise is not mediated by humanistic value commitments it may lead toward the state of technocracy and, through international conflicts, result in final catastrophe. Ideologists of technocratic society assume that the 'technical man' is needed to save us. They believe he should replace the <u>homo economicus</u> who since the beginning of modern ages has dominated societies. One of them pathetically wrote: "The race's only salvation is in the creation of technological man".[20]

We are also arguing that <u>homo economicus</u> should be replaced with a more human "Homo". However, a "technological homo" is not more human than a <u>homo economicus</u>. The philosophy of those who promote a future model of man determined by highly technological qualifications seems to be based on three intellectual inclinations: first, to identify science and technology; second, to recall 18th-century mechanistic materialism; and third, to construct the image of social reality in accordance with the dogma of naturalism.

The answer which should be given to these views by a humanist sociology is developing along the following lines:

(1) Twentieth-century technology is so heavily based on science that it gives a misleading impression of their kinship. Logical analysis as well as historical and sociological scrutiny of those two phenomena, however, shows an essential difference in their nature and purpose. The fact that today science cannot progress (at least in the present direction) without technology and that further technological development is impossible without permanent application of the new data of scientific discoveries, does not diminish the actual difference between them. Science initially

grew primarily out of human intellectual curiosity and in its pure form can develop itself without any applicability. Technology grows out of people's practical needs. The first step of the former is reflection. The first step of the latter is action.

(2) Mechanical materialism, rejected even by Marx, penetrates the ideology of technocracy. It was a progressive outlook in the 18th century, but in the 20th century it presents a regression in philosophical comprehension of world phenomena and is particularly dangerous in its application to the social world.

(3) Naturalism, a foundation of one-sided philosophies, is blocking efforts to understand the entire nature of man which developed within social and cultural processes. The understanding of man's nature in all its dimensions is desperately needed today in our struggle against the dehumanization of the individual, society, western civilization, and international relations.

The needs of technological advancement in world industrial production and international communication on the one hand, and in the armament race on the other, has caused the voice of ideologists of technology to be too willingly heard both in democratic and communistic countries by managers as well as by semi-educated masses interested mainly in further improvement of living conditions. Now, however, a humanistic response to these suicidal ideologies is urgently needed. We should realize that the conflict of ideological and political orientations is in its essence a conflict of different systems of values. Within the frames of each culture, systems of values had been transferred from generation to generation by tradition and education. So, our global crisis is brought about by the interruption in the continuity of cultural tradition on the one hand, and related critical changes in education on the other hand.

Until the present age, prevailing value-systems within Western civilization have been rooted on the one side in Graeco-Roman traditions of secular life and in the Christian religion on the other. These combined traditions determined our social life for centuries until almost World War I. However, since the French Revolution secularization together with the rapidly growing demands for experts and specialists allowed for an encroachment into educational curriculum of a particular emphasis on technical and scientific training. Moral education, the immanent part of humanistic education, began to lose ground. The knowledge of history, a familiarity with Graeco-Roman culture as well as religious training have become less and less important. Fewer and fewer individuals learn Latin and Greek and possess a working knowledge of the great literary and philosophical works on which western civilization was built up. Few have read Homer whose heroes embodied the basic secular values of western societies and who were living ideals for ruling-class men during two millennia. Plutarch's Lives is practically unknown in 20th-century society whereas, in the past, a familiarity with its pages was commonplace for the educated person. The reading of the Bible as the greatest stimulation for moral reflection lost its significance in educational training.

In sum, education previously served as a source of moral unity for western civilization. The two great functions of education--creating a continuity of values and knowledge between generations and providing a morally integrating effect for existing peoples--have become progressively disrupted. The continuity of the western civilization is seriously undermined for the first time after twenty-five centuries of development.[21] And, although this statement expresses only our Euro-American-ethnocentrism, we have to remind the reader that despite all failures and sins of the western civilization it was the only one which produced and elaborated great ideas such as "freedom", "equality", and the "rights to favorable conditions for personal development". Although, today, the two conflicting ideologies (communism and capitalism) assign different priorities for the actualization of these ideals and propose various programs for their realization, both promise these ends will be accomplished. It is, finally, western civilization's science and technology which has become at least a potential common platform for the future global security: the peaceful unification of the human race. Furthermore, it is science and technology, which (in spite of all our own criticism) may be the only forces if properly used, that can prevent potential world catastrophy.

Citizens of affluent societies who are becoming more and more aware of this critical development have a right to ask whether the present educational systems are preparing the new generation to deal with the era of great **transition** and whether these systems will enable them to build more humane societies in the world of scarcity?

Is it not a rhetorical question? Since we know that only essential structural changes in social, economic and political relations among the nations and within each of them, can bring us peacefully to the postindustrial era, humanistic sociology should contribute by analysis and creative criticism of the present educational ideas and systems.

How do educators view the future education as shown by some leading educators? Maybe the most symptomatic is the perspective Professor Thorsten Husen, an UNESCO expert on education, expressed in his Education in the Year 2000.[22] In reviewing educational problems of the approaching era, he did not even mention the basic dilemma of our secular civilization: the problem of moral education. This implies a naive optimism that in our technologized social life morality will no longer be a matter of human concern. Of course, there is no discussion on humanistic aspects of education.

It is an interesting paradox that in the socialist countries which have not yet entered the post-industrial era and are still highly interested in full exploitation of modern technology, the emphasis on the humanistic aspects of education is greater than in the affluent West. This might partially be explained by the fact that the agricultural part of the 19th century produced a social stratum of the intelligentsia (particularly in Russia and Poland). The intelligentsia possessed limited opportunities for careers in business or industry and inherited the lifestyles, traditions, and manners of the nobility. For this reason, they were more interested in humanistic education than the bourgeoisie of industrialized countries. Thus, in societies in which the educational system was determined by the demands of the intelligentsia, humanistic attitudes were so strongly rooted that even communist upheavals were unable to erase them. Three years ago, for example, Bogdan Suchodolski, one of the leading theoreticians of education in Eastern Europe, wrote:

> ...in the epoch, when praxeological skills of men are under the heaviest test, when the governing of material and social growth demands to the same extent the knowledge of computer science as the modern people--the humanistic culture is becoming a peculiar and distinctive need of people.[23]

We are in full agreement with Suchodolski's opinion that the mission of humanistic culture is to "teach people how to organize the world, which they are creating and in which they are living, in a 'humane' way".[24]

One can speak today about new paradigms of knowledge because our education must aim toward new and different goals than those of the past. However, to achieve them we need to organize the development of science and technology from a humanistic perspective. As Willis E. Harmon points out, this would mean that "Instead of being an eager servant of industry and the military, the new science would actively assist society in formulating new dominant goals for the whole culture".[25]

Thus, if we do not wish the coming epoch of global society to be deprived of all that which offers the highest human value and has been produced in the cradles of national cultures, we must solve a great dilemma: how to unite mankind in the frame of a global civilization which will not reduce national cultures to the level of ethnic customs, but will instead support their flowering.

However, to clarify our views in this matter for those who may criticize us by saying that our arguments sound similar to those of "modernization theorists", further explanation is needed. Despite the Anglo-Saxon proclivity to do so, in this work we are not identifying culture and civilization. The distinction which we are making between these terms has a long tradition in continental social thought. However, each author has defined terms according to the needs of his ideas or system. This distinction was rooted in the Greek concept of paideia, popularized in Europe by the French language, which until the 20th century reserved the usage of la culture for spiritual expression mainly in arts and letters, and la civilization for economic and technological standard of living. This distinction came to sociology particularly with the help of German authors. Marx spoke about "superstructure" and "base" which, although not identical, are very close to the French distinction. Oswald Spengler, foreseeing a decline of the West, distinguished historical stages of "creative culture" and that of the material comfort of "civilization".[26] Alfred Weber distinguished between the "movement of culture" and "process of civilization".[27] Mannheim followed him in general, but realized that there are some essential philosophical and historical problems which do not fit either the category of culture or civilization.[28] Some American writers such as Robert MacIver did attempt to introduce the distinction between culture and civilization into American social thought but it never received the attention or emphasis it deserved.

In our consideration, civilization differs from culture not only because the former has mainly materialistic dimensions while the latter is spiritual in its essence, but also because the phenomenon of a civilization is much larger than that of culture. Within each civilization many divergent cultures exist and develop. We define culture as a set of values, moral norms and psychic characteristics which determine the way of life, artistic and literary expressions and styles, inclinations and preferences of social groups among which the nation is the largest and includes various ethnic and religious groups with their subcultures. All cultural goods are appreciated as such for the expression of values and psychic-emotional power which have called them into existence.

There is a deep gap dividing cultural goods and products of civilization. The former are unrepeatable and individualized (even if created by generations--like medieval cathedrals). The latter are repeatable and anonymous. A product of civilization could be a highly sophisticated instrument but still might serve barbarian purposes, while a piece of authentic culture, no matter how primitive, is designed to serve, to stimulate, or at least to bring to mind those values and psychic-emotions from which it grew up. This distinction between culture and civilization though far from the American inclination and habit of thinking designed by the Anglo-

Saxon tradition of "cultural anthropology" which failed to recognize the essential difference in origin and function of the bow and decoration carved on it, between hunting and a picture of it made on the wall of a cave.

The conflict between culture (in this old sense of the term) and civilization though neglected by sociologists, is one of perilous dilemmas of our time. The triumphant progress of civilization is so fast that the development of culture cannot keep pace. In these spheres of social life in which humanistic education, humanistic attitudes or humanistic policy is neglected, the victorious civilization helps to replace culture by mass culture. This conflict is most dramatic where the native culture of so-called "underdeveloped" (what an ideologically loaded term!) country receives benefits of the great powers' civilization.

On the American continent this problem should be particularly well known. The history of the American movement from the east to the west coast was, to a large extent, characterized by the conflict between a more highly developed white man civilization and a primitive civilization of Indians. The latter, however, often had a high standard of culture. Without idealizing Indian cultures, it is easy to understand that the trappers, goldminers and fur-traders who spearheaded the westward expansion came to dominate the native American inhabitants through the ownership and control of the beneficiary products of civilization and not that of culture. The same process is repeated today, for example, when American or Canadian workers who come in contact with aboriginal Eskimos impress or amuse them with the gadgets of our civilization but not with their command of cultural values. Too often, the penetrating power of modern civilization results in the destruction of small traditional cultures. Similar problems appear very often when and where an American federal agency, even if directed by the most humanitarian spirit, brings technological know-how and financial aid to nations proud of their great cultural heritage. The famous "Marshall Plan", which virtually rebuilt western Europe awakened an anti-American spirit in those nations which received American aid because, together with this great help, came the impact of American civilization which was too large to be digested and adopted without unwanted and sickly effects on the culture of the benefited countries.

Even in the United States this conflict between culture and civilization is observable. The uncontrolled progress of technology is destroying the necessary balance between these two spheres of human life, between material welfare and spiritual harmony. Unbreathable air, undrinkable water, the horror of crime, drug and narcotic abuse, the failures of mass education--these are but a few results of the rapid growth of civilization which has undermined the essential values of American culture.

In the currently developing international situation, this conflict between culture and civilization acquires a particular significance. On one hand, the great powers represent the greatest achievements of modern civilization and possess the means to save the world's population from a catastrophy resulting from uncontained growth of population and the exhaustion of resources. On the other hand, however, the balance between culture and civilization is deeply disrupted by the processes of mechanization, industrialization, and depersonalization of life which are most highly developed in the great power societies.

Some political scientists have observed this phenomenon. For example, Zbigniew Brzezinski has written about the "conflict between the irrational personalism of the 'humanists' and the impersonal rationality of the 'modernizers': "...the emerging rational humanism is historically contingent in the sense that it does not involve--as was the case with the nineteenth-century ideology--universally prescriptive concepts of social organization but stresses cultural and economic global diversity".[29] He believes that a synthesis of those two orientations is possible. Although Brzezinski himself, as a former director of the "Trilateral Commission" (which aims to solve global problems by the collaboration of the greatest managers of business and industry from America, Western Europe and Japan), belongs formally to the group of "modernizers", nevertheless he expressed views to which any fair-minded humanist can ascribe:

> The technological thrust and the economic wealth of the United States now make it possible to give the concept of liberty and equality to a broader meaning, going beyond the procedural and external to the personal and inner spheres of man's social existence. By focusing more deliberately on these qualitative aspects of life, America may avoid the depersonalizing dangers inherent in the self-generating but philosophically meaningless mechanization of environment and build a social framework for a synthesis of man's external and inner dimensions.[30]

If this social framework for a new synthesis will be elaborated within the United States, Americans could not only restore their prestige in the world community but also contribute to the decrease of neo-nationalism in our global village. It is not generally recognized that the conflict between culture and civilization in its universal dimension is related to the well-known phenomenon of the revival of nationalisms. The Anglo-Saxon reader is usually familiar with all kinds of social and international dramas brought about by the excesses of nationalisms, but is not equally well informed about the causes of the current growth of nationalisms. He is inclined to believe that the causes of nationalistic ferment are basically economic and political.

However, it is easy to observe that beside countries which were deprived of independence by Soviet expansion and the newly awakened countries of the Third World, there are several nations in the western hemisphere which have lived more or less harmoniously within the frames of larger political organisms but are desperately fighting for independence. Within the political boundaries of the affluent part of the globe the Irish, Flemish, Baskian, Quebecian and Scottish independence movements cannot be explained solely as responses to economic and political oppression. In part, these smaller nations are attempting to preserve their <u>cultural</u> identity which is threatened by the ubiquitous penetration of modern civilization. Therefore, one of the greatest tasks before us is to reconcile the independent growth of national cultures and the progress of world civilization.

The humanistic ideal of education is to develop all human potentialities individually and generally. However, there are various philosophies of education and it is a moral duty of contemporary sociologists to consider and support those forms of education which can most effectively defend humankind against the processes of depersonalization which result from the domination of culture by civilizations. To make this statement clearer, we have to say that that which is forming a greatness of civilization, like the highest achievements of technology (e.g., the steps beyond the orbit of Earth, electronic microscopes or radar telescopes) do not effect our everyday life and do not play a negative role in our personal development. Only by-products of these great steps of civilization before which we are yielding to the most appalling forms of vulgar materialism, at home and in social life.

Paul Tillich cogently observes that "the revolutionary movements of the 20th century tried to return to the medieval combination of technical with inductive education".[31] This is a cultural task of humanistic sociologists: to defend the ideal of humanistic type of education in opposition to the present trend which is evident not only in totalitarian states but in the pragmatically oriented schooling programs of democracies as well.

Humanistic sociologists should help deepen the understanding of the significance of national cultures within a framework of global civilization because, even though national cultures contribute to the growth of different value-systems (or at least different hierarchies of values), they nevertheless constitute the only viable ground for the cultivation of humane values and the growth of humanist culture. The 'world culture' is nothing else but a great treasure of the best cultural values and goals produced by national cultures.

CHAPTER XI FOOTNOTES

1. Michael Katz, Class, Bureaucracy and Schools: The Illusion of Educational Change in America (New York: Praeger Publishers, 1973), p. 124.

2. Thorstein Veblen, The Higher Learning in America: A Memorandum on the Conduct of Universities by Business Men (New York: B. W. Auebsch, 1918).

3. Joel H. Spring, Education and the Rise of the Corporate State (Boston: Beacon Press, 1972), p. 149.

4. G. Bruce Dearing, "Education for Humane Living in an Age of Automation", in William W. Brickman and Stanley Lehrer, eds., Automation, Education and Human Values (New York: School and Society Books, 1966), p. 99.

5. For an understanding of the philosophical and social ethos behind his educational views, see John Dewey, Democracy and Education (New York: Macmillan Company, 1916).

6. Jacques Ellul, The Technological Society (New York: Vintage Books, 1967), p. 348.

7. For an account of the Paris protest, see The New York Times (April 12, 1976), p. 1.

8. Erich Fromm, foreward to A. S. Neill, Summerhill: A Radical Approach to Child Rearing (New York: Hart Publishing Company, 1960), p. x.

9. A. S. Neill, ibidem. For other statements of an humanistic educational perspective, see Ivan Illich, Deschooling Society (New York: Harper and Row, 1971); Paul Goodman, The Community of Scholars (New York: Random House, 1962) and Compulsory Miseducation (New York: Horizon Press, 1964).

10. Carl R. Rogers, Freedom to Learn (Columbus, Ohio: Charles E. Merrill Publishing Company, 1969), p. 304.

11. Judith Wechsler, "Some Thoughts About the Humanities at M.I.T.", in Phillip C. Ritterbush, Technology as Institutionally Related to Human Values (Washington, D.C.: Acropolis Books, Ltd., 1974), p. 29.

12. Burton R. Clark, Educating the Expert Society (San Francisco, California: Chandler Publishing Company, 1962), pp. 290-291.

13. John Martin Rich, Humanistic Foundations of Education (Worthington, Ohio: Charles A. Jones Publishing Company, 1971), pp. 309-319.

14. Rose explicates the inevitable relationship between scientific activity and social repercussions. See David J. Rose, "Engineers and Humanists", in Phillip C. Ritterbush, op. cit., pp. 19-23.

15. Don K. Price, "Science and Technology in a Democratic Society: Educating for a Scientific Age", in Kingman Brewster, et al., Educating for the Twenty-first Century (Urbana: University of Illinois Press, 1969)

16. For a summary of the proceedings and policies at the Woods Hole Conference, see Jerome S. Bruner, The Process of Education (Cambridge, Massachusetts: Harvard University Press, 1962).

17. Glenys G. Unruh, Responsive Curriculum Development: Theory and Action (Berkeley, California: McCutchan Publishing Company, 1975), p. 55.

18. John L. Reed, The Newest Whore of Babylon: The Emergence of Technocracy (Boston: Branden Press, 1975), p. 179.

19. Max Weber, Wirtschaft and Gesellschaft, excerpted in H. H. Gerth and C. Wright Mills, From Max Weber: Essays in Sociology (New York: Oxford University Press, 1971), p. 243.

20. Victor C. Ferkiss, Technological Man: The Myth and Reality (New York: George Braziller, 1969). Ferkiss' book is particularly interesting for us because his goals are not far from ours. He, however, trusts technology in a way and to an extent which are in collision with our understanding of a humanistic model of man.

21. Peter Drucker in his The Age of Discontinuity (New York: Harper and Row, 1968) pointed out four important discontinuities, which eight years later Willis W. Harmon found obsolete "because new discontinuities have appeared", that are at least as significant as the ones he [Drucker] had identified. See: Willis W. Harmon, An Incomplete Guide to the Future (San Francisco: Book Company, Inc., 1976), p. 2.

22. Thorsten Husen, Education in the Year 2000 (Stockholm: National Board of Education, 1971).

23. Bogdan Suchodolski, *Problem Wychowania i cywilizacji nowoczesnej* (Warszawa: PWN, 1974), p. 194.

24. *Ibidem*, p. 193.

25. Willis W. Harmon, *op. cit.*, p. 123.

26. Oswald Spengler, *Der Untergang des Abendlandes* (Munich, 1918).

27. Alfred Weber, "Principielles zur Kultursoziologie: Gessellschaftsprozess, Zivilizationsprozess und Kulturbewegung", *Archiv fur Sozialwissenschaft und Sozialpolitik*, vol. 47 (1920).

28. Gunther Remmling wrote that "Philosophical and historical analysis has its own evolutionary dynamics which Mannheim characterizes in analogy to Hegel as dialectical rational development in which problems not merely recur, but in which a succession of new systematizing centers of awareness provides them with novel modes of systematization and organization". *The Sociology of Karl Mannheim* (London: Routledge and Kegan-Paul, 1975), p. 33.

29. Zbigniew Brzezinski, *Between Two Ages, America's Role in the Technotronic Era* (New York: Viking Press, 1970), p. 272.

30. *Ibidem*, p. 270.

31. Paul Tillich, *Theology of Culture* (London, Oxford, New York: Oxford University Press, 1959), p. 146.

CHAPTER XII

CLOSING REMARKS

After having critically reviewed the present development of science, analyzing the humanistic elements in the works of four outstanding representatives of classical sociology and reflecting upon the current problems and trends in humanistic sociology, we are still not ready to give a recipe for the construction of a new system of humanistic sociology adequate for our epoch. Indeed, we do not feel that such a system is needed. What is actually needed, instead, is a further criticism of existing schools of sociology from the humanistic viewpoint and the introduction of the humanistic approach into present developments in sociology. The strictly humanistic field within the present body of sociological specializations should recieve the status of basic studies. It is the task and calling of humanistically oriented members of the sociological community to scrutinize current trends in the social sciences and to analyze the development of sociology as a component of a general intellectual endeavor. An effort must be made: to understand the phenomena of social life in its complexity going far beyond the nationalistic framework; to relate sociological developments to other social disciplines as well as to various achievements in both natural science and the humanities; and to study the responsive character of sociology in its relation to social, political, economic, and technological changes and processes. In addition to these tasks, humanistic sociologists should impregnate current sociological trends with philosophical reflection and defend the role of history as a background for analysis which, when neglected, usually creates many weaknesses in modern sociological thought.

A sociologist who strives to fulfill the role of a humanist in his discipline also has particular duties as a citizen. Because a humanist is a person who is concerned with human affairs in general, in our own time he must be particularly alert to many trends and events far beyond his own discipline. If sociology is to help address the global crisis which mankind is now facing, there are severla key problems which humanistic sociologists should undertake, all of which are related to the current process of transformation taking place throughout the entire world: the emergence of the global civilization out of the mixture of certain durable elements from declining local civilizations united through the network of science and technology.

To make our reasoning clear, we have to refer to the explantion made in Chapter XII. We distinguish there between culture and civilization saying that the term "culture" designates the sum total of individual and collective achievements of a spiritual nature, while civilization refers to the material hemisphere of human life, obtaining the sum total of material goods, organization of their production, and distribution.[1]

Another important distinction worth noting in this discussion is that between "local" and "global" civilization. Local civilizations created in the past in various regions of the earth are declining and forging a place for a global civilization which is developing for the first time in human history.

One does not need to be a prophet or futurologist to understand that the formative period of the global civilization will be very dramatic.

Generally we know the differences and relation between a local civilization and cultures developed within its frames. But even the most cogent studies of these relations cannot tell us about future relations between 'global civilization' and national cultures. Is a 'global _culture_' possible and could it develop parallel to the global civilization?

The tensions and crises caused by the atrophy of old civilizations and the struggle for survival of national cultures may bring the most horrifying conflicts. The wave of neo-nationalisms observable in our days is not only a reaction against the coming Unavoidable. It is stimulated above all by a conflict between national cultures of the old world and the expanding global civilization. It is amazing how this conflict develops unnoted by columnists and unrecognized by political scientists.

The conflict has many dimensions. One of the most interesting for humanistic sociologists is that, while we can more or less foresee the structure of global civilization (i.e., the world equalized and somehow united in the basis of modern technology and scientific know-how), no one as yet knows how to produce "global Culture". Mass culture is not a substitute for actual culture. The problem is whether the Culture (conceived as a set of values and norms which form the framework for spiritual life and creativity, expressed in the works of great writers, thinkers, poets and artists), may be produced without the background of national tradition. Thousands of years of historical experience have taught us that cultural values and goals are products of national life. We can speak of "universal" or "global" culture as the sum total of national cultures only. Therefore, a great problem of the future is to recognize and protect nationally rooted cultures within the frames of global civilization.

We know that science and technology have no national character. Although they can be more highly developed under one set of socio-historical conditions than another, they cannot be closed by the boundaries of any political system for very long. They are born out of cultural contacts, exchange, and the shared experience of many nations. Thus, science and technology are universal by their very nature.

In the developing global civilization, the role and function of science and technology are becoming as dominant ideologically and socially as religion was in the past. Despite the different nature and purpose of science and tehcnology, they began to form an undividable complex: one cannot advance without the other. But, can the techno-scientific complex produce substitutes for those spheres of human needs and cravings which have been satisfied by cultural creativity?

Similar to science and technology, most religious and political ideologies, although produced in the womb of one or another nation, usually have a stronger or weaker tendency to spread beyond national boundaries and form religious or ideological blocs.

The matter is different in the case of culture. Marx's 19th-century ideology was successfully adopted (with certain adjustments) even in 20th-century China. But a similar planting of Goethe's poetry or Mozart's music in Chinese soil would not be possible because cultural development is dependent upon and closely linked to national character not only by tradition but often by psychic and physiological characteristics. Therefore, the unification of culture is incomparably more complex and difficult than that of civilization.

Although the possibility of unification of national cultures into one global culture belongs to a far and not yet visible future, one aspect of this larger problem has the most significant meaning for our period of great transition. It is the problem of common values in various national cultures. The 19th- and 20th-centuries' cultural and ethical relativism has been blocking the sociological imagination in this field.

There is now time to realize that we can no longer pay deference to the positivistic slogan that there is no logical passage from statements about facts to statements about values. It is unimportant whether the links between facts and values have logical or extra-logical character, and this is not the place for such a discussion. What is essential for us to understand is that this old idea of David Hume played a significant role in the epoch when science began to liberate itself from the domination of religion and the control of the Church, because it served as a shield for scientists in all areas where scientific exploration was suspected to undermine religious views. However, now the situation is entirely changed. Science has won the greatest prestige comparable to that of religion during the Middle Ages. Taking this fact into account, we should consider the possibility of a scientific search for a certain fundamental set of values common for all humankind; because if a set of core values of universal meaning for social welfare would be pointed out with the help of science, they would be respected like religious values were respected in the epoch dominated by religion.[2]

However, one can say that epochs ruled by religious values were in many respect more inhumane than our secular age. But the answer is that the values which great religions brought about were not responsible for the cruelty of the past, but rather the historical circumstances, prejudices, and the level of cultivation of human societies. So, we should not be afraid of general acceptation of some core values, especially if they will be carefully reflected in scientific procedure as those which do not limit people's independence but help individual growth and harmony of societal life.

The positivists' belief that the relativism of intrinsic values is so great that we cannot find any value or norm accepted by all people in all times should be empirically verified before we accept it. Until now, this conviction has been based only on fragmentary ethnographic and cultural-anthropoligical studies which focused on cultural differences. It is more probable that, through the use of modern technology and research devices, today we can successfully search for a set of common core values. However, we should make it clear: we do not suggest finding or establishing <u>one system</u> of values for all mankind. This could lead first to world totalitarianism and, in consequence, to the total atrophy of culture. What seems most worthy of scientific exploration is: (1) what is common to all value-systems; and (2) which social values are most directly related to the cravings and needs of the human personality, as Robert Lynd proposed it thirty years ago.[3]

Of course, a thousand doubts and questions may be raised. What is personality? How many types of personality exist? Do they share similar cravings? Does not the hierarchy of cravings vary from person to person? The answers to these fully appropriate questions depend upon the level of reduction. For example, there are as many personalities as there are people. Each personality, therefore, is unique and humanists should have a particular respect for this uniqueness. Here, however, we are looking only for those basic elements which are common for all people. Just as the basic physical characteristics are shared by Homo sapiens-- each must breathe, act, and rest--so too there exist certain shared psychic and social characteristics. And it is time now to call for a grand interdisciplinary research on a global scale in order to discover the fundamental relations between these human characteristics and a set of core values which people have to respect if they want to survive.

The modern idea of relativism imposed upon our intellectual community a conviction that any search for universals is a regression into medieval philosophy, that it creates a threat to freedom and undermines the great idea of relativism itself. But this is only one more of our "scientific" prejudices. A knowledge of universals is just as important as the knowledge of relativity in the social and cultural world. One idea should not replace or remove the other. Because relativity exists parallel to universality, they are recognizable on different levels of reduction.

The philosophical search for universals in the past was determined by historical conditions. Medieval Europe was virtually a closed fortress, a hemisphere of one Christian system of beliefs braided with Greco-Latin culture. Later, the idea of relativism was fed by geographical discoveries and related ethnographical studies. It became dogma under the influence of the 'theory of relativity', and although this theory was formulated for the explanation of natural phenomena again the prestige of natural sciences called upon the fate of social sciences.

In this way the great idea of cultural relativism began to stretch beyond its own field and has been identified with an ideology called ethical relativism. Today, however, the developing "global village" inclines us, for practical reasons, to think more about that which is common to humanity than about that which divides it. Conditions are incomparably better at the present time to undertake a search for social universals than those under which the scholastics labored in their search for philosophical universals.

It would be great naivete to believe that scientific findings of such a set of core values with the prestige of science behind them can bring us to the core of totally peaceful and harmonious life on the earth. The human free will should not and even cannot be limited; it always will be a source of conflicts and upon conflicts essential progress is dependent. However, in our time of great transition some general frames of human activity are as needed as red and green lights on highways in the hour of heavy traffic.

Today, as never in human history, a chance exists that with the help of contemporary mass communication media, computer data processing and instantaneous knowledge-retrieval systems, our search for human nature, personality, and social values, if taken on a global scale, could allow us to reduce human behaviors and beliefs to common denominators, which we call "core values" of human existence. These findings might eventually aid us in securing the old humane dream of a peaceful world where, despite the plurality of cultures, people have respect for one another. The urgent need of a sociological search for common values is becoming more obvious if we keep in mind the seriousness of a new political tension growing within our global village.

Among the causes of international tensions of our time, one which should be considered by humanistic sociology is the question of how to protect the grassroots of Culture. The answer may be found only in the cooperation of sociologists and political scientists, because this question is realted to the political problem of the domination of many relatively unadvanced nations by the few advanced nations. The lopsided economic and technological progress of the advanced nations in comparison to those less technologically developed reminds us of Malthus' view on the growth of population and food which is geometrical on one side and arithmetic on the other. Small and poor nations cry about the imperialism of the big and rich because economically less advanced nations are not always culturally unadvanced. The actual situation is often reversed. Small and poor nations resent the imperialism of the big and rich nations partially because the former are often culturally more advanced. The mass culture, a product of the giant techno-industrial complexes of super-powers, is threatening cultural development in all smaller nations. Over four centuries ago, Nicolas Copernicus discovered that less valuable currency tends to displace more valuable currency within the marketplace. (This is known in the history of economics as "Gresham's Law".) Contemporary sociologists could apply this law to the cultural market where the products of mass culture are displacing the products of authentic cultures. This is one reason for the antagonistic posture of developing nations toward encroaching superpowers, even if the latter offer them enormous economic aid as in the case of the Marshall Plan for West European nations or the case of American aid for Third or Fourth World countries. (Of course, in these cases it is only *one* of the essential causes.) The need to maintain cultural identity is motivated not only by the threat of mass culture but, above all, by a more rudimentary concern for the negative impact of growing techno-scientific civilization on local value systems.

Each national value system is determined by group life-conditions on the one hand and a religious and philosophical tradition on the other hand. Therefore, they are not monolithic. For example, in all European national value-systems for centuries a mixture of the secular element originating in the Greek tradition with religious values of the Christian tradition is evident. Value-systems of several nations belonging to the same circle of civilization are distinguishable mainly by a different accentuation or different hierarchization of the same or quite similar values. Nations which belong to different civilizations are more essentially divided by their value-systems.

In our world full of conflicting interests and political tensions, a new line of division is growing. This is due to the bare fact that most of the yet-unexhausted minerals needed for maintaining industrial production of the advanced countries lie in the soil of the developing countries. Very soon they will be tempted to exploit their former exploiters as ruthlessly as they were in the past. Is a new age of wars, conquests and the code of brute strength unavoidable?

The alternatives should be found by these countries which for centuries have enjoyed privileged conditions of development. On the one hand they are guilty of exploitation of the weaker countries, but on the other hand they produced the highest forms of civilization and some of culture. If in the appearance of the global civilization one can see a hope, it is yet a long way to its peaceful civilization. Nevertheless, humanistic sociologists should visualize the emerging new situation. The global civilization can save us by solving dramatic international conflicts and mitigate the calamities brought about by exhaustion of resources only if some set of universal values will be found and supported by the prestige of science as the old value-systems within particular national cultures were supported by religion and national tradition.

In the world-wide discussion on the first and second Report of the Club of Rome, in one of the most interesting and convincing criterion of both reports, Eric Ashby, a great British naturalist, set forth statements which particularly fit to our way of reasoning. He writes,

> I suggest that one important--I would call it essential--educational response to the threatened shortages of non-removable resources is to provide, for industry and government service, men who can establish a rapport with those countries which are likely to become the capitalists of the 21st century, a rapport based not just on trading for their cobalt or tin or phosphate or oil, but on sympathetic understanding of their style of life.[4]

In closing this work devoted to the defense of the humanistic approach in sociology, we must express a kind of apology to science as far as it can be free from positivistic bias. The integration of science with the humanistic perspective is necessary for our earthly salvation.

It should be made clear that the transcendental type of humanism (see Chapter I) has never been in conflict with science (though it is in opposition to scientism). The same is true of technology insofar as it does not become an ideology. If transcendental or anti-naturalistic humanism finds the essence of humanness in mankind's permanent effort to overstep the limits of its earthly nature and the physical environment of a given time, then, from a humanistic viewpoint, an uninterrupted effort of scientists to go beyond the present horizon must be recognized as the most human enterprise.

The present-day humanist should not simply condemn science for the social injustices stemming from the application of scientific developments to capitalist forms of industry; rather, he should defend science against the encroachments of industry and the technocratic mentality. We should not forget the central lesson of the 19th century that social evils were caused by the egoistic application of science and technology to industry for the extension of income and benefits of the capitalist-industrial establishment and not by the rapid growth of science itself.

We are also aware of a growing wave of scepticism toward the scientific achievements of our times even among those who are not looking at it from a strictly humanistic perspective. A legitimate question is whether the scientific-technological progress of today is in a collision with the progress of human beings or not? Day after day newspapers and TV news are learning information about conflicts with or collision between the application of some new products of techno-scientific industry (pharmacists, chemical or energetic) and the interest of men and their natural environment. Under heavy criticism are preparations of national budgets: those for scientific discoveries and those for direct human needs.[5] The most common is the fear of possible "scientific" intervention into human genetic heritage. For the first time the problem, 'what is the human being in its essense', appears as a practical question.

These views on the role of science in present times inclines us to support a new rationalism which takes into account human sentiments, the irrational aspects of behavior, psychic and psychological needs, and the power of emotions because these are dynamic forces of culture. Therefore, humanistic sociologists should study this complexity of social reality which, to a large extent, is created by modern science.

In Greek mythology Prometheus delivered to the people the art of fire stolen from the house of Hephaestos and Athens. However, Zeus realized that it is not enough to endow people with fire which is the base of all technology. He knew that they also needed some basic elements of morality in order to live together and survive. Plato expressed the essence of the old myth concerning the origin of moral and legal order:

> ...the desire of self-preservation gathered them into cities; but when they were gathered together, having no art of government, they entreated one another, and were again in process of dispersion and destruction. Zeus feared that the entire race would be exterminated, and so he sent Hermes to them, bearing reverence and justice to be the ordering principles of cities and the bonds of friendship and conciliation. Hermes asked Zeus how he should impart justice and reverence among men:--Should he distribute them as the arts are distributed; that is to say, to a favoured few only, one skilled individual having enough of medicine or of any other art for many unskilled ones? "Shall this be the manner in which I am to distribute justice and reverence among men, or shall I give them to all?" "To all", said Zeus; "I should like them all to have a share; for cities cannot exist, if a few only share in the virtues, as in the arts. And further, make a law by my order, that he who has no part in reverence and justice shall be put to death, for he is a plague of the State".[6]

In other words, science and technology are indispensable tools if we are to successfully meet the coming world crisis. However, without a humanistic approach and the infusion of humanistically informed knowledge, the proliferation of the techno-scientific complex may result in the emergence of an inhuman civilization.

CHAPTER XII FOOTNOTES

1. It seems worth knowing that Pufendorf, in his efforts to use the term <u>culture</u> as an independent notion and not only in its Latin sense, contrasted <u>culture</u> and <u>nature</u> just as we are contrasting it with civilization. See: Samuel Pufendorf, <u>De jure naturae et gentium</u> (London: Scanoruin, 1672; Oxford: Clandon Press, 1934).

2. Aleksander Gella, "Can Our Search for Social Values Be Supported by Science", <u>Organon</u>, 1968.

3. Robert Lynd, <u>Knowledge For What?</u> (Princeton: Princeton University Press, 1939).

4. Eric Ashby, "A Second Look at Doom", <u>Encounter</u>, p. 21.

5. Lubbe, <u>Tages-Anzeiger</u>, January 4th, 1977.

6. Plato, "Protagoras", <u>The Works of Plato</u>, Selected and Edited by Irwin Edman, (New York: The Modern Library, 1928), p. 208-209.

APPENDIX

THE HUMANISTIC TREND IN RECENT SOCIOLOGICAL THEORY: A GUIDE TO THE ISSUES AND LITERATURE

Sociology must be defined by the questions it asks, both those that are trans-historical and those that our contemporary history 'places on the agenda' for us. A subtle interplay between the trans-historical problems and their embodiment in the structure of the historical individuals we directly confront is the hallmark of the work of the great theorists of the recent past. The requirements of this interplay make the abstract, logically formal models we find in physics of only secondary relevance to our particular enterprise. It therefore seems to me a grave error if sociologists create a model of human nature, even if they do so with heuristic intent, that is, in effect, a caricature.

Dennis Wrong[1]

The Question of Human Nature

"What is Man?" Most of the representatives of the 'classic tradition' in sociology felt the question posed by the Hebrew prophet, Job, warranted their attention. However, the generation that followed did not share this priority. Indeed, in the era dominated by what Rollo May has referred to as the "methodolatry" of logical positivism, a sociologist could not raise such a question without risking scorn.[2] 'Antiquated', 'pre-scientific', 'philosophical': these were the labels that were likely to be pejoratively appended to the work of any intrepid inquirer who defied this convention. But, as Karl Mannheim has pointed out, the logical positivists could not escape the problems of philosophy simply be issuing a proclamation abolishing them.[3] Whether the sociologist overtly examines the image of humankind that lies at the center of his or her work or covertly smuggles it in through the medium of metaphor or the method of operationalism, it is this image which largely determines the character of the theories he or she will construct. The late Ernest Becker emphasized this point when he wrote:

> ...the shape of our science must be largely influenced by the Image of Man as its center. Say that man is good--and you have one kind of social theory; say that he is bad--and you have a philosophy that more or less determines how you will formulate your hypotheses about man and society...whatever progress we might be making in theoretical and empirical work, as solid as it might seem, is being constructed on a base of shifting sand. Without an agreed portrait of basic human nature, our best theoretical and empirical work is rootless, anecdotal, disjointed, peripheral. And even worse: it is based on an image that is implicit, disguised, ideological. In a word, it is the erection of a scientific edifice on an unexamined central core, a heap of fact, theory and data that reposes on an unexamined belief...The fact is that the science of man _began_ with this question, and must one day return to it--or expire because of betrayed hopes.[4]

Dennis Wrong also underscores the importance of examining the role conceptions of human nature play in sociological theory. Wrong contends, "I cannot conceive of any sociological theory or interpretation, as distinct from sheer description and reporting of data, that does not rely at least implicitly on such assumptions".[5] By emphasizing the learning of theoretical assumptions on the methods of measuring socio-cultural phenomena, Aaron Cicourel extends the horizon of our argument: "I further assume--as suggested by Dennis Wrong's excellent paper--that any views on method and measurement presuppose a certain kind of actor..." (p. 189).[6]

In this epilogue we will examine some of the models of human nature which have been incorporated in the writings of the representatives of several influential schools of sociological or social psychological thought. In locating the concerns we have professed in this book within the context of the dialogue of recent theoretical discourse, we paint in very bold strokes. We therefore acknowledge that the comrades we embrace may not always be comfortable in our arms. The particulars of our respective definitions of a humanistic sociology may differ and some of us may disagree on the proper role of a humanistic sociology in confronting contemporary world problems. Nevertheless, we will attempt to show that during the past decade there has been a dramatic decline in enthusiasm among Western sociologists for the elaboration of conceptual systems in which humankind is depicted as the passive victim of external forces. Conversely, there is evidence that an increasing number of sociologists endorse theoretical perspectives which portrary the human actor as a creative agent who in interaction with others plays an active role in the construction of social reality. Thomas Wilson has described this shift in terms of the Kuhnian thesis characterizing it as a paradigmatic shift from a "normative" to an "interpretive" discipline matrix--a transition from a paradigm which emphasizes (a) the concensus of externalized norms, and (b) presupposes that sociological explanation should follow the deductive form characteristic of the nature sciences; to a paradigm which (a) conceives of "interaction as an essentially interpretative process in which meanings evolve and change over the course of interaction", and (b) holds that "depictions of interaction in terms of the meanings of the actions whether these depictions be the participants own or the researchers, must be construed as intepretive descriptions" therefore "the characteristics of interpretive description are incompatible with the logic of deductive reasoning".[7] That is, "interpretive" sociologists have rediscovered the problem of reification.[8] They are now in the process of attempting to escape the delusion that the ship is the port.[9] Therefore, they have made a deep methodological commitment to study social phenomena on its own terms: to use observational procedures and analytic tools which retain "the integrity of the phenomena". Michael Phillipson, a phenomenological sociologist, describes his understanding of the imperatives of this new commitment from the perspective of his own theoretic stance:

> In developing new methods of investigation and in rephrasing sociological questions Wright Mills' exhortation to sociologists again become relevant; in recommending avoidance of the "fetishism of method and technique" he suggests the following precept:
>
>> 'Let every man be his own methodologist, let every man be his own theorist; let theory and method again become part of a craft.'
>
> Abandoning the dogma of conventional theory and method in favour of the open horizons of phenomenological sociology facilitates the implementation of Wright Mills' exhortation.[11]

We regard the growing support of the "interpretive paradigm" as a <u>potential</u> harbinger of the advent of the era of creative growth in sociology prophetisized by P.A. Sorokin.[12] Less equivocably, we see this development as part of the broad movement to "rehumanize" science and culture which has been so eloquently described by Polanyi, Maslow and Matson. Therefore, despite the many issues dividing the partisans of these viewpoints, we regard such recent developments in sociological theory as the formulation of the dramaturgical approach, the emergence of ethnomethodology, the regeneration of symbolic interactionism, and the rediscovery of the young Marx and Alfred Schutz by critical and phenomenological sociologists, respectively, as sharing a common concern with what might be called the "liberation" of the image of humankind from the constraints which were imposed upon the range of sociological discourse by the dominance of the organismic and mechanistic image of man promulgated by the positivistic, neo-positivistic, and behavioristic schools of sociology.

As humanistic sociologists we celebrate the emergence of a sociological paradigm which champions a transcendent image of humankind: a holistic image in which man's distinctly human capacities, needs and aspirations occupy center stage. We share Lewis Mumford's conviction that:

> Not the Power Man, not the Profit Man, not the Mechanical Man, but the Whole Man, Man in Person, so to say, must be the central actor in the new drama of civilization...If technics is not to play a wholly destructive part in the future of Western Civilization we must now ask ourselves, for the first time, what sort of society and what kind of man are we seeking to produce?[13]

Our own epistemological reservations regarding the normative approach were shared by Kurt Riezler. In <u>Man: Mutable and Immutable</u>, written over a quarter of a century ago, he presented an eloquent critique of the prevailing currents of modern scholarship which discard

> ...eternal man and cut mutable man into pieces to be inquired into by different sciences, each of which claims autonomy. The pieces fit into one another less and less. A relatively immutable remnant, called human nature, is left to the care of a biology that speaks the language of physics and chemistry. In this language, the mammal we call Man is meaningless to himself.[14]

> The science of man today defines science by the
> scientific method...The results of this science
> of man are meager. Sooner or later people will
> inquire whether such meagerness is really due
> merely to the youth of this scientific enter-
> prise or not rather to the dictates of a method
> that disregards the specific nature of the sub-
> ject matter, or perhaps even to some meta-physical
> assumption inherent in the method.[15]

But, if we have learned anything from Dilthey, Weber, Sorokin, Znaniecki, Mannheim, and the great tradition of humanism which they represent it is to deplore all absolutist claims. Thus, we assert no claim to a hegemony of theoretic perspective, method, model or set of priorities. Unlike Ernest Becker, we contend that a fully humanistic perspective defends the co-exis- tence of a diversity of 'images' of human nature within sociologi- cal scholarship for <u>the contingency of being is a "base of shifting sand"</u>.[16] With Max Weber, we profess a "polytheism of values". We share the conviction of his colleague, Ernst Troeltsch, that truth manifests itself in many different "forms and kinds".

We see the Schutzian conception of "multiple realities" as largely in harmony with this perspective. The most significant contribution of the ethnomethodologists may be their effort to sensitize students of society to the profound significance of the multiple reality thesis, i.e., Harold Garfinkel's early writ- ings. Erving Goffman's much neglected <u>Frame Analysis</u> (1974) adds depth to this thesis by providing a provocative survey of some of the realities of being, 'everyday life', dreams, rituals, fictive planes, etc., which man-in-person, "someone of particular biographical identity" inhabits.[17] If reality is multi-dimensional and 'truth' is multi-form common-sense dictates that we should attempt to approach social reality from as many different vantage points and with as many different tools as possible. Paul Feyera- bend's espousal of an "anarchy of method" not only seems warranted, but when viewed in this context, his 'radical' program can be regarded as a moderating force--a prophylaxis against the prolifer- ation of uni-dimenisional accounts. Within recent sociological discourse, the perspective of the sociology of everyday life and ethnomethodology have presented the most comprehensive accounts of the way in which neo-positivistic methods of sociological analy- sis simplify or "gloss" the complexity of social phenomena. Aaron Cicourel's attempt to develop a sociology of language and meaning seems especially relevant to our concerns: particularly, his ef- forts to disentangle the perspective of the observer from the observed; his attempt to extend Frake's conception of "contrastive analysis"; and his own notion of "indefinite triangulation".[18]

We remind the reader of our earlier endorsement of Santayana's dictum: humanism always identifies with the suppressed sides of human nature therefore as the ruling conventions change, the humanist's sympathies must also change. Thus, while the 'interpretive' model of man has received relatively little systematic articulation in American sociology during the past half-century, we acknowledge that it is conceivable but most unlikely[19] that the pendulum could swing too far in that direction. Certainly the Promethean image of man was overelaborated in extreme forms of German idealism as Dilthey, Weber, and Simmel readily acknowledged. Similarly, the 'reflexivity' which contemporary phenomenological sociologists have introduced into sociological discourse degenerates into solipsism when pursued to excess for "Methodological self-consciousness that is full, immediate, and persistent sets aside all study and analysis except that of the reflexive problem, thereby displacing fields of inquiry instead of contributing to them".[20] But we do not believe the current period of theoretical and methodological self-consciousness is merely an orgy of "bizarre navel-gazing".[21] Rather we maintain that it can be a period of renewal and growth. It is in this spirit that we proceed with our description of several families of the modern species, "Homo Sociologicus".[22]

Behavioristic and Normative Paradigms: The Manufacture of Homonucleus

Behaviorism emerged as a protest against the 'introspective' schools which had strongly influenced nineteenth century psychology and sociology. As such, it may be conceived as a deliberate inversion of the program for the human studies outlined by Wilhelm Dilthey and Max Weber.

John B. Watson issued the clarion call for the development of behaviorism in 1913 with the publication of "Psychology as a Behaviorist Views It". Pavlov's discovery of the conditioned reflex served as Watson's immediate inspiration. Watson urged modern psychology to abandon all concern with mentalistic concepts and images including introspection and the study of consciousness and its contents. He maintained, "'consciousness' is neither a definable or usable concept...it is merely another word for the 'soul' of more ancient times".[23] Watson called upon psychologists to limit their study to "things that can be observed and formulate laws concerning only those things".[24]

The pioneers of behaviorism believed their enterprise would bring about a revolution in human knowledge--in the enthusiastic words of Clark Hull, "a development comparable to that manifested by the physical sciences in the age of Copernicus, Kepler, Galileo, and Newton".[25] This revolutionary breakthrough was thought to be contingent upon the assumption of an objectivist perspective.

Therefore, machine theory became the dominant paradigm (or metaphor) of the behaviorist outlook.[26] Watson, for instance, described man as "an assembled organic machine ready to run", while Hull exhorted his fellow psychologists to purge themselves of "anthropomorphic subjectivism" by adopting as a heuristic device the practice of regarding the object of their study--the human being--as "a completely self-maintaining robot, constructed of material as unlike ourselves as may be ".[27] Hull believed that ultimately mechanical laws underlying human behavior would be discovered and fully articulated through the language of mathematics.

The emphasis behaviorism placed upon objectivity, operationalism, and statistical analysis made it especially appealing to American sociologists who, like their colleagues in psychology, saw it as a means of achieving true scientific status. As early as the writing of Franklin Giddings, the impact of behaviorism on sociology was evident.[28] Even George Herbert Mead called himself a behaviorist but his version of behaviorism was far removed from that of his contemporary, Watson. Mead reflecting the tutelage of Wundt, attempted to integrate the concepts of attitude, motive and value into a theory derived from the observation of overt behavior.[29]

By the mid-1930's the influence of behaviorism upon sociology was so pervasive that Karl Mannheim expressed alarm at the fact that behaviorism had strongly encouraged the tendency to study only external factors and to "construct a world of facts in which there will exist only measurable data".[30] Mannheim prophesized, "It is possible, even probable, that sociology must pass through this stage in which its contents will undergo a mechanistic dehumanization and formalization, just as psychology did, so that out of devotion to an ideal of narrow exactitude nothing will remain except statistical data, tests, surveys, etc., and in the end every significant formulation of a problem will be excluded".[31]

The tendency to which Mannheim referred reached its classic expression in the programmatic volume of George Lundberg, <u>Can Science Save Us?</u> (1947). Lundberg called upon sociologists to mobilize their quantitative techniques and get on with the business of human engineering. When chided about his neglect of "the human factor", Lundberg responded, "We know what we know about these factors through observation of human behavior and what more we need or want to know is learned in that way and no other."[32] Science, he believed, would show that the human factor is, "no factor at all, but merely a vague word designating a great variety of behavior which social scientists have hitherto been too lazy or ignorant to approach by the same methods that have clarified the factors in other phenomena of nature".[33]

The model for science which Lundberg so enthusiastically celebrated was constructed by the Logical Positivists, Operationalists, and Neo-Pragmatists. In fairness, it should be noted that some of the finest philosophical minds of the twentieth century addressed themselves to the issues involved in formalizing the methodology of science and, similarly, that the most intelligent and severe criticism of Logical Positivism has come from those who have at one time or another been members of the movement. However, the model for science which sociologists and psychologists (largely at the behest of the influential Hull) imported for their purposes was at best a caricature of the already flawed original. Sigmund Koch maintains that it was the authority of these ideas not their content that appealed to psychologists: "The large methodological literature by which they were conveyed from the glittering areas of their origin to psychology was prescriptive and zealous but, when written by psychologists, marked by modest orders of philosophical sophistication...What seems to have been imparted to the typical psychologist might be characterized as an ocean of awe surrounding a few islands of sloganized information..."[34] Koch's remarks are, of course, equally applicable to sociologists especially those who in addition to Lundberg made up the vanguard of the sociologistic version of Logical Positivism--Dodd, Stouffer, Lewin, and J.F. Brown.[35]

Robert Friedrichs reports that shortly before Lundberg's death, the battle-weary champion of operationalism recognized Talcott Parsons as a theoretical "brother-in-arms".[36] Although Parsons' early work strongly reflected the humanistic influence of Weberian sociology, by 1953 he had abandoned this position to the point where he was willing to acknowledge that his theory of action could explain sub-human behavior and might be articulated in "modified behavioristic terms".[37]

The congruences of B.F. Skinner's psychology and George Homans' sociology have been widely commented upon. In his search for an alterntive to the discredited functionalist paradigm, Homans turned to behavioristic psychology. His conception of social behavior as an exchange involves a hedonistic notion remarkably similar to Skinner's pleasure-pain nexus. Homans maintains that the fundamental variables for social behavior will probably be derived from biology.[38]

The Neo-Behaviorism of B.F. Skinner openly espouses the manipulation and control of human behavior.[39] Skinner proposed an even more rigid definition of behavior than his predecessors and completely eliminated all reference to psychic events or inner states--in his lexicon, 'meaning', 'intent', and 'understanding' are obsolete terms. Skinner combats anthropomorphism by studying rats and pigeons. The rodent, he writes, "has the advantage over man of submitting to the experimental control of its drives and routines of living".[41] According to Skinner, the behaviorist must not only predict the future; he must control it in order to insure the "survival" of the species. He acknowledges that behaviorism is in conflict with a philosophy of personal freedom: "A scientific analysis of behavior disposes autonomous man and turns the control he has been said to exert over to the environment".[42] In the name of his own idiosyncratic version of humanism, Skinner announces, "It is the autonomous inner man who is abolished, and that is a step forward."[43]

Behaviorism has distinguished itself among 'schools' of learned thought by its seemingly unparalleled capacity to inspire controversy: some distinguished criticism, much bombast, and occasional intellectual distemper.[44] However, Koch contends that it will never be possible to present a "final and crushing refutation of behaviorist epistemology" because behaviorism is often advanced as a metaphysical position as well as a methodological thesis.[43] As a metaphysical thesis, it entails something like an inverted Kierkegaardian leap of faith--the true-believer simply maintains against all evidence that 'mind' does not exist. Koch argues that metaphysical as well as methodological behaviorism are fundamentally irrational positions which start with the denial of basic tenet of common-sense which can, "in the abstract, be 'rationally' defended for however long one wishes to persist in one's superordinate irrationality, but which cannot be implemented without brooking self-contradiction".[46] He believes that the nearest we can come to refuting behaviorism is to demonstrate such self-contradictions and thereby exhibit the shaky and sometimes ludicrous foundations upon which the vast apparatus of the behaviorist enterprise has been built.[47]

Michael Polanyi argues that all attempts to use mechanistic models to explain human learning must (i) limit the subject matter to the most rudimentary types of learning, and (ii) exploit the ambiguity inherent in the "impersonal terms" so that they will appear to apply to the activities of the living being who remains covertly in the mind of the experimenter.[48] The major critiques of behaviorism have revolved around these two points.

In his monumental work, The Act of Creation (1964), Arthur Koestler focuses upon the first point and demonstrates the total inadequacy of behavioristic approaches in attempting to deal with the phenomenon of creativity. Watson maintained that new verbal creations, poems, novels, and other literary forms are the result of a mere manipulation of words, of shifting elements about until a new pattern is hit upon. Guthrie regards the original solution to a problem as belonging within the province of 'luck' and therefore beyond the concerns of science. "Insight" is among the words banished from the Skinnerian vocabulary. In Skinner's view, the solution of novel problems is merely a matter of 'manipulating variables' which may lead to the 'emission of a new response'--it involves no new factor of originality. Koestler concludes that to the behaviorists creation is synonymous with manipulation, "a random activity, which, through elimination of useless movements by the trial-and-error method, gradually develops into ordered habits...It is expressly denied that...the poet, or painter has any 'picture of his mind' of the kind of thing he is planning; he simply goes on manipulating the units until the model, poem, or drama is 'hit upon'. At that moment the stimulus 'to arouse admiration and condemnation' ceases to be active, and manipulation stops--'the equivalence of the rat's finding food'."[49] In their zealous campaign to exorcise the anthropomorphic view of the rat from their laboratories, Koestler maintains that American psychologists "substituted the rattomorphic view of man".[50]

Joseph Wood Krutch (The Measure of Man, 1953) referred to the tendency to which Koestler alludes as indulging the "Idol of the Laboratory". The underlying assumption of this "Idol" is that any entity is illusionary unless it is amenable to measurement and experimentation by the same methods which have demonstrated their utility in dealing with mechanical phenomena. He maintains that many psychologists and sociologists denounce as an 'anthropomorphism' "every attempt to interpret even human behavior on the assumption that men are men".[51] Behavioristic methodologies required that they proceed as if humans were "animals at most, even if not mere machines in the end"--Krutch asks, "But how can Anthropos be understood except in anthropomorphic terms? Or should we assume that the mechanomorphic error is not really an error at all?"[52]

Some of the most outspoken criticism of behaviorism has come from within the ranks of psychology itself. The so-called "third force" (a large and loosely-knit group of individuals of highly diverse theoretical persuasions) who, under the leadership of the late Abraham Maslow and Carl Rogers, have vehemently fought the hegemony of the behaviorist paradigm within psychology.[53] However, many experimental psychologists have also decried the reductionism of extreme behaviorism. C.E. Osgood charged that, "Many present-day psychologists are loath to attribute to humans any characteristic that cannot be demonstrated in lower animals."[54] And, more than a half-century ago, Kurt Lashley warned, "the essence of behaviorism is the belief that the study of man will reveal nothing except what is adequately describable in the concept of mechanics and chemistry".[55]

In The Human Condition (1958), Hannah Arendt echoed a similar sentiment. She characterized the interdisciplinary reductionism of behaviorism as, "the all-comprehensive pretension of the social sciences which, as 'behavioral sciences', aim to reduce man as a whole, in all his activities, to the level of a conditioned and behaving animal".[56]

In his now classic essay reviewing B.F. Skinner's <u>Verbal Behavior</u>, Noam Chomsky addressed Michael Polanyi's second point carefully documenting the ways in which Skinner is led astray by his own verbal behavior. Others, of course, have noted Skinner's gymnastic jostlings with jargonese; however, Chomsky's exegesis is distinguished by the fact that its author is equipped with the linguistic tools which enable him to systematically and authoritatively unravel the tortured paths which words are forced to negotiate when they are translated into Skinnerisms. The object of Skinner's book is to offer a means to the prediction and control of 'verbal behavior' through the observation and manipulation of the external environment. Skinner minimizes the contribution of the speaker and maintains that precise prediction of verbal behavior involves merely the specification of a limited number of external factors that he has isolated experimentally in lower animals. Chomsky counters Skinner's claim with the statement that, "The magnitude of the failure of this attempt to account for verbal behavior serves as a kind of measure of the importance of the factors omitted from consideration, and an indication of how little is really known about this remarkably complex phenomena."[57] Chomsky's examination of Skinner's terminological transmogrifications of such concepts as "stimulus", "control", "response", and "strength" lead him to the conclusion that, "The way in which these terms are brought to bear on the actual data indicates that we must interpret them as mere paraphrases for the popular vocabulary commonly used to describe behavior, and as having no particular connection with the homonymous expressions used in the description of laboratory experiments. Naturally, this terminological revision adds no objectivity to the familiar 'mentalistic' mode of description".[58] Or, in popular vocabulary, Skinner's usage possesses no special claim to <u>scientific</u> authority and except for its extraordinary obtuseness, it does not differ from ordinary educated discourse.

In effect, critics argue that behaviorism, like positivism and physicalism, has imitated the methods but not the spirit of the natural sciences.[59] It has borrowed the apparatus, the jargon and the procedures, but in the process it has betrayed the integrity of the quest for truth unbound. Arthur Koestler ironically remarks that attempts to construct a universal theory of learning from observations of pigeons who have been taught to play ping-pong through the process of 'stamping-in' are in grevious "danger of confusing a travelling circus with Plato's Academy".[60]

Karl Mannheim presents a more sobering characterization of behaviorism. He draws an analogy between behaviorism and fascism: "It is not as though behaviorism itself is fascist, but rather that fascism in the political sphere is to a large extent behaviouristic...Fascism creates an apparatus of social coercion which integrates every possible kind of behavior or at least brings it into an external harmony by force. Fascism in its ideology eulogizes the instinctive forces in man, but in fact it does not penetrate to the depth of human personality or do justice to its genuine complexity. It has, however, an abstract ordering principle which changes man through the maximum combination of external coercion and suggestion with no wider aim than the regulation of outward behavior and the integration of the sentiments".[61] In a similar vein, Sigmund Koch points out that psychology is probably more influential than any other branch of the scholarly community in shaping humankind's image of itself. Yet, the image of human nature projected by modern psychology is demeaning and simplistic. He contends that psychology has played a significant role in implementing and supporting "the mass dehumanization process which characterizes our time--the simplification of sensibility, homogenization of taste, [and] attenuation of the capacity for experience".[62]

Behaviorism offers an external model for the explanation of internal phenomena--a physicalistic interpretation of mentalistic experience. The Existentialist, Albert Camus (whose Notebooks reveal that he was influenced by Dilthey) contends that, "Understanding the world for man is reducing it to the human, stamping it with his seal. The cat's universe is not the universe of the anthill. The truism 'All thought is anthropomorphic' has no other meaning. Likewise, the mind that aims to understand reality can consider itself satisfied only by reducing it to the terms of thought."[63] One of the recurrent themes of Camus' work is man's dependence upon and imprisonment in a physical body--he is keenly aware of the physical nature of man; but he argues that its study can never fully explain the 'human'. Polanyi goes a step further in the celebration of anthropomorphism: "Behaviorists teach that in observing an animal we must refrain above all from trying to imagine what we would do if placed in the animal's position. I suggest, on the contrary, that nothing at all could be known about an animal that would be of the slightest interest to physiology, and still less to psychology, except by following the opposite maxim of identifying ourselves with a centre of action in the animal and criticizing its performance by standards set up for it by ourselves."[64]

Whereas critics argue that behaviorism incorporates a debased conception of human nature; opponents of the normative perspective in sociology point out that the latter approach tends to ignore human nature almost entirely. The concept of 'human nature' was among the first sacrificial offering which neo-positivistic sociologies placed upon the altar of scientism. Words like 'system', 'pattern variables', 'motives', seemed to denote far more prestigious preoccupations.

By the late nineteen-fifties, however, a conviction was growing among some sociologists that the normative paradigm had degenerated into an empty scholasticism whereby not only the relevant problems of modern societies but also humankind itself had eluded the system-makers. Ralf Dahrendorf ("Out of Utopia: Toward a Reorientation of Sociological Analysis", 1959) contended that the obsessive concern with physicalism had deformed the discipline so completely that it had lost its "problem consciousness":

> Although what we still tend to call 'theory' has failed as miserably in tackling real problems as Plato's blueprint, we have so far not admitted defeat.
>
> The social system, like utopia, has not grown out of familiar reality. Instead of abstracting a limited number of variables and postulating their relevance for the explanation of a particular problem, it represents a huge and allegedly all-embracing superstructure of concepts that do not describe, propositions that do not explain, and models from which nothing follows. At least they do not describe or explain (or underline explanations of) the real world with which we are concerned.[65]

Dahrendorf concludes the 'social system' of the structural-functionalists is a utopia. But where literary utopias were at least expressions of moral critiques of existing societies; contemporary sociology surrendered all concern with moral imperatives in its pursuit of scientific respectability. The system-makers' inherent conservatism and corresponding complacency with the status quo denies their model of society of the humanism of more traditional genres of utopian critical thought.

Alfred Baldwin, who identifies Talcott Parson's work as representative of the approach of functionalist sociology and contemporary sociology (normative) in general, argues that,

> One consequence of his approach is that personality theory is not intrinsically very important to him [Parsons]. His real commitment is to the problem of stability and change in a complex social system, not the conceptualization of individual personality...From such a viewpoint the most relevant features of individual personality are those that effect his social functioning.[66]

But is was Dennis Wrong who sketched most deftly the profile of the functionalist actor as a passive pawn enmeshed in an omnipotent system. In commenting on Baldwin's remarks, Wrong outlines the essential features of the "oversocialized" view of humankind upon which the premises of normative sociology are founded:

> ...the tendency of structural-functional sociologists to stress the primacy of society and consensus on values over conflicts of interest and to define society itself as a 'boundary-maintaining system' with built-in processes preserving its equilibrium, inclines them to reliance on a generalized view of man as a thoroughly oversocialized, conformist creature. In this sense an oversocialized view of man complements the overintegrated conception of society in structural-functional theory that has been so roundly --and I think, effectively--criticized for its relative neglect of change, group conflict, and the role of coercion as opposed to consent in human society.[67]

Wrong does not confine his critique of scientific deformations of the image of humankind to normative sociology. He argues that the orthodox Marxist view is similarly vulnerable since "a Marxist view which treats the individual as the creature of his economic class and reifies 'history' as an all-determining entity in the same manner that Parsonians reify the 'social system', ultimately presents a no less oversocialized conception of human nature than structural-functionalism".[68]

Even George Homans engaged in the rhetoric of relevance upon abandoning the sinking ship of the structural-functionalists in order to embrace a behavioristic perspective. In his 1964 Presidential Address to the American Sociological Association entitled "Bringing Men Back In", Homans contends that the functionalists have never produced a theory that provides an explanation of the real behavior of human beings in society. He maintains that,

> If a serious effort is made to construct theories that will even begin to explain social phenomena, it turns out that their general propositions are not about the equilibrium of societies but about the behavior of men. This is true even of some good functionalists, though they will not admit it. They keep psychological explanations under the table and bring them out furtively like a bottle of whiskey, to use when they really need help.

> What I ask is that we bring what we say about
> theory into line with what we actually do
> and so put an end to our intellectual hypocrisy.[69]

Elsewhere, Homans points out the "Modern social science has been so sensitive to the charge that its findings are old and obvious, so ready to go out of its way to show how common-sense explanations are wrong, that it has ended by painting a picture of man that man cannot recognize".[70] Homans offers some sobering advice to theorists: "No one will go far wrong theoretically who remains in close touch with and seeks to understand a body of concrete phenomena."[71] As we have already emphatically indicated, we cannot share Homans' conviction that a behavioristic perspective can provide a viable solution to the dilemmas of the normative approach; we nevertheless recognize the lucidity of his description of those dilemmas.

With the publication of The Coming Crisis of Western Sociology (1970), Alvin Gouldner emerged as one of the most formidable critics of the structural-functionalist approach. He also regards Talcott Parsons as the chief dragon to be slain. On the question of human nature, Gouldner draws a parallel between the work of Parsons and Comte:

> Parsons, however, does not speak of 'human nature' but instead moves toward more behavioristic distinctions between types of social action. Insofar as these entail imputed states of mind they are not, of course, any more behavioristic or 'empirical' than attributes of human nature. The shift, however, does imply an emphasis on the great variety of concrete ends that men may pursue; it implies a drift toward a more relativistic image of man.
>
> Very importantly, it also implies a more sociologistic picture of man. While Parsons' voluntarism places a great importance on man's effort to realize certain ends, it is paradoxically true that these ends are no longer seen as derived from him; though they reside in him, they derive from social systems. Man is a hollowed-out, empty being filled with substance only by society. Man thus is seen as an entirely social being, and the possibility of conflict between man and society is thereby reduced. Man now has and is nothing of his own that need be counterposed to society.[72]

In a long neglected dialogue with the logical positivists, Alfred Schutz described sociologistic man as a unique species. Schutz annointed the abstraction which is the product of the generalizing process of the scientific enterprise, "homunculi".[73] Taking a leaf from the notebook of Alfred North Whitehead, Schutz reminds scholars of the limits of theory. He points out that our scientific models are inherently artificial and limited. Consonant with the tradition of Dilthey, Simmel, and Weber; Schutz emphasized that the observational field of the social scientist, unlike that of the natural scientist, is pre-structured: "It has a particular meaning and relevance structure for the human beings living, thinking, and acting therein."[74] Thus we cannot fully escape our own reflection in the mirrors of social reality we construct. Schutz maintains,

> ...these models of actors are not human beings living within their biographical situation in the social world of everyday life. Strictly speaking, they do not have any biography or any history, and the situation into which they are placed is not a situation defined by them but defined by their creator, the social scientist. He has created these puppets or homunculi to manipulate them for his purpose...It is...the social scientist, who sets the stage, who distributes the roles, who gives the cues, who defines when an 'action' starts and when it ends and who determines, thus, the 'span of projects' involved...In such a simplified model of the social world pure rational acts, rational choices from rational motives are possible because all the difficulties encumbering the real actor in the everyday life-world have been eliminated.[75]

Schutz draws an analogy between the relationship of the scientist and his puppet and the ancient problem of theology and metaphysics, the relationship between God and his creatures:

> The puppet exists and acts merely by grace of the scientist; it cannot act otherwise than according to the purpose which the scientist's wisdom has determined it to carry out. Nevertheless, it is supposed to act as if it were not determined consciousness bestowed upon the puppet and the pre-constituted environment within which it is supposed to act freely, to make rational choices and decisions. This harmony is possible only because both the puppet and its reduced

> environment, are the creation of the scientist.
> And by keeping to the principles which guided him,
> the scientist succeeds, indeed, in discovering
> within the universe, thus created, the perfect
> harmony established by himself.[76]

The implications of Schutz's work for sociology were not explored in any comprehensive way until the ethnomethodologists took up the cause. Harold Garfinkel, the grand satrap of the ethnomethodological enterprise, holds an image of humankind which is remarkably similar to and perhaps derivative of that of the great poets of the absurd, Baudelaire and Mallarme.[77] Like the poets, Garfinkel sees humankind entrapped in a cage of reason, the creator and creation of Logos. Garfinkel maintains that what we regard as objective characteristics of social reality are objective only because we choose to describe them in objective terms, i.e., in terms of their common properties.[78] These common properties do not necessarily inhere in the events or objects themselves, but are created through the process of description. Thus the established forms of sociological explanation must be seen as a coding vocabulary which accentuates the common properties of the phenomena of social reality and directs attention away from its unique properties. Garfinkel contends that this process of objectification is a feature of all explanation. In his view, the process of explanation is therefore synonymous with the process of constructing social reality: when members account for their actions in a rational way, they are thereby making those actions rational. It is only in this way that a coherent and comprehensible reality emerges. Viewed from this perspective, sociologistic man must be regarded as a particularly arrogant, yet naive and simplistic fiction. Garfinkel calls this fiction, "a cultural dope":

> By 'cultural dope' I refer to the man-in-the-
> sociologist's-society who produces the stable
> features of the society by acting in compliance with
> pre-established and legitimate alternatives of ac-
> tion that the common culture provides. The 'psy-
> chological dope' is the man-in-the-psychologist's-
> society who produces the stable features of the society
> by the choices among alternative courses of action
> that are compelled on the grounds of psychiatric bio-
> graphy, conditioning history, and the variables of
> mental functioning. The common feature in the use
> of these 'models of man' is the fact that courses
> of common sense rationalities of judgment which
> involve the person's use of common sense knowledge
> of social structures over the temporal 'succession'
> of here and now situations are treated as ephiphenomenal.[79]

Like Schutz and Garfinkel, Aaron Cicourel also expresses profound dissatisfaction with the image of humankind generated by the deductive systems of the behaviorists and functionalists.[80] Thus Cicourel points out that, "To assume that the only valuable framework is the one that imposes a denotative structure determined by the researcher and divorced from members' actual intention and usage reduces the actor to a rather simple 'dummy'."[81] The ethnomethodologists share Schutz's conviction that the data of sociology is of a different order than the data of the natural sciences and therefore requires a different set of methodological commitments and procedures. In this respect, their work can be seen as deriving from the humanistic tradition of Dilthey. However, most ethnomethodologists have yet to discover their ancestry. A humanistic sociology supports diversity and discourages intellectual imperialism. We recognize and respect some ethnomethodologists' desire to see their work as a separatist enterprise, i.e., Mehan and Wood conclude their recent introduction to ethnomethology by asserting,

> That my understanding is radically unlike contemporary social science seems a virtue to me. In commiting itself above all to reporting, social science has shown itself to be a form of life that denigrates the integrity of non-Western, nomale, nonliberal, nontechnological realities.
>
> My vision of ethnomethodology undermines this practice. I do not suggest that social scientists cease studying human phenomena, only that they begin to use methods that are more becoming to the mysterious phenomena ethnomethodology has unearthed. To become one's own phenomenon is such a method.[82]

Our interest in the implications of their work is born of desire to learn and share rather than to co-opt and conquer. We are in deep sympathy with Mehan and Wood's value commitments. And while we are aware of the limitations of the ethnomethodological perspective as it has been developed thus far,[83] we nevertheless endorse the exploratory spirit in which many of the inquiries are conceived. However, we also support with similar enthusiasm other efforts to discover an uncorrupted social science.

The Interpretative Paradigm and the Rediscovery of Homo Loquens

R.S. Broadhead contends that the extreme reaction against the oversocialized conception of man has produced its dialectical counterpart, the "undersocialized" conception of man present in certain recent versions of existential sociology.[84] While this may be a rhetorical overstatement, the emergence of the "interpretive" discipline matrix of sociology has been accompanied by the elaboration of "creative" images of human nature.[85] Within the theoretical frameworks of phenomenology, symbolic interaction, neo-symbolic interaction, ethnomethodology, and the 'sociology of the absurd'; the position of homunculi has been usurped by a model of an actor who is active in creating social reality through interpretive interaction with others.

During the ascendency of structural-functionalism, the Chicago School of Symbolic Interactionism became somewhat of a beseiged protectorate of the humanistic model of man.[86] Under the influence of Herbert Blumer, the Meadian conception of the "self" was counterposed against the deterministic stance of neo-positivism. Blumer unequivocably championed a voluntaristic perspective: "The human being is not a mere responding organism, only responding to the play of factors from his world or from himself; he is an acting organism who has to cope with and handle such factors and who, in so doing, has to forge and direct his line of action."[87] Ralph Turner further developed the notion of role-construction, which is present but not fully developed in Meadian social psychology. Turner emphasizes the creative and modifying aspect of "role-taking" and "role-making". Turner contrasts his approach with that which has currency within the normative approach: "The idea of role-taking shifts emphasis away from the simple process of enacting a prescribed role to devising a performance on the basis of an imputed other role."[88] Thus in his view, "The actor is not the occupant of a status for which there is a neat set of rules--a culture or set of norms--but a person who must act in the perspective supplied in part by his relationship to others whose actions reflect roles he must identify."[89] He therefore maintains, "it is this tendency to shape the phenomenal world into roles which is the key to role-taking as a core process of interaction".[90] However, it was Erving Goffman, whom Alvin Gouldner once referred to as "the William Blake of sociology", who played an especially crucial role in bringing sociologists back to the realities of everyday life and in pointing out that role construction takes place during the process of interactions.[91] Goffman focuses on the underside of the social system emphasizing the significance of individual skills of "impression management". He describes a model of the person who "gets by" in a dehumanized and alienated society. T.R. Young contends Goffman's work implies a critique of the conditions which make impression management (inauthenticity) necessary.[92] One does not have to search very far through the pages of the Goffman corpus to discover its inherent humanism: his empathy for those whose "masks" slip:

> In spite of the fact that performers and audience
> employ all of these techniques of impression
> management, and many others as well, we know, of
> course, that incidents do occur and that audiences
> are inadvertently given glimpses behind the scenes
> of a performance. When such an incident occurs,
> the members of an audience sometimes learn an
> important lesson, more important to them than the
> aggressive pleasure they can obtain by discovering
> someone's dark, entrusted, inside or strategic
> secrets. The members of the audience may discover
> a fundamental democracy that is usually well hidden.
> Whether the character that is being presented is
> sober or carefree, of high station or low, the
> individual who performs the character will be
> seen for what he largely is, a solitary player in-
> volved in a harried concern for his production.
> Behind many masks and many characters, each per-
> former tends to wear a single look, a naked un-
> socialized look, a look of concentration, a look
> of one who is privately engaged in a difficult
> treacherous task.[93]
>
> Shared staging problems; concern for the way
> things appear; warranted and unwarranted feelings
> of shame; ambivalence about oneself and one's
> audience: these are some of the dramaturgic
> elements of the human condition.[94]

Howard Becker and David Matza have brought a similar humanism to the study of deviancy through their respective emphasis on consciousness and intentionality.[95] We acknowledge the legitimacy of Cicourel's methodological critique of Goffman (and by implication Becker's and Matza's) work: that it cannot serve as an exemplar for the sociology of everyday life because it does not specify the "interpretive procedures" through which the gap between the sociologist's "reconstructed logic" and the actor's "logic-in-use" is bridged.[96] However, we believe that there is room within a humanistic sociology to accommodate the insights of a "William Blake" although we recognize that few of us have the talents to aspire to that mantle.

No account of the development of a humanistic perspective within contemporary sociological theory would be adequate without some mention of the influence of the ghost of young Marx. The re-discovery of Marx's early writings has inspired a vigorous dialogue among academics and intellectuals generally. A full account of this controversy and its many implications for humanistic sociology is beyond the scope of the present chapter. We will therefore merely briefly outline the relevance and extreme importance of the work of such phenomenologically oriented critical theorists as Jurgen Habermas, Alvin Gouldner, and John O'Neill.

John Horton as astutely observed that alienation is the "utopian concept of the radical left": it challenges economic liberalism from the "futuristic perspective" of the deprived classes.[97] The concept is developed within the context of naturalistic and historical immance. Horton regards it as an attempt to translate the ideas of German idealism and the Enlightenment into the tradition of historical and scientific research.

> Marx stressed the human and the active side of of the man-society relationship and ultimately denied the dualism of man-society. Man's human and social activity is labour, and the products of labour, including society, are the extensions of man's own nature. Thus, man is his activity, his objects, man *is* society. Any reification of men's objects, any transcendence of men's products over men so that they do not see their interests, powers, and abilities affirmed and expressed therein, is evidence of the alienation of man from his self-activity, his objects, and himself. The whole notion of social alienation presupposes this immanent conception of human nature. Alienation is an historical state which will ultimately be overcome as man approaches freedom.[98]

The critique of reification which impells contemporary phenomenological-critical theory derives via Lukacs from Simmelian-Weberian sociology.[99] Thus Habermas, Gouldner, and O'Neill consistently punctuate their works with attempts to demystify the scientistic claims of positivistic social science.

Habermas points out that the role played by mythical, religious, and metaphysical interpretations of reality as legitimating agents in traditional societies has been usurped in modern societies by ideological apologetics for science and technology.[100] Habermas also sees science and technology as a leading productive force under advanced capitalism:

> With the advent of large-scale industrial research, science, technology and industrial utilization were fused into a system. Since then, industrial research has been linked up with research under government contract, which primarily promotes scientific and technical progress in the military sector. From

> there information flows back into the sectors
> of civilian production. Thus technology and
> science become a leading productive force, ren-
> dering inoperative the conditions for Marx's
> labor theory of value.[101]

Political problems are increasingly defined as technical problems.
Under the ideology of the "technocratic intent", the social life-
world and normative-evaluative aspects of the institutional framework are transformed:

> It is a singular achievement of this ideology
> to detach society's self-understanding from the
> frame of reference of communicative action and
> from the concepts of symbolic interaction and
> replace it with a scientific model. Accordingly
> the culturally defined self-understanding of a
> social life-world is replaced by the self-reflec-
> tion of men under categories of purposive-rational
> action and adaptive behavior.[102]

Technical and behavioral controls replace moral standards as norms
for social action:

> The model according to which the planned recon-
> struction of society is to proceed is taken
> from systems analysis. It is possible in prin-
> ciple to comprehend and analyze individual enter-
> prises and organizations, even political or
> economic subsystems and social systems as a
> whole, according to the pattern of self-regulated
> systems...the transferral of the analytic model
> to the level of social organization is implied
> by the very approach taken by systems analysis...
> If, with Arnold Gehlen, one were to see the inner
> logic of technical development as the step-by-
> step disconnection of the behavioral system of pur-
> posive-rational action from the human organism
> and its transferral to machines, then the tech-
> nocratic intention could be understood as the
> last stage of this development. For the first
> time man cannot only, as _homo faber_, completely
> objectify himself and confront the achievements
> that have taken on an independent life in his
> products; he can in addition, as _homo fabricatus_,
> be integrated into his technical apparatus if the
> structure of purposive-rational action can be

> successfully reproduced on the level of social systems. According to this idea the institutional framework of society--which previously was rooted in a different type of action--would now, in a fundamental reversal, be <u>absorbed</u> by the subsystems of purposive-rational action, which were embedded in it.[103]

The "technocratic intention" thus serves as ideology for the new politics:

> The manifest domination of the authoritarian state gives way to the manipulative compulsions of technical-operational administration...The industrially most advanced societies seem to approximate the model of behavioral control steered by external stimuli rather than guided by norms.[104]

Habermas agrees with Herbert Marcuse that the ideology of science is deeply implicated in the process of political domination in modern societies.[105] However, unlike Marcuse, Habermas does not regard science as necessarily entailing political domination. Habermas distinguishes three modes of scientific inquiry: the natural sciences, the hermeneutic sciences, and the emancipatory or critical sciences. He agrees with Marcuse's assessment of positivism as being essentially guided by a technical interest in control. But Habermas contends that this interest may be wholly justified as an absolute requirement for the maintenance of life within modern industrial societies. Habermas therefore regards the advances of the natural sciences as providing important and humane contributions to the alleviation of human suffering. He believes Marcuse's conception of science as a partnership with nature would jeopardize these contributions. Thus his critique of the impact of positivism is confined to the social sciences. Under the guise of objectivity and neutrality, positivism in the social sciences provides the ideological base for the emergence of technocracy. Habermas underscores the dangers of an exclusively technical civilization: "It is threatened by the splitting of its consciousness, and by the splitting of human beings into two classes--the social engineers and the inmates of closed institutions."[106]

Habermas therefore calls for a new orientation in the social sciences, the creation of an "emancipatory science". Farganis outlines the dimensions of Habermas' utopia:

> What Habermas envisions is the eventual revitalization of the sphere of communicative action, the sphere of values with the critique of ideology and the emergence of a fuller, substantive democratic order characterized by the 'critical interaction' between scientists and politicians. With free communication, the public may be repoliticized and allowed to determine the substantive ends towards which its resources will be put...an emancipatory social science based on the principles of critical theory provides a critique of science as ideology and, in so doing, joins the epistemological and political questions. Once established, an emancipatory science would 'steer' the further development of the institutional framework and provide the preconditions for a 'substantive' as opposed to a formal democracy. The infusion of a critical social science into the communication system of society would revitalize the function of the public, making it more knowledgeable about the issues while casting them in a framework different from the 'scientism' that acts as an ideological subterfuge. Habermas is thus hopeful that the process of depoliticalization and the elitist control projected by the technocratic intention can be avoided.[107]

Habermas casts the scientific community in the role of a new vanguard bringing about the reunification of theory and practice: "the vindicating superiority of those who do the enlightening over those who are to be enlightened is theoretically unavoidable, but at the same time it is fictive and requires self-correction: in a process of enlightenment there can be only participants".[108]

Alvin Gouldner rejects "the historically limited, elite-distorted character of traditional humanism" in favor of his own version of emancipatory social science, "Reflexive Sociology":

> ...I have stressed that a Reflexive Sociology requires a radical character. To say that a Reflexive Sociology is radical does not mean, however, that it is only a nay-saying or 'critical sociology'; it should be just as much concerned with the positive formulation of new societies, of utopias, in which men might live better, as it is concerned with a criticism of the present.[109]

Gouldner's utopia requires the generation of an "extraordinary sociology" because emancipation from the old society and the creation of new humane forms of social organization will only be possible through "the construction of a total counterculture, including new social theories".[110] The Reflexive Sociology envisioned by Gouldner is an explicitly "moral sociology" which embodies and advances certain specific values.[111] He contends that a "program" for a Reflexive Sociology implies that:

> (1) The conduct of researchers is only a necessary but not a sufficient condition for the maturation of the sociological enterprise. What is needed is a new praxis that transforms the person of the sociologist. (2) The ultimate goal of a Reflexive Sociology is the deepening of the sociologist's own awareness, of who and what he is, in a specific society at any given time, and of how both his social role and his personal praxis affect his work as a sociologist. (3) Its work seeks to deepen the sociologist's self-awareness as well as his ability to produce valid-reliable bits of information about the social world of others. (4) Therefore, a Reflexive Sociology requires not only valid-reliable bits of information about the world of sociology, and not only a methodology or a set of technical skills for procuring this. It also requires a persistent commitment to the value of that awareness which expresses itself through all stages of work, as well as auxiliary skills or arrangements that will enable the sociologist's self to be open to hostile information.[112]

He maintains that a Reflexive Sociology "prefers the seeming naivete of 'soul-searching' to the genuine vulgarity of [the] 'soul-selling'" which has been a trademark of recent successful versions of neo-positivism.[113] Gouldner repudiates the natural science paradigm in sociology because "it 'thingafied' man".[114] He contends that "from the viewpoint of much of the sociology dominant in the United States today, it is not man but society that is the measure".[115] Gouldner points out that whereas "Conventional Positivism promises that the self is treacherous and that, so long as it remains in contact with the information system, its primary effect is to bias or distort it"; "what Relfexive Sociology seeks is not an insulation but a transformation of the sociologist's self, and hence of his praxis in the world".[116] Thus Gouldner, like Michael Polanyi and C. Wright Mills, recognizes that private or personal truth is the only authentic base from which public truth can be reached. If Gouldner's sociology is occasionally exhortative: "In truth, a Reflexive Sociology is concerned more with the creativity than the reliability of an intellectual performance: it shuns the domestication of the intellectual life"; it is nevertheless also vigorously and consistently pervaded by a commitment to a humane perspective.[117] He maintains:

> A Reflexive Sociology means that we sociologists must--at the very least--acquire the ingrained <u>habit</u> of viewing our own beliefs as we now view those held by others...Much of our noble talk about the importance of 'truth for its own sake' is often a tacit way of saying that we want the truth about <u>others</u>, at whatever cost it may be to <u>them</u>. A Reflexive Sociology, however, implies that sociologists must surrender the assumption, as wrong-headed as it is human, that others believe out of need while we believe--only or primarily--because of the dictates of logic and evidence.
>
> A systematic and dogged insistence upon seeing ourselves as we see others would, I have suggested, transform not only our view of ourselves but also our view of others. We would increasingly recognize the depth of our kinship with those whom we study. They would no longer be viewable as alien others or as mere objects for our superior technique and insight; they could, instead, be seen as brother sociologists, each attempting with his varying degree of skill, energy, and talent to understand social reality...The development of a Reflexive Sociology, in sum, requires that sociologists cease acting as if they thought of subjects and objects, sociologists who study and 'laymen' who are studied, as two distinct breeds of men. There is only one breed of man.[118]

Gouldner, then, fully acknowledges that, "knowledge of society is not something simply found or 'discovered'"; but rather "it is something forged, constructed in the community of common-language-speaking men".[119] Thus he regards sociologists as:

> ...in the business of proposing and fashioning ways of looking at, thinking, and talking about--and hence contributing to the <u>very constitution</u> of--social objects and social worlds.

> They are not simply <u>studying</u> a social world--
> apart, but are contributing to the construction
> and destruction of social objects. To say
> social theorists are concept-creators that
> they are not merely in the <u>knowledge</u>-creating
> business, but above all, in the <u>language</u>-
> reform and language-creating business. In
> other words, they are from the beginning involved
> in creating a new <u>culture</u>.[120]

This formulation clearly provides the sociologist with a mandate to begin experimenting with new forms of expression as a part of the search for the "ideal speech situation" that the Habermasian version of emancipatory sociology requires.[121]

A number of other sociologists have independently discovered this 'mandate': Garfinkel (ironically and perversely), Alan Blum, Mehan and Wood, and John O'Neill are notable examples.[122] We will confine our attention to O'Neill's work because it exemplifies this innovative trend in a highly creative and, for our interests, relevant way. As a political theorist, philosopher, translator, and sociologist, O'Neill displays a mastery of humanistic learning more characteristic of a nineteenth century German philologist than a twentieth century North American sociologist. It is therefore not surprising that O'Neill seeks to re-invent sociology within the philological tradition of Giambattista Vico. The basic message espoused in the essays collected under the title, <u>Sociology as a Skin Trade</u> (1972), is that the "basic norm of liberal captialism is contained in the pattern of scientific and technological rationality which legitimates a corporate agenda of the overprivatization of all social resources, including individual knowledge and conduct".[123] In developing this theme, O'Neill acknowledges his intellectual debt to Hanna Arendt, Herbert Marcuse, C. Wright Mills, Paul Baran, C.B. Macpherson, Hegel, Marx, Peter Berger, Erving Goffman, Merleau-Ponty, and Alfred Schutz respectively. O'Neill is concerned with the consequences of "repressive communication" within the context of the social and political framework of contemporary society. However, O'Neill is also actively engaged in a concerted campaign to destroy the intrusions of repressive communication in his own writing. This effort has led him to develop a unique rhetorical style and a compelling program for a humanistic sociology:

> In calling sociology a skin trade I want to
> restore its symbiotic connections with the
> body-politic and to situate it in relation to
> the exchange of organic needs and utopian
> celebration of libidinal community which
> surpasses all understanding. This means that

> the rhetoric of scientism in sociology as well
> as its humanism must be tested against the
> common sense relevance of everyday life. It
> is a reminder that society is richer than so-
> ciology and that for all our science the world
> is still the mystery and passion of being with
> our fellow men.[124]

O'Neill asserts universal truth is "the trick of university, newspaper, and tourist culture".[125] He therefore rejects Husserl's attempt to construct an eidetic science. Instead, he posits the notion of "reflexivity as institution":

> We need...a conception of the auspices of philo-
> sophical reflexivity that is consistent with
> 'poetic invention' (<u>Dichtung</u>), as well as with
> the community in which we philosophize. Such a
> notion may be present to us in the concept of
> <u>reflexivity as institution</u> rather than as trans-
> cendental constitution. By means of the notion
> of institution we may furnish a conception of
> reflexivity which, instead of resting upon a
> transcendental subjectivity, is given in a field
> of presence and coexistence which situates reflex-
> ivity and truth as sedimentation and search.[126]

The work of the critical theorist is seen as grounded in the community: in language, work, and politics. O'Neill shares Merleau-Ponty's conviction that,

> There is no serious humanism except the one which
> looks for man's effective recognition by his fellow
> man throughout the world. Consequently, it
> could not possibly precede the moment when humanity
> gives itself its means of communication and communion.[127]

Because "man is nothing else than the way he talks about himself"; the project of O'Neill's "wild sociology" is a "call for the renewal of the springs of languages dried out in an age of precision and clarity".[128] O'Neill regards "care" as "the domicile of our being together".[129] The vocation of the wild sociologist is existential--a quest for an "indwelling" in the "house of being":

> For we must know where we are at home if ever
> we are to be able to look elsewhere. We cannot

> distinguish other ways or see other places
> unless we know our own.[130]

O'Neill acknowledges that "sociology is the poorest of sciences" but it is inherently humanistic, the "brother to man unless it tricks him with the power of politics or the promise of history".[131] Thus he warns,

> ...it may well be that the daily practice of sociology encourages arrogance upon the part of its members, undermining the very resources of humanism and numb professionalism or the shrill cry of ideology. If this is not to happen wild sociology must make a place for itself, and to accomplish this it must engage hope and utopia. Hope is the time it takes to make the place in which men think and talk and work together. Thus wild sociology is essentially engaged in the education of the oppressed.[132]

It is difficult for conventional sociologists to assess O'Neill's rediscovery of rhetoric because our praxis is pervaded by the habits of the repressive communication that he would reverse. His utopia, like Habermas' and Gouldner's, locates the potential for human freedom in the discovery of a communal basis for unfettered dialogue. For each, humankind is <u>Homo loquens</u>, a talker, a symbol monger. O'Neill celebrates Paulo Freire portrayal of human nature:

> Human existence cannot be silent, nor can it be nourished by false words, but only by true words, with which men transform it. Once named, the world in turn reappears to the namers as a problem and requires of them a new <u>naming</u>. Men are not built in silence, but in word, in action-reflection.[133]

Freire's words succinctly capture the project of hermeneutic sociology. In place of 'positive' knowledge, it offers 'accounts' but it also acknowledges "there are some human encounters that can never be brought to account even though they are remembered by us and shape our conscience".[134] Its claims to 'objectivity' are tempered by the failures of its fathers. It seeks "trans-situational" knowledge but does not claim to 'discover' universals.[135] If it wears the mantel of science at all, it clearly specifies the limits of its currency. Thus most recognize that the empirical basis for macrosociological theories remains problematic while the problems addressed at this level are most compelling.[136] Some conclude with O'Neill that "cultural revolution must always be the work of poets and artists and can never be trusted solely to Marxists and social scientists".[137] Others assume a less political stance. They look to the humanistic traditions of philosophy and history which shaped the genius of a Gibbon, a Burckhardt, a Weber, to provide a renewal of our scholarly resources. But all share Simmel's resolute conviction that,

> ...there is no doubt that all societal processes and instincts have their seats in minds and that sociation is, as a consequence, a physical phenomenon. In the world of bodies, not even an analogy to the fundamental fact of sociation exists...Whatever external occurrences we might designate as societal would be a puppet show, no more understandable and significant than the merging of clouds or the entanglement of tree branches, if we did not, as a matter of course, recognize psychic motivations--feelings, thoughts, and needs--and recognized them not merely as bearers of those external relations but also as their essence, as what really and solely interests us.[138]

Conclusion: The Paradox of Our Praxis

Thus, we find ourselves locked into an uncomfrotable paradox. We simultaneously defend diversity and denounce the dominion of the mechanical man. Yet, we have no real quarrel with those who pursue their truths under the umbrella of the normative paradigm. Unquestionably their methods reveal a truth, a construction of reality consistent with the assumptions of their epistemology. However, we do vigorously object to the extravagant claims which their epistemology allows them to make for their findings. We locate a greater authenticity in O'Neill's polymorphous perversity than in the repressive communication mandated by the forms of discourse prescribed by positivistic epistemologies. Moreover, we acknowledge that the work of many positivists and neo-positivists is born of deep humanitarian commitments.[139] We further acknowledge that the 'information' provided by such conventional sociological methods as the survey questionnarie is often indispensable to the rational functioning of industrial societies. We support attempts such as Cicourel's to refine these methods in a direction consistent with the presuppositions of an interpretive perspective. While the information provided by these methods, under current practices, is used primarily to

serve the interests of the status quo: occasionally it also
underscores the disparities between the prevailing ideology
and the realities experienced by oppressed minorities. When
such information inspires attempts to rectify such oppression,
it serves the interests of a humanistic philosophy. Thus unlike
some of our ethnomethodological colleagues, we cannot repudiate
normative sociologists _en masse_ nor can we affirm the residual
positivistic sympathies of those phenomenological sociologists
who yearn for a _specific_ methodological recipe.[140] While our
own 'theism' is centered in the hermeneutic tradition, we accept
the claim of Rene Dubos, a physical scientist who is actively
engaged in the elaboration of a humanistic version of the philosophy
of science: "Reality has multiple facets and, therefore, can be
apprehended only if seen from different points of view".[141]
Nevertheless, we cannot abandon the critique of the _dogmatic_
epistemological premises upon which normative sociologies are
premised because we share Roche's conviction that,

> ...both as 'abstracted empiricism' (now, 'sci-
> entifically' serving the agencies of government
> and big business) and as 'grand theory' (now with
> an alleged added ingredient--'application to the
> world') they are still firmly entrenched in the
> tribal beliefs and practices of the American
> sociological profession...<u>In spite of the growing
> political and methodological critiques of these
> beliefs and practices, their loss of power has not
> yet anywhere near matched their loss of authority</u>.
> However, their loss of authority means that both
> humanism and Marxism, long repressed, are now at
> least heard in sociology.[142]

Similarly, we must continuously re-examine our own efforts. We
acknowledge that we are no less vulnerable to ideological-
critique than our brothers and sisters.[143] Roches cogently
describes the _plight and the pride_ of a humanistic sociology:

> ...forms of consciousness, given that they are
> intrinsically social,...have a degree of autonomy
> and integrity in their internal structures of
> meaning. A humanistic sociology lives with the
> complexity that this imposes on its so-called
> 'sociology of knowledge', without dissipating
> or reducing that complexity.[144]

If, in conclusion, we must isolate a quality which distinguishes humanistic approaches to social reality, we would describe

the quality quite simply as--caring. Humanistic sociologies from Dilthey to O'Neill, have involved an existential quest. Mannheim expressed the nature of this quest concisely when he called upon social scientists to "risk themselves" because it is not disinterest, but interest, not detachment but concern, which makes knowledge of social reality possible.[145] In a recent book (1976) entitled, Caring, Willard Gaylin, a humanistic psychiatrist argues that within the context of our present political technological and ecological crisis, caring can make the difference. Gaylin specifies the conception of human nature which lies at the center of his thesis:

> I do not despair at the state of the world; I despair at the current state of passive disenchantment and self-denigration. Part of the uniqueness and the wonder of the human species is our ability to redefine our nature. What we are is in the great part up to us. In a Medieval Talmudic text, we read that 'Man, alone amongst animals, is created incomplete, but with the capacity to complete himself'. We are the executors of our future.[146]

Our understanding of humanistic sociology, as well as our personal "despair" and hope, are premised upon the same image of humankind.

APPENDIX FOOTNOTES

1. Dennis H. Wrong, "Human Nature and the Perspective of Sociology", Social Research 30 (1963), p. 318.

2. May cited by Matson in The Broken Image, op. cit., p. 237.

3. Kurt H. Wolff, "Introduction", to From Karl Mannheim (New York: Oxford University Press, 1971) p. xxxiv.

4. Ernest Becker, "What is Basic Human Nature? Further Notes on the Central Problem of the Science of Man', in Angel in Armor (New York: The Free Press, 1969), pp. 159-161.

5. Wrong, op. cit., p. 303.

6. Aaron V. Cicourel, Method and Measurement in Sociology (Glencoe: The Free Press, 1964), p. 189.

7. Thomas P. Wilson, "Normative and Interpretive Paradigms in Sociology", in Understanding Everyday Life, edited by Jack D. Douglas (Chicago: Aldine, 1970) pp. 67 and 70.

8. A problem explored in a comprehensive way by Marx, Simmel, and Lukacs.

9. Simmel used this metaphor to distinguish his own intellectual quests from that of his colleagues in a letter to Marianne Weber, see Simmel, et al., Essays on Sociology, Philosophy, and Aesthetics (New York: Harper and Row, 1965), p. 242.

10. Blumer, Goffman, and Douglas have all described the necessity of such a commitment.

11. Michael Phillipson, "Phenomenological Philosophy and Sociology", in Paul Filmer, Michael Phillipson, David Silverman and David Walsh, New Directions in Sociological Theory (Cambridge The MIT Press, 1973) p. 120.

12. P.A. Sorokin, "Sociology of Yesterday, Today and Tomorrow", American Sociological Review (December 1965) Vol. 30, No. 6.

13. Mumford quoted by Matson, The Broken Image, op. cit., frontispiece.

14. Kurt Reizler, Man: Mutable and Immutable (Chicago: Henry Regnery Co., 1950), p. vii).

15. Ibid., p. 279.

16. Becker, op. cit., p. 160.

17. Erving Goffman, *Frame Analysis* (New York: Harper and Row Publishers, 1974).

18. Aaron Cicourel, *Cognitive Sociology* (New York: The Free Press, 1974).

19. It is unlikely for pragmatic reasons, i.e., large-scale funding of social science research is linked to the apparatus and ideology of the 'hard science' approach. In addition, the impact of present retrenchment policies in higher education will probably affect the ethnomethodological enterprise adversely since the age profile of ethnomethodologists would indicate that they are overrepresented among the ranks of the youngest faculty. See Helmut R. Wagner, "Sociologists of Phenomenological Orientations: Their Place in American Sociology", *The American Sociologist*, Vol. 10, No. 3, (August 1975) pp. 179-186.

20. Goffman, *Frame Analysis*, op. cit., p. 12.

21. Gouldner contends Flacks, Bottomore and Hinkel regard a sociology of sociology as a form of navel-gazing. "The Politics of Mind", in *For Sociology* (New York: Basic Books, Inc., Publishers, 1973), p. 84.

22. Ralf Dahrendorf coined the neologism, "Homo Sociologicus", in *Essays in the Theory of Society* (Stanford: Stanford University Press, 1968).

23. John Watson, *Behaviorism* (Chicago: University of Chicago Press, 1958), p. 6.

24. Ibid. Watson maintains, "The rule, or measuring rod, which the behaviorist puts in front of him always is: Can I describe this bit of behavior I see in terms of 'stimulus and response'?" Of course, only the most elemental behavior could be described in these terms (and even this entailed unwarranted causal imputations).

25. Clark L. Hull, *Principles of Behavior* (New York: Appleton-Century) p. 400.

26. Arthur Koestler remarks, "How, just at a time when the mechanistic conceptions of the nineteenth century had been abandoned in all branches of science, from physics to embryology; how just at that time, in the 1920's, the concept of man as a rigid mechanism of chained reflexes could become fashion-

able in cultures as different as the United States and the Soviet Union is a fascinating problem for the historian of science. The Pavlovian School in Russia, and the Watsonian brand of behaviorism in America, were the twentieth-century postscript to the nineteenth-century's mechanic materialism, its belated and most consistent attempt to describe living organisms in terms of machine theory." The Act of Creation (New York: Dell Publ. Co., Inc., 1967), p. 557.

27. Watson, Behaviorism, p. 269. Hull, Principles of Behavior, p. 27.

28. Giddings defined sociology as "the psychology of society"-- "the scientific study of 'pluralistic behavior', defined as the predictable responses of a 'plurel' [sic] or group to objective stimuli". Giddings quoted by Floyd W. Matson, The Broken Image (Garden City: Doubleday and Company, 1966), p. 67.

29. Dorian Apple Sweetser, "Behaviourism", in A Dictionary of the Social Sciences (Glencoe: The Free Press, 1964), edited by Julius Gould and William L. Kolb, p. 68.

30. Karl Mannheim, Ideology and Utopia (New York: Harcourt and Brace, 1959), p. 39.

31. Ibid. Elsewhere, Mannheim notes that this emphasis is particularly pronounced in American sociology which is distinguished by its "methodological asceticism"--the tendency to "aim in the first place at being exact, and only in the second place at conveying a knowledge of things". "American Sociology" in Sociology on Trial (Englewood Cliffs: Prentice-Hall, 1963), edited by Maurice Stein and Arthur Vidich, p. 7.

32. George Lundberg, Can Science Save Us? (London: Longman, 1947) p. 28.

33. Ibid., p. 41.

34. Sigmund Koch, "Psychology and Emerging Conceptions of Knowledge as Unitary", in Behaviorism and Pheonomenology (Chicago: Rice University and the University of Chicago Press, 1964) Edited by T.W. Wann, p. 11.

35. Pitirim Sorokin, Fads and Foibles in Modern Sociology (Chicago: Henry Regnery Company, 1956). It might be noted that the activities of "robot psychologists" inspired Sorokin to vent one of his more vociferous verbalisms: "...the ritualistic procedures of this cult: with mechanical tests...and statistical operations...always delivering to us 'objective, quantitatively-precise knowledge' of all the mysteries of

the human soul and mind...'mathematical models of robots', and pseudo-experimental studies of mechanical man and his 'mindless mind', 'emotionless emotions', 'will-less mind', all 'the invariant variables' of man's behavior and psychological processes...the unhesitating extension upon man of conditioned reflexes or the mechanisms of learning observed in rats, mice, dogs, rabbits, or other animals...the still more mechanistic interpretation of man's psychology and behavior by the principles of cybernetics, with its 'feed back' and extension of control and communication in the machine upon man...p. 195.

36. Robert W. Friedrichs, A Sociology of Sociology (New York: The Free Press, 1970) p. 232.

37. Ibid.

38. Friedrichs predicts that Neo-Behaviorism is likely to have a significant influence upon the development of sociology in the immediate future due to the attractiveness of the Skinnerian framework to funding agencies and the strategic placement of sympathetic scholars within the American academic and sociological establishment (specifically, Homans at Harvard and Coleman at Chicago). He contends that the basic tenet of the Skinnerian paradigm is compatible with the fundamental assumptions of the sociological perspective-- "that the behavior of the individual is to be viewed as dependent variable, that of the environing social context the independent variable". "The Potential Impact of B.F. Skinner upon American Sociology", The American Sociologist 9 (February 1974) p. 6.

39. The impulse toward 'benevolent' manipulation is not absent from the work of Watson and Hull. With Skinner, however, it becomes the dominant motif.

40. B.F. Skinner, The Behavior of Organisms (New York: Appleton-Century, 1938, p. 5). Skinner defines behavior as "what an organism is doing--or more accurately what it is observed by another organism to be doing". Also cited by Matson who presents a good discussion of Skinner's attempt to exorcise mentalistic words from his vocabulary. The Broken Image, pp. 54-56.

41. Ibid, p. 47.

42. Skinner, Beyond Freedom and Dignity, p. 196.

43. Ibid., p. 205.

44. Criticism of the presuppositions of behaviorism was launched as early as 1896 by John Dewey in an article, "The Reflex Arc Concept of Psychology", Psychological Review, Vol. III, pp. 357-370.

45. Koch, "Psychology and Conceptions of Knowledge", p. 6.

46. Ibid.

47. Koch points out that this is a difficult task because behaviorists often anticipate and cover up these discrepancies through the use of deliberately obscure language. He particularly faults Skinner in this respect.
    Skinner himself presents an excellent catalogue of the objections which have been raised to behaviorism in his most recent book, About Behaviorism (1974). Among these, he lists the following: "It ignores consciousness, feelings, and states of mind...It formulates behavior simply as a set of responses to stimuli, thus representing a person as an automaton, robot, puppet, or machine...It does not attempt to account for cognitive processes...It has no place for intention or purpose...It assigns no role to a self or sense of self...It limits itself to the prediction and control of behavior and misses the essential nature of being of man...It dehumanizes man; it is reductionistic and destroys man qua man...It regards abstract ideas such as morality or justice as fictions...It is indifferent to the warmth and richness of human life, and it is incompatible with the creation and enjoyment of art, music and literature and with love for one's fellow man.
    Skinner says, "They are all, I believe, wrong...These contentions represent, I believe, an extraordinary misunderstanding of the achievements and significance of a scientific enterprise." Excerpts from Skinner contained in Willard F. Day, "A Defense of Skinner's Behaviorism", The Humanist (March-April 1975) p. 29.

48. Michael Polanyi, Personal Knowledge (Chicago: The University of Chicago Press, 1958).

49. Koestler, The Act of Creation, p. 558.

50. Ibid., p. 560.

51. Joseph Wood Krutch, The Measure of Man (Indianapolis: The Bobbs-Merrill Company, 1953) p. 106.

52. Ibid.

53. Although it is beyond the scope of the present paper, humanistic sociologists should attempt to build bridges to humanistic psychology since both approaches seek a wholistic image of humankind in contrast to the fragmented images projected by the reductionist methodologies of positivists, physicalists, and behaviorists.

54. Osgood quoted by Koestler, The Act of Creation, p. 559.

55. Lashley quoted by Matson, The Broken Image, p. 252, n. 67.

56. Hannah Arendt, The Human Condition (Chicago: The University of Chicago Press, 1958), p. 45.

57. Noam Chomsky, "Verbal Behavior of B.F. Skinner: A Review", Language 35 (1959) p. 28.

58. Ibid., p. 36.

59. F.A. Hayek, The Counter-Revolution of Science (Glencoe: The Free Press, 1964).

60. Koestler, The Act of Creation, p. 512.

61. Karl Mannheim, Man and Society in an Age of Reconstruction (New York: Harcourt, Brace and Co., 1949), p. 216.

62. Koch, "Psychology and Conceptions of Knowledge", p. 38.

63. Albert Camus, Notebooks: 1935-1942 (New York: The Modern Library, 1963), p. 142. Camus, The Myth of Sisyphus (New York: Random House, 1955), p. 13.

64. Polanyi, Personal Knowledge, p. 364.

65. Ralf Dahrendorf, "Out of Utopia", The American Journal of Sociology, Vol. LXIV (September 1958) p. 119.

66. Alfred Baldwin, "The Parsonian Theory of Personality", in The Social Theories of Talcott Parsons, edited by Max Black (Englewood Cliffs: Prentice-Hall, 1961) pp. 153-154. Also cited by Wrong, op. cit., p. 305.

67. Wrong, op. cit., pp. 305-306.

68. Ibid., p. 306.

69. George C. Homans, "Bringing Men Back In", American Sociological Review, Vol. 29, No. 5 (December 1964) p. 818.

70. George C. Homans, Social Behavior: Its Elementary Forms (New York: Harcourt, Brace and World, 1961), p. 13.

71. George C. Homans, "Contemporary Theory in Sociology", in Handbook of Modern Sociology, edited by Robert E.L. Faris (Chicago: Rand McNally and Co., 1964), p. 976.

72. Alvin Gouldner, The Coming Crisis of Western Sociology (New York: Basic Books, 1970) pp. 205-206.

73. Schutz apparently adopted this notion from Santayana. For Santayana's portrayal of "Homunocleus", see Santayana on America edited by Richard C. Lyons (New York: Harcourt, Brace and World, 1968).

74. Alfred Schutz, "Common Sense and Scientific Interpretation of Human Action", in Maurice Natanson, Philosophy of the Social Sciences (New York: Random House, 1963) p. 305.

75. Ibid., 341-343.

76. Ibid., p. 346.

77. Both Goffman and R.S. Broadhead contend that aesthetics of the absurd provided the essential insight of ethnomethodology. See Goffman, op. cit., and R.S. Broadhead, "Notes on the Sociology of the Absurd: An Undersocialized Conception of man", Pacific Sociological Reivew, 17 (1974) pp. 35-45.

78. In addition to Garfinkel's own writings, we have relied heavily on secondary sources in our interpretation of Garfinkel. The interpretation here is a summary on Paul Filmer's excellent essay, "On Harold Garfinkel's Ethnomethodology", in Filmer, et al., New Directions in Sociological Theory, op. cit., p. 210.

79. Harold Garfinkel, Studies in Ethnomethodology (Englewood Cliffs: Prentice-Hall, 1967) p. 68.

80. Thomas Wilson demonstrates that inspite of the claims by behaviorists that their approach is essentially inductive; their theoretical approach is deductive. Wilson, "Normative and Interpretive Paradigms", op. cit.

81. Aaron Cicourel, "The Acquisition of Social Structure", in Douglas, Understanding Everyday Life, op. cit., p. 160.

82. Hugh Mehan and Houston Wood, The Reality of Ethnomethodology (New York: John Wiley and Sons, 1975) p. 238.

83. See Z. Bauman, "On the Philosophical Status of Ethnomethodology", *The Sociological Reivew*, 1973, Vol. 21, No. 5, and Robert Gorman, *The Dual Visions: Alfred Schutz and the Myth of Phenomenological Social Science* (London and Boston: Routledge and Kegan Paul, 1976).

84. R.S. Broadhead, "Notes on the Sociology of the Absurd: An Undersocialized Conception of Man", *Pacific Sociological Review*, 17 (1974) pp. 35-45.

85. Morris points out that Broadhead, inspite of his otherwise trenchant criticism of Lyman and Scott's *Sociology of the Absurd*, fails to understand the importance the latter attack to interaction with others in the process of creating the social world. Morris presents the best brief review available of what she calls "creative sociology". See Monica B. Morris, "Creative Sociology: Conservative or Revolutionary?" *The American Sociologist,* 10 (1975) pp. 168-178.

86. In contrast, the Iowa School embrace logical positivism and sought to 'operationalize' the concepts of symbolic interactionism.

87. Herbert Blumer, *Symbolic Interactionism: Perspective and Method* (Englewood-Cliffs: Prentice-Hall, 1969) p. 55.

88. Turner quoted by Wilson, op. cit., p. 66.

89. Ibid.

90. Ibid., pp. 66-67.

91. Alvin Gouldner, "Anti-Minotaur: The Myth of Value-Free Sociology", in *For Sociology: Renewal and Critique in Sociology Today* (New York: Basic Books, 1973) p. 17.

92. Young argues, "Goffman should be read as a radical sociologist and he will open radical vistas that are impossible to come by when reading him as apolitical." T.R. Young, "The Politics of Sociology: Gouldner, Goffman, and Garfinkel", *The American Sociologist* 6 (1971) p. 278. Also cited by Morris, op. cit., p. 174.

93. Erving Goffman, *The Presentation of Self in Everyday Life* (Garden City: Doubleday Anchor, 1959) p. 235.

94. Ibid., p. 237.

95. Howard Becker, *Outsiders* (New York: Free Press, 1963). And David Matza, *Becoming Deviant* (Englewood Cliffs, New Jersey: Prentice Hall, 1969).

96. Aaron Cicourel, "Interpretive Procedures and Normative Rules in the Negotiation of Status and Role", in Cognitive Sociology, op. cit., pp. 23-24. Jack Douglas explicitly specifies Matza's methodological distance from the "sociology of everyday life", in <u>Understanding Everyday Life</u> (Chicago: Aldine, 1970) pp. 19-21.

97. John Horton, "The Dehumanization of Anomie and Alienation: A Problem in the Ideology of Sociology" in <u>Humanistic Society: Today's Challenges to Sociology</u> edited by John F. Glass and John R. Staude (Pacific Palisades: Goodyear Publishing, 1972) p. 141.

98. Ibid.

99. Gouldner affirms this link in "Comments on History and Class Consciousness", in <u>For Sociology</u>, op. cit., p. 415.

100. In addition to Habermas' corpus itself we have relied heavily on James Farganis' excellent article, "A Preface to Critical Theory". When an interpretation was dubious, we yielded to Farganis superior knowledge of critical theory. See <u>Theory and Society</u> 2 (1975) pp. 483-508.

101. Habermas quoted by Farganis, op. cit., p. 498.

102. Ibid., p. 499.

103. Jurgen Habermas, <u>Toward a Rational Society</u> (Boston: Beacon, 1971) p. 106. Also quoted in part by Farganis, op. cit., p. 499.

104. Ibid., p. 107.

105. Farganis presents a lucid comparison of Marcuse and Habermas, largely summarized here.

106. Habermas, <u>Theory and Practice</u> (Boston: Beacon, 1974) p. 282.

107. Farganis, op. cit., p. 502.

108. Habermas quoted by Farganis, p. 503.

109. Gouldner, <u>The Coming Crisis in Western Sociology</u>, op. cit. p. 503.

110. Ibid., p. 5.

111. Ibid., p. 491.

112. Ibid., p. 494-495.

113. Ibid., p. 499.

114. Ibid., p. 492.

115. Ibid., p. 508.

116. Ibid., p. 495.

117. Ibid., p. 504.

118. Ibid., p. 490.

119. Gouldner, "The Politics of Mind", in *For Sociology*, op. cit., p. 104.

120. Ibid., p. 105.

121. Gouldner describes the elements "crucial for the practical production of Habermas' ideal speech situation--(1) no violence, (2) permeable boundaries between public and private speech, (3) allowance of traditional symbols and rules of discourse to be made problematic, and (4) insistence on equal opportunities to speak". Gouldner, *The Dialectic of Ideology and Technology* (New York: Seabury Press, 1976, p. 142.

122. Garfinkel's irony parodies the problem by compounding it.

123. John O'Neill, *Sociology as a Skin Trade* (New York: Harper and Row, 1972), p. xi.

124. Ibid., p. 10.

125. John O'Neill, *Making Sense Together: An Introduction to Wild Sociology* (New York: Harper Torchbooks, 1974), p. 24.

126. O'Neill, *Sociology as a Skin Trade*, op. cit., pp. 230-231.

127. Merleau-Ponty quoted by O'Neill in *Sociology as a Skin Trade*, op. cit., p. 103n.

128. O'Neill, *Making Sense Together*, op. cit., p. 35.

129. Ibid., p. 64.

130. Ibid., p. 81 and p. 76, respectively.

131. Ibid., p. 81.

132. Ibid., p. 80.

133. Ibid., p. 79.

134. Ibid., p. 71.

135. Douglas discusses the trans-situational conception of objectivity in his <u>Understanding Everyday Life</u>, op. cit., pp. 31-35.

136. Douglas, op. cit., pp. 11-12.

137. O'Neill, <u>Sociology as a Skin Trade</u>, p. 57.

138. Georg Simmel, "The Problem of Sociology", in <u>The Sociology of Georg Simmel</u> (New York: Free Press, 1950) edited by Kurt H. Wolff, p. 329.

139. Thus for example, Anatol Rapoport, whose research program (as indicated in his "Foreward" to Walter Buckley's <u>Modern Systems Research for the Behavioral Scientist</u>) can only be interpreted by the humanistic sociologist as a surrealistic cybernetic update of "homonucleus", was awarded the 1975 Lentz International Peace Research Award for his outstanding contributions in the field of peace research.

140. Filmer faults Berger and Luckmann for failing to "attempt to deal with the crucial methodological implications of their critique", "On Harold Garfinkel's Ethnomethodology" in Filmer, et al., <u>New Directions in Sociological Theory</u> op. cit., p. 205. In contrast, Maurice Roche repeatedly reiterates, a humanist sociology presupposes a personalist ontology. See <u>Roche, Phenomenology, Language and the Social Sciences</u> (London and Boston: Routledge and Kegan Paul, 1973).

141. Rene Dubos, <u>The Dreams of Reason: Science and Utopia</u> (New York: Columbia University Press, 1961) p. 165.

142. Roche, op. cit., p. 315. See also note 38.

143. We already have some reservations regarding a possible leap back into a disguised positivism by some sociologists who are devoted enthusiasts of Chomsky's generative-transformational grammar and Levi-Strauss structuralism. And humanism itself has been used as an ideology of repression in the third world as Franz Fanon so eloquently documents. Dennis Wrong points out that the label 'humanistic' has recently "acquired a certain self-congratulatory auro, a 'more-caring-about-people-than-thou flavor'. This is doubtless partly due to the 'humanistic psychology' movement, which not only extols emotion at the expense of reason but regards publicly expressed and even group-induced emotion as the measure of the genuinely 'human'--a fashionable therapeutic version of

an oversocialized conception of man. Some sociologists also use 'humanistic' as a virtual synonym for an engage sociology aligned politically with the Left". Skeptical Sociology (New York: Columbia University Press, 1976), p. 2.

The writer of this epilogue is uncomfortably suspicious that her own prose may be vulnerable to at least one of the lapses cited by Wrong: the "more-caring-about-people-than-thou" syndrome--if so, such a pretension is without merit.

144. Roche, op. cit., p. ix.

145. We agree with Floyd Matson's reading of Mannheim on this point. See The Broken Image, op. cit., pp. 242-243. It is interesting to note that Maslow drew similar conclusions. See particularly his discussion of "caring objectivity" in The Psychology of Science, op. cit.

146. Willard Gaylin, Caring (New York: Alfred A. Knopf, 1976). Cited here from pre-publication excerpt printed in Psychology Today under the title, "Caring Makes the Difference", (August 1976), p. 39.

INDEX OF NAMES

Abel, Theodor, 85n, 86n
Adams, E. Merle, 138n
Adelman, Frederick J., 23n
Allport, Gordon, 68n
Anderle, Othmar F., 137n
Angel, Ernest, 137n
Arendt, Hannah, 53n, 210, 227, 239n
Aron, Raymond, 89n
Ashby, Eric, 198, 201n

Babbitt, Irving, 5-8, 10, 17n, 52n, 157n
Bacon, Francis, 26, 29n, 53n
Baier, Kurt, 174n
Baldwin, Alfred, 214, 239n
Barrett, William, 29n, 77, 87n
Bart, Pauline, 23n
Bauman, Z., 241n
Beard, Charles, 133
Beck, L. J. 29n
Becker, Carl, 131
Becker, Ernest, 132, 203, 206
Becker, Howard, 221, 241n
Beckett, Samuel, 15
Bell, Daniel, 30n
Bendix, Reinhard, 86n
Berger, Peter, 45-47, 55n, 70n, 175n, 244n
Bergson, Henri, 78, 83n, 92, 93
Berkhan, W., 115
Bierstedt, Robert, 45, 54n, 92, 114n
Blum, Alan, 228
Blum, F. H., 76, 79
Blumer, Herbert, 220, 234, 241n
Bochenski, I. M., 13, 22n
Bottomore, T., 30n
Boulding, Kenneth, 162, 165, 173n
Bridgeman, Percy, 39n

Broadhead, R. S., 219, 240n, 241n
Bronowski, J. R., xi, xii-n
Brouwer, L.E.G., 34
Brown, J. F., 209
Bruner, Jerome S., 190
Bruyn, Severyn, 47, 55n
Brzezinski, Zbigniew, 187, 191n
Buckley, Walter, 244n
Burke, Edmund, 38n

Camus, Albert, 136n, 213, 239n
Carleton, William, 170
Chalasinski, Jozef, 114n
Chomsky, Noam, 146, 156n, 212, 239n, 244n
Cicero, 1, 2, 3
Cicourel, Aaron, 203, 206, 219, 231, 235n, 240n, 241n
Clark, Burton, 179, 190n
Coldhamer, Herbert, 173n
Comte, Auguste, 9, chapter II, 57, 148
Confucius, 1
Cooley, Charles Horton, 37, 75
Crane, Diane, 89n
Curry, D. A., 174n

Dahrendorf, Ralf, 214, 235n, 239n
Davis, Arthur K., 132, 137n
da Vinci, Leonardo, 18n
Day, Willard, 238n
Dearing, G. Bruce, 189n
de Chardin, Pierre Teilhard, 163
Descartes, Rene, 26, 29n
Dewey, John, 177, 189n, 238n
Dilthey, Wilhelm, chapter V, 71, 72, 83n, 141, 169, 170, 206, 233
Dostoevsky, Fyodor, 78

246

Douglas, Jack, 163, 173n, 242n, 244n
Drucker, Peter, 190n
Dubos, Rene, 232, 245n
Dulczewski, Zygmunt, 115n
Durkheim, Emile, 27, 90n, 148

Einstein, Albert, 33
Eiseley, Loren, 164
Eliot, T. S., 6, 7, 17n, 20n, 36, 42, 52n, 157n
Ellul, Jacques, 165, 174n, 177, 178
Engels, Friedrich, 31n
Erasmus, 3
Esslin, Martin, 23n
Etcheverry, A., 21n

Fanon, Franz, 15, 244n
Farganis, James, 224, 242n
Ferkiss, Victor C., 190n
Fermi, Laura, 118n
Feyerabend, Paul, ix, xii-n, 35, 39n, 206
Finch, H., 86n
Ford, Joseph B., 135n
Francis of Assisi, 3
Frankel, Charles, 155n
Freire, Paulo, 230
Freud, Sigmund, 27
Friedrichs, Robert, 209, 237n
Fromm, Erich, 135n, 163, 174n, 175n, 178

Galilei, Galileo, 29n, 33
Garfinkel, Harold, 206, 218, 240n, 241n, 243, 245n
Gasset, Ortega y, 152
Gay, Peter, 154
Gaylin, Willard, 233, 245n
Gella, Aleksander, 21n, 38n, 53n, 56n, 156n, 201n
George, Stefan, 78
Giddings, Anthony, 236
Glass, John, 48, 55n
Goethe, 83n
Goffman, Erving, 206, 221, 235n, 240n, 241n
Goodman, Mark, 74, 85n
Goodman, Paul, 189n

Gorman, Robert, 241n
Gough, Kathleen, 36, 40n
Gouldner, Alvin, 40n, 87n, 170, 175n, 216, 225, 226, 227, 240n, 241n, 242n, 243n
Green, Martin, 156n
Gross, Llewellyn, 54n
Gumplowicz, Ludwik, 94
Gundolf, Friedrich, 140
Gurvitch, Georges, 84n

Habermas, Jurgen, 222, 224, 243n
Harmon, Willis W., 190n
Harton, Hector, 21n
Hayek, F. H., 239n
Hegel, Frederich, 24
Heidegger, Martin, 2, 17n, 78
Hilbert, David, 33
Hodges, H. A., 59, 63, 67n
Holborn, Hajo, 67n
Homans, George, 209, 215, 239n, 240n
Honigsheim, Paul, 78, 88n, 145
Horkheimer, Max, 139
Horowitz, Irving Louis, 54n
Horton, John, 222, 242n
Hughes, H. Stuart, 27, 30n
Hull, Clark, 207-209, 235n
Hume, David, 26, 29n, 33, 195
Husen, Thorsten, 183, 190n
Husserl, Edmund, 139, 229

Illich, Ivan, 189n

Jaeger, Werner, 1, 17n
Jaspers, Karl, 59, 67n, 78, 79, 81, 90n, 145
Jay, Martin, 153n
Jesser, Clinton Joyce, 83n
Job, 202

Kantorowicz, Ernst, 140
Kaplan, Abraham, xii-n
Katz, Michael, 189n
Kidd, Benjamin, 148
Kierkegaard, Soren, 78, 80
Kimmel, William, 134n
Kloskowska, Antonina, 114n
Koch, Sigmund, 213, 236n, 238n

Koestler, Arthur, 210, 212, 235n, 238n, 239n
Kolakowski, Leszek, 18n, 29n
Korac, Veljko, 175n
Krutch, Joseph Wood, 211, 238n
Krynski, Waclaw, 114n
Kubler-Ross, Elisabeth, 175n
Kuhn, Thomas, ix, xii-n, 40n
Kurtz, Paul, 21n
Kusch, Polykarp, 39n

Lakatos, Imre, ix, xii-n
Lask, Emil, 139
Lazarsfeld, Paul, 86n
Lederer, Emil, 140
Lee, Alfred McClung, 49, 56n
Lenin, Nikolai, 22n, 108, 131
Lewin, Kurt, 209
Levy, Marion, 164, 174
Levy-Strauss, Claude, 244n
Lichtheim, George, 59, 68n
Lipset, Seymour M., 31n
Lobachevski, Nicholas I., 34
Lopata, Helena, 112n, 117n
Lowe, Adolph, 140
Lowenthal, Leo, 140
Luckmann, Thomas, 47, 244n
Lukacs, George, 139, 142, 154n
Lukasiewicz, J., 34
Lundberg, George, 76, 208, 209
Lyman, S., 241n
Lynd, Robert, ix, xii-n, 201n

Machajski, Waclaw, 105, 118n
MacIver, Robert, 37, 138n, 185
Malthus, Thomas, 164, 197
Mannheim, Karl, 14, 22n, 40n, 87n, chapter IX, 185, 202, 208, 212, 233, 239n, 245n
Marcuse, Herbert, 40n, 224
Markley, O. W., 174n
Maritain, Jacques, 11
Martin, David, 139, 140, 153n
Martindale, Don, 47
Marx, Karl, 4, 6, 10, 24, 57, 58, 94, 141, 205, 221
Maslow, Abraham, ix, 153n, 205, 211, 245n
Masur, Gerhard, 72, 84n, 89n
Matson, Floyd, xiii-n, 9, 21n, 239n, 245n
Matter, Joseph Allen, 136n
Matza, David, 221, 241n, 242n
May, Rollo, 79, 89n, 136n, 202
McKee, James, 168, 175n
Mead, George Herbert, 208
Mehan, Hugh, 240n
Menniecke, Karl, 140
Merleau-Ponty, Maurice, 13, 134n, 243n
Michels, Robert, 132
Mills, C. Wright, 39n, 40n, 43-44, 54n, 147, 152, 226
Mitzman, Arthur, 40n, 89n
Mokrzycki, Edmund, 49, 56n, 70n, 75, 76, 85n
Mommsen, Wolfgang, 40n
Moore, Wilbert E., 84n
Morgan, Robin, 16, 23n
Morris, Monica, 241n
Mounier, Emmanuel, 11, 12
Muller, Herbert J., 174n
Mullins, Nicholas, 89n
Mumford, Lewis, 136n, 163, 166, 174n
Mussolini, Benito, 108
Murray, Gilbert, 9
Murry, J. Middleton, 140
Myers, Bernard S., 88n

Nader, Ralph, 164
Natanson, Maurice, 135n
Neill, A. S., 178, 189
Nicolaus, Martin, 134n
Nietzsche, Friedrich, 46, 78, 80, 104
Nisbet, Robert, 45, 55n, 159, 173n

Okinski, W., 114n
O'Neill, John, xi, 167, 174n, 222, 228, 243n, 244n
Oldham, Joseph, 140
Orwell, George, 177
Osgood, C. E., 211, 239
Ossowski, Stanislaw, 69n

Pareto, Vilfredo, 27, 33
Parsons, Talcott, 87n, 132, 214, 216

Pascal, Blaise, 6
Paul VI, 13
Peirce, Charles Sanders, 39n
Pelz, Werner, xi, 85n
Petrarch, 3
Pfuetze, Paul, 87n
Phillipson, Michael, 204, 234
Piotrowski, Jerzy, 114n
Plato, 200, 201n
Polanyi, Michael, ix, 205, 210, 213, 238n
Popper, Karl, ix
Powell, Elwin H., 138n
Price, Don K., 180, 190n
Protagoras, 2, 5, 94
Psathas, George, 135n

Quinney, Richard, 134n

Radin, Paul, 68n
Rappaport, Anatol, 244n
Raushing, Herman, 119n
Read, Herbert, 13
Reed, John L., 163, 173n
Regush, Nicholas, 27, 30n
Rembrandt, 14
Remmling, Gunther, 35, 141, 155n, 191n
Rhine, J. B., 136n
Rich, John Martin, 179, 190
Rich, Vera, 89n
Rickert, Heinrich, chapter V, 71, 72
Rickman, H. P., 61
Riemann, Georg F. B., 33, 34
Riezler, Kurt, 140, 205, 235n
Rilke, Rainer Maria, 139
Rink, D. L., 174n
Ritterbush, Phillip C., 189n
Roche, Maurice, 48, 55n, 244n, 245n
Rogers, Carl, 178, 189n, 211
Rose, David J., 190n
Roth, Guenther, 90n, 134n
Ryan, William, 162, 173n
Rybicki, Pawel, 116n

Saint-Simon, Henri de, 12, 22n, 148
Salomon, Albert, 16, 37, 73, 83n, 84n
Santayana, George, 6, 7, 17n, 20n, 36, 42, 52n, 207, 240n
Sartre, Jean-Paul, 15, 17n, 23n, 87n
Schaff, Adam, 12
Scheler, Max, 11, 141
Schiller, F.C.S., 5, 19n, 94
Schutz, Alfred, 37, 73, 74, 75, 84n, 204, 217, 218, 240n
Scott, Marvin, 241n
Seaborg, Glenn, 169
Sellars, R. W., 4, 19n
Shattuck, Roger, 14, 22n
Shils, Edward, 86n, 153n
Silverman, David, 136n
Simmel, Georg, 59, 71, 74, 83n, 92, 132, 231, 234, 244n
Simpson, George, 67n
Sinzheimer, Hugo, 139
Skinner, B. F., 9, 209, 210, 212, 238n
Skolimowski, Henryk, xi, xiii-n, 30n, 38n
Sorel, Georges, 108
Sorokin, Pitirim A., 102, 131, 163, 169, 205, 206, 235n, 236n
Speer, Albert, 173n
Spencer, Herbert, 130
Spengler, Oswald, 185
Spranger, Edward, 142, 154n
Spring, Joel, 176, 189n
Staude, John, 242n
Suchodolski, Bogdan, 184, 191n
Sullivan, John E., 63, 70n
Sweetser, Dorian Apple, 236n
Szczepanski, Jan, 42, 52n, 107, 114n, 118n
Szczurkiewicz, Tadeusz, 114n

Tagore, Rabindranath, 15
Tatarkiewicz, Wladyslaw, 29n, 67n
Taylor, Stanley, 154
Thomas, W. I., 37, 92, 93, 111, 114n
Tillich, Paul, 139, 140, 188, 191

Tiryakian, Edward A., 87n, 89n, 137n
Toynbee, Arnold, 133, 134n
Trew, V.C.G., 29n
Troeltsch, Ernst, 73
Turner, Ralph, 220, 241n
Tuttle, Howard Nelson, 62, 69n

Unruh, Glenys, 180, 190n

Varro, 1, 2
Veblen, Thorstein, 132, 176, 189n
Vico, Giambattista, 228
Vonnegut, Kurt, x
von Neuman, John, 33

Waller, Willard, 132
Watson, John B., 207, 208, 235n, 236n
Weber, Alfred, 37, 185
Weber, Max, 59, chapter VI, 116n, 132, 138n, 155n, 169, 180, 190n, 206
Wechsler, Judith, 179, 189n
Weil, Herman, 33
White, H. V. 69n
Whitehead, Alfred North, 130, 217
Wicker, Tom, 136n
Wiles, Jean, 134n
Wilkinson, John, 20n
Wilson, Thomas P., 204, 234n, 240n
Windelband, Wilhelm, chapter V, 71
Wolff, Kurt, 53n, 141, 144, 154n, 157n, 234n, 244n
Wood, Houston, 240n
Wood, Margaret Mary, 175n
Woolf, Virginia, 15
Wrong, Dennis, 202, 203, 215, 234n, 239n, 244n, 245n

Young, T. R., 220, 241n

Zalia, Bela, 139
Zeitlin, Irving, 86n
Zimmerman, C. C., 175n
Zinoviev, Alexander, 157n

Znaniecki, Florian, 75, chapter VII, 169, 206
Znaniecki-Lopata, Helena, 112n, 117n